SOCIAL CHANGE IN LATIN AMERICA TODAY

Its Implications for United States Policy

SOCIAL CHANGE IN LATIN AMERICA TODAY

Its Implications for United States Policy

RICHARD N. ADAMS · JOHN P. GILLIN

ALLAN R. HOLMBERG · OSCAR LEWIS

RICHARD W. PATCH · CHARLES WAGLEY

Introduction by

LYMAN BRYSON

Published for the
COUNCIL ON FOREIGN RELATIONS
by
HARPER & BROTHERS
New York

The Council on Foreign Relations is a non-profit institution devoted to study of the international aspects of American political, economic and strategic problems. It takes no stand, expressed or implied, on American policy.

The authors of books published under the auspices of the Council are responsible for their statements of fact and expressions of opinion. The Council is responsible only for determining that they should be presented to the public.

Published in Great Britain and the British
Commonwealth, excluding Canada, by
London: Oxford University Press

FOREWORD

In the years since World War II both makers and thinkers of foreign policy have been more acutely aware than before that the interaction of states and peoples does not take place on some abstract plane of equal and identical nationhood but against a background of wide cultural and social diversity. "Nationalism," "equality," "progress," "democracy"—these and other words take on different meanings in different settings. To understand these differences has become important, even vital, to the thinking and conduct of policy in a rapidly changing, some say a "revolutionary," stage of history.

How can social anthropologists, who have made great strides in the past generation in broadening our understanding of cultural patterns and social forces, best contribute to the essential fund of our knowledge of new processes of social and political change? And how can political analysts and policy-makers best draw upon the anthropologists' accumulated findings and fresh insights? The Council's project on Social Change in Latin America was undertaken, in some part, to serve as a case study in the interaction of anthropological research and political science and, in larger part, to fill a gap in the tool kit with which North Americans approach the crucial problems of U.S. relations with the peoples of Latin America.

What lies behind the rise and fall of *caudillos,* the stagnation of many peasant regions, the gap which divides Indians from *mestizos,* the brilliant rise of great cities, the new restlessness which brings a Castro or an Arbenz to power on a wave of anti-gringoism? What factors of social change are working for a wider sharing of economic and cultural opportunities, for an orderly participation of larger and larger segments of the people in the management of their governments? These six essays, introduced by the late Lyman Bryson, provide some striking answers, necessarily incomplete though they may be, to these and related questions. Of necessity, they do not offer recipes for day-to-day decisions. They may, we hope, help provide a part of the background for understanding the sources of social and ideological turmoil and the ever-changing challenge to political wisdom.

Each of the six participating authors is an authority in his own field. Each has devoted many years to the grass-roots study of several regions and nations of Latin America. All of them have become conscious of the potential importance for policy of their research findings. Several of them, particularly Allan R. Holmberg, have planned or participated in programs for promoting or inducing social change. Whether as observers or doers, they have placed their emphasis on the meaning, both for the peoples concerned and for the United States, of the profound social changes that are reshaping so much of Latin American life in our own generation.

John P. Gillin, author of "Some Signposts for Policy," Dean of Social Sciences at the University of Pittsburgh, has carried out numerous field studies in some six countries of Spanish America. Allan R. Holmberg, professor of anthropology at Cornell University, has been the moving spirit in a fruitful enterprise of scientific collaboration between Latin American and North American anthropologists, especially in the Vicos experiment, which he describes in "Changing Community Attitudes and Values in Peru: A Case Study in Guided Change." Richard W. Patch, a member of the American Universities Field Staff, has carried out extensive studies of both village and national society in Bolivia since the revolution of 1952. In this volume he analyzes "Bolivia: U.S. Assistance in a

Revolutionary Setting." Charles Wagley, professor of anthropology at Columbia University, has been intimately
concerned for twenty years with the study of Brazilian
society; he has also pioneered in large-scale regional and
village studies carried on jointly by Brazilian and U.S.
social scientists. His "The Brazilian Revolution: Social
Changes Since 1930" summarizes a generation of intensive
and original work. Richard N. Adams, professor of anthropology at Michigan State University and formerly a
staff member of the World Health Organization and Institute of Social Anthropology, has carried out his investigations of "Social Change in Guatemala and U.S. Policy"
before, during, and since the Arbenz regime. Oscar Lewis,
professor of anthropology at the University of Illinois and
author of "Mexico Since Cárdenas," has made careful
studies of the processes of social change in several rural
regions of Mexico and of the growth of Mexico City, and
is completing a new study of the emerging middle class
and its role in Mexican society.

The Council on Foreign Relations wishes to thank each
of the six authors for the enthusiasm with which they responded to its invitation to interpret their research findings
in the light of present and prospective challenges to U.S.
policy in this hemisphere, for their stimulating contributions to the meetings of the Council's Discussion Group,
and for the patience with which they have elaborated and
updated their essays for presentation in this volume. The
authors join with the Council and its staff in expressing
their gratitude to their chairman, the late Lyman Bryson,
for the skill and grace with which he challenged both anthropologists and political scientists to identify areas of
blended or at least common discourse, and their regret
that he is no longer in our midst to inspire and guide
our efforts to peer into the future.

Under Lyman Bryson's chairmanship the Discussion
Group held six meetings. Its members, in addition to the
six authors, were: Miron Burgin, John C. Campbell, Dana
S. Creel, Charles Dollard, Phanor J. Eder, David M. Freu-

denthal, Berent Friele, Samuel P. Hayes, Jr., Stacy May, Paul R. Miller, Jr., Philip E. Mosely, Dana G. Munro, Joshua B. Powers, Clarence Senior, Carleton Sprague Smith, Frank Tannenbaum, Charles Temple, Kenneth W. Thompson, and Edward L. Tinker. Guests at individual meetings were: Adolf A. Berle, Jr., Lewis S. Gannett, Carter Goodrich, Otto Klineberg, William W. Marvel, Charles Shipman Payson, Ernest V. Siracusa, Leo D. Welch, Arthur P. Whitaker, and Bryce Wood. The group also expresses its thanks to Peter Davies, Stanley Leyden, and Roberto E. Socas, who served as rapporteurs.

The planning of this volume was carried on by Philip E. Mosely, Director of Studies, and in this he benefited greatly from the wise and generous counsel of John W. Gardner and Charles Wagley. Mr. Mosely also edited the volume for publication. William Diebold, Jr., Director of Economic Studies, and Helena Stalson, Research Associate, provided invaluable guidance and assistance in the difficult problems of economics and demography. Byron Dexter read the complete drafts and made many valuable suggestions of substance and style. Lorna Brennan carried out the arduous task of copy editing and supervised the copying of numerous drafts. The staff of the Library, particularly Janet Rigney, were very helpful in supplying information and checking numerous references. Elizabeth Kridl Valkenier prepared the index with her usual skill.

The reporting of facts and the statements of opinion are, as usual, the responsibility of the authors, not of the members of the Discussion Group, in which many diverse opinions were expressed, or of the Council on Foreign Relations. The Council on Foreign Relations presents these studies as a contribution to the study and formulation of U.S. policy toward the new Latin America that is emerging under our very eyes to a world-wide role of perhaps decisive importance.

CONTENTS

INTRODUCTION
by LYMAN BRYSON

MOST POLICIES in international relations, even for a country like ours whose interests have expanded so fast, are based on ancient ideas. Some of these old ideas are, of course, historical facts of lasting significance. Some of them are encrusted prejudices. We are lucky when our acquaintance with some region of world importance is made up mostly of innocent ignorance because there is in that case a chance to found our policy on fresh and genuine knowledge.

As regards Latin America, the policy of the United States has been largely improvised and there is still time to ignore the past and found a lasting policy on knowledge acquired by the modern methods of social science. The anthropologists can tell us facts about the peoples of Latin America which were not accurately known about any peoples when most of the old notions of diplomacy were formulated and sanctified. This region is bound to play a great role in our affairs. It has been studied by trained observers and we now have the beginnings at least of something like real acquaintance. It would be a great loss to miss this chance, and the purpose of this book is to call the attention of policy-makers and public opinion in the United States to the kind of information they can use if they will.

The scientists who have written the six essays here assembled, and who engaged in long discussions with the members of the study group organized by the Council on

Foreign Relations, do not offer definite suggestions as to what our Latin American policy ought to be. They do venture, in a few instances, to point to what they believe have been glaring errors. But they cannot, as scientists, pretend to be policy-makers. Their role is different, more fundamental and not less difficult. They can help policy-makers know better the peoples with whom they deal. In fact, the anthropologists demonstrate in these essays that they can provide information which the ordinary working staff of an embassy could never hope to get, no matter how well trained or how energetic. The anthropologist has a different approach. He is trained to get into the skins of strange peoples, insofar as that can be done, and to free himself of the assumptions which make him a member of his own tribe at home. This is much more than a knowledge of the languages, although that skill is generally more firmly exercised by the scientist than by the diplomat. It involves searching and friendly inquiries outside the high circles of government and national affairs. It comprises also a rigorous training in the relativity of cultural assumptions and the relativity of value systems. The anthropologist is an expert in helping others learn to be less "culture-bound."

A reading of these six papers indicates that one fundamental fact we now know about Latin America is that all of the countries to the south of us, in varying degrees but all in some measure, are undergoing social, economic, and political changes which pain and bewilder their people and make them more difficult to deal with.

In many places, the changes cannot be measured. It is only a complicated country that can describe itself or be described in comparative measures because only highly developed countries collect statistics. The simple annals of a Guatemalan village or a Bolivian mining town are not complicated, but they are not easy to locate. It takes patience and sympathy and well-trained skill to see under the surface, or even under the current impressions which the villages themselves may have of what is going on.

But the sweep of basic change cannot be mistaken. It is affecting the lives of Latin Americans in at least four ways, as Mr. Gillin shows in his comprehensive essay.

There are, first, changes in the relations among the more primitive tribal organizations and the new forms of nationalism and national unity. Nations are being made up of more or less interrelated groups. The locus of patriotism is being shifted in many places. Closely intertwined with the changes shown in the unification of tribes into nations is another set of changes in the relations among different races. The population of Latin America is much less European in its racial mixtures than the populations of the United States and Canada, as we well know. But the proportion of Indians—that is, Indians by cultural habits as well as by blood—differs greatly in different countries. In some places the Indians are moving into more sophisticated ways, or at least the ways of their white neighbors, and this generally means an upward movement economically if not socially. It is likely also to mean a greater participation in the rather unstable systems of self-government.

These two kinds of shifting in indigenous patterns, in tribal organizations, and in racial integrations complicate a third kind of change which is not peculiar to Latin America. Indeed, it is going on in most parts of the world. The Latin Americans are moving into the cities and building up power industry. Agriculture is still the chief industry in Latin American countries, even in Mexico where modern technology is making swift progress. But the big cities are getting bigger. Mexico City is now the second largest city in the two Americas; it contains 13 per cent of all Mexicans. São Paulo, Buenos Aires, and Rio de Janeiro are close behind. And these cities comprise a large proportion of the population of their respective countries. Smaller places that are still big enough to have the living and working conditions of urban centers are also growing in size and number. And in these cities and large towns the factories are going up. Industry demands orderly labor

in a money economy, and its demands shatter the imme-
morial patterns of primitive life.

These three sets of changes must necessarily make
changes also in the attitudes of both governments and peoples toward the United States. The people look at their
powerful northern neighbor sometimes more kindly,
sometimes less kindly, than do the governments of the
moment. When there is conflict in the voices we hear from
one of these countries it is difficult to avoid the stock fal-
lacies of international intercourse. A country under a
dictator always speaks with one voice and has the look of
either friendship or hostility, simple and evident. When a
country is in a tumult of political change, it may give forth
confused noises of almost every emotional suggestion. But
when a country is really free, or has made substantial steps
toward freedom, it will always show a somewhat mixed
attitude toward a neighbor. In other words, what we have
to take carefully into account is that an uncertain attitude
toward ourselves in any country may be the result of confusion and undigested changes, or it may be the sign that
free speech has been achieved. To find an example in more
distant nations, we get a clear picture of hostility from
official Russian contacts, whatever the Russian people may
really feel toward us. We get on all occasions a mixed
chorus of boos and cheers from the friendly but free-
speaking British.

Our six essays cover the general drift of change in five
areas of special interest: Brazil, Peru and Bolivia, Guatemala and Mexico. Brazil is an area of broad changes which
are being made without some of the strains seen in other
countries, but Mr. Wagley still finds it appropriate to describe its change as a "revolution." Peru is also slowly
being transformed in social and economic institutions. In
Bolivia the pace is so swift that violent revolution has been
barely prevented and may still break out if the demands of
the long-suffering people are not met. In Guatemala the
conflict appears to be more ideological than economic and
takes overt political forms. In Mexico we have conditions

closer to those we are used to in the United States, a technological revolution in a somewhat earlier stage than our own. For that reason the chapter on Mexico gives us more statistical information on the nation's economy than we could possibly get from the other areas.

The materials on which these papers were based were collected by all the techniques of the modern social scientist. Where there were records, they were studied. The opinions of the city dwellers, heavily charged with prejudices for or against the United States, imbued with European learning and experience, were gathered but were not mistaken for the voices of the people. This does not mean that the intellectuals of the Latin countries are ignored. Indeed, it is strongly recommended that we give the artists and scholars and philosophers the same respectful hearing they receive from their own countrymen. We need to listen to them, to cultivate their good will, and to enlarge generously the interchanges between the intellectual institutions of Latin America and our own.

But the anthropologist goes also into the slums of the newly aggregated industrial towns, into the mines and villages, and also into the remote feudal estates where life is simple, hard, and removed, but emotionally secure. He traces the changing patterns of the farmer who begins to drop off Indian customs, of the peasant who tries to live in the unfamiliar city, the outraged worker who listens to revolutionary talk, the newly rich and the ancient poor. He watches living men and women moving through these patterns in the confusions modern life has created.

The Latin American peasant or miner may look outside for a villain to blame for his troubles and find him in the North American capitalist. He may even look outside for a friend and find him in the Kremlin-inspired Communist. He may find the word both use, "democracy," too empty of content to be reassuring. The anthropologist studies the shifting meanings and demands that go through the minds of these people. He is politically aware as well as scientifically observant. He has mastered and evaluated large

quantities of material, on which to base his cautious conclusions.

It is not, as I said, the business of the specialist to make
policy decisions. He is able to point out the relevance of
his findings to policy considerations, but he can do this
only if called on and listened to. Underlying much of the
scholarly caution of these papers there is a well-disciplined
impatience with bureaucratic impenetrability. In fact, the
tape-bound bureaucrat is one kind of human being the
anthropologists seem to understand least of all. They do
not see the reasons for his troubles; sometimes they fail
even to try to learn his language. But as time goes on, the
anthropologist's usefulness becomes more apparent and
the knowledge of the foreign relations officer in the social
sciences is enlarged. A partnership useful to both and
greatly useful to the rest of us is being forged. The diplomatic mind is getting to be less "culture-bound." The
scientific mind may be getting more practical also, although this is not necessarily the case since the role of the
scientist is still to project theories, to collect and interpret
facts. Only when asked can he help in discovering their
relevance to high policy.

This kind of knowledge may enable the representatives
of our government in foreign lands, and especially in countries now undergoing profound transformations, to get at
levels of the population not reached before and scarcely
ever understood. In the case of most Latin American areas,
the new levels of power and understanding are just coming
into existence. Mr. Gillin calls them the "middle mass"
and that term is usefully descriptive. The middle mass is
not a class in the usual meaning of that European word.
It is not yet fully self-conscious and it is not rigidly organized. But it is a real force and its power grows.

It is a conviction of my own, for which I cannot blame
any of the contributors to this volume, that the slow progress of democratic ideas in many of the countries which
seem to our eyes politically backward is caused by the lack
of a class of "operators" and our own compounding failure

to recognize and strengthen the operators where they exist. We cannot be sure that we perceive an interacting association in theory between democracy and modern industrialism, but we act as if we believed they were inextricable. We approach the countries where we hope to make friends for our own international policies of peace and freedom with the tools of material advancement, with new capital, and with technical advisers. There seems to be an unacknowledged assumption that, if we could share our engineering and business know-how, our beneficiaries would thereby know how to vote. There is certainly this much truth in this unstated principle. Poverty-stricken people want material help and they can see political values best in ready cash. Our own attitudes toward our own prosperity and our own freedom would indicate that this is natural, although it may be more sophisticated in its Western forms.

Whatever we think of this partnership between freedom and machines, we ought to face the fact that most of the poor countries we are trying to persuade into freedom have no middle class. They have never needed one. A middle class, a middle mass, is produced by growing economic and technological activity and is required by further progress of that kind. The poor countries, such as those in the Middle East, for example, which are now making us so much trouble, have had masses of the very poor and a thin scum of the very rich on top. Their leaders, like Nasser, can rule by the pressure of street mobs because the streets are full of uneducated, unoccupied, unemployed, and unrewarded men. In medieval times, when those social patterns were created, the mass below toiled without rest or comfort at the simplest tasks, by the oldest methods. The rich made meager proportionate profits on their holdings but were luxurious because they held enormous estates. The only operators needed in such a system were the slave overseers of the owners and a few more or less subservient merchants. I am aware that I am not now describing Latin America but the parallel is real. Poor countries are slow to

learn the uses of democracy because they have had no
middle group of the kind that does the more skilled work
of the economy, manages the machines as they are created,
provides a hospitable group into which the gifted poor
man can climb, mediates between ignorant poverty and
blind wealth, and gets personal benefit out of increasing
freedom and self-government.

The Middle East (and I believe Latin America also) has
long had idealists of freedom. Their intellectuals, their
poets and philosophers have expressed freedom as well and
in many cases better than their Western contemporaries.
But no implementation of freedom is possible without a
democratic-minded and democratically ambitious middle
group, those whom I have called the operators. They are
not only necessary to the economy; they are also necessary
to democracy.

On this account, and to the extent that I am right, it is
of the greatest significance that Mr. Gillin sees in Mexico
especially, but more or less everywhere, the growth of the
middle mass. In Mexico, which is the most advanced of
the Latin countries, judged by our standards, the middle
mass has most clearly emerged. In other countries, Bolivia
for example, as described by Mr. Patch, the cultural
changes are not yet effective in bringing these middle
groups into power and revolutions seem more likely than
democracy.

We would be making another mistake, however, if we
took it for granted that the cultural invasion of machines
and self-government, as North American imports, will inevitably and immediately make for friendliness toward us,
even where they are accepted. It is the opinion of our
specialists, variously expressed, that the movement of
North American aid, machines, and political ideas into
many places increases hostility. This may be, of course, a
natural result of more freedom of expression. As I have
already said, the hostilities of a growing democratic movement toward an older and more powerful democracy are
in part the mere emergence of free-speaking.

There is more to it than that, however. There is one kind of hostility toward another power which is the natural outcome of continued dependence. In their first contacts with an industrially stronger power, a poor country is generally eager for help and looks upon capital invasions as benefits. It is much like the farmer who asks a loan from the village banker. It begs. But gratitude toward a creditor or an invading capitalist soon vanishes because the benefits are taken for granted and dependency is observed to be unpleasant. The banker who was once the giver of ready cash is now the creditor who wants it back, with interest. The poor country, not so poor now perhaps and forgetful, wants to get back the old freedom and still keep the new benefits. This is the kind of dependent's hostility that we are used to and are more or less prepared to bear.

Dependent economies are very likely, however, if the metropolitan country has capital and technical knowledge to spare, to become independent. Economic empires break up for the same reason as do political empires; the parts grow to be too strong and break away. In Mexico and Brazil, at least, and perhaps in much smaller measure in other Latin American countries, the economy has grown out of independence into rivalry. The resentment of the debtor and the dependent have been replaced by the more vigorous and self-respecting hostility of the rival. This is an immense gain for the Latin American country. It is a problem for American policy; will it end finally in gain or loss to us?

The first essay, Mr. Gillin's survey of the general situation is, as already pointed out, an indication of the part which is being played in all the various "revolutions" by the growing middle mass. We may easily exaggerate the similarity between this new industrially active and democratically inclined group and our own dominant socioeconomic group, the middle class in the United States. In North America, that is, in the United States and Canada, this class is not only typical, economically powerful, and politically dominant, it is also the numerically largest component of the total populations. It does not need to have ideological self-consciousness to determine the trends in North American culture or North American power. Whether or not it is manipulated by capitalistic controls and standardizing mass media, as some think, this immense group of men and women in the United States and Canada has strong traits of generosity mixed with occasional fits of parochialism, peacefulness with convulsive fits of belligerence, tolerance with strange prejudices, and friendliness tinged with suspicion. The government of the United States has its own constituency as well as the Latin Americans to deal with in solving the problems of hemispheric brotherhood.

The new middle mass in Latin America is different in ways that may persist for a long time. The frontier with its individualistic ideals has persistently colored the ideals of North America. In Latin America, feudalism, with the emotional dependence of little men on their patrons and strong personal bonds among persons of rigidly marked class differences, will likewise persist. Mr. Gillin lists nine dominant values which will be more or less carried over into middle-mass life no matter how much shift there may be to urban living and wage economies. They do not sound like the values of an average North American and they are not. The Latin American cares more than the North American for personal dignity, for family cohesion and social hierarchy, perhaps even more for tangible possessions, although materialism is a trait in both groups of cultures. The other five values which are stronger in our southern neighbors than in ourselves are shown in an interest in spiritual experience and in emotional expression, a tendency to fatalism, a strong sense of propriety or decency in mode of life, and a scorn for manual labor.

Our government is dominated by American middle-class values. For it to deal generously and effectively with any government which speaks honestly for a new middle mass which holds these different values will take patient translation of cultural assumptions and a tolerance too deep

for condescension. The present gap in our understanding
is illustrated vividly in Mr. Holmberg's study of the processes and strains of social change among the Indians of
Peru.

In describing both the traditionally isolated and depressed way of life of the Indians of the Peruvian highlands, Mr. Holmberg makes it clear that a do-nothing
policy can only lead to social and political catastrophe. As
he and his Peruvian and North American colleagues have
demonstrated through their remarkable experiment in the
sierra community of Vicos, only an all-round integrated
approach to the entire complex of problems—better production, education, health care—can overcome the lethargy
left behind by centuries of neglect. And, as his report shows
vividly, these goals cannot be imposed from without by
government, however benevolent. The ambition and the
means to achieve them must be assisted to grow from
within the community, through developing new concepts
and new types of local leadership.

In his essay on Bolivia, Mr. Patch makes two highly
significant points which bear on other parts of the South
American continent as well as on his chosen area of study.
First, he shows that incipient civil war in Bolivia has been
on the verge of developing into large-scale violence for the
reason that has been behind all the classical revolutionary
patterns in world history, land hunger. And his second
point, resting on that, is that our government has never
realized the extent to which the real power in Bolivia now
rests ultimately in the hands of the *campesinos,* the farmers. They represent the bulk of the people of Bolivia and
are certain in the long run to have their own way.

We have not, Mr. Patch says, done a skillful job of helping Bolivia get out of its deep economic morass up to now,
in spite of having spent large sums of money in aid. We
have not given our help in such a way as to improve the
actual living of the *campesinos,* and they cannot see much
political value in a foreign system, like our kind of democracy, if it gives them no quick relief. Both the farmers and

the miners want immediate action, not long-range plans, and they may wreck any scheme of intergovernmental co-operation which sacrifices present needs to future possibilities. The future of Bolivia, like the future of many other parts of South America, may be brilliant; the critical present must in the meantime be lived through.

Mr. Wagley's account of the changes in Brazil exemplifies most of the trends indicated in the general survey. Much of the discomfort which makes the urban and rural proletariats of Brazil politically restless, and at least mildly attracted to left-wing ideas, seems to come from social changes rather than from intentional exploitation. If more peasants come into the cities than can be housed and fed, they will be disturbed even though their situation in the slums is better and more exciting than their ancient primitive village life and they do not want to go home again.

It is not surprising perhaps that Mr. Adams tells us most about the political or ideological shifts in Guatemala in his description of the present state of that country. We have read a good deal in newspaper accounts of political governmental upheavals there and of Communist threats. If there has been the possibility of a Communist salient in the Western world it has been in part, Mr. Adams believes, because we have made the mistake of vigorous action in ignorance. It is the same story here as elsewhere. There is no reason, Mr. Adams says, why we should "convey the impression that Guatemalans and other Latin Americans ought to seek a gringo utopia." But we create the impression that this is what we expect because we have never demonstrated a positive interest in the values held by the Latins themselves.

In the Mexican essay, Mr. Lewis gives us a full documentation in brief compass of the assertion that hostilities caused by dependence may change into hostilities caused by rivalry. This sense of rivalry is not as fantastic as some complacent northern neighbors might assume. Mr. Lewis shows that the per capita increase in production is greater in Mexico than it has been in the United States, and in

spite of continuing bad distribution the whole population
is rising in its demands and in its purchasing power. Here
as elsewhere the middle mass grows and in spite of suffering and inequalities there is a fair promise of continuing
political governmental stability.

We can sum up the truth which we hope will be taken
into account by the makers of North American policy in
words used by Mr. Wagley. He applies them to Brazil;
they can be applied to all the countries south of the Rio
Grande: ". . . Only now is Brazil going through the same
kind of social and economic revolution that most Western
European countries experienced in the nineteenth century. But with this important difference: Brazil is undergoing its revolution in the midst of the accelerated changes
and profound tensions of the mid-twentieth century."

The countries to the south of us have the advantage of
our experience, the help of our capital and technical skills,
the stimulation of our nearby example. They have the disadvantages of mixed populations, ancient and deeply based
feudal customs, and poverty. We can help them if we do
not overwhelm them with the wrong kind of aid, by selfish
capital invasions, or with rigidly defined political ideas
which they cannot adapt to their own thinking. There are
evidently principles which will guide a wise policy toward
the Latin countries as a group, modified, of course, by the
differences. These differences seem to be largely in the
stage that each has arrived at in the journey they are all
making in the one direction, toward freedom and welfare.

One

SOME SIGNPOSTS FOR POLICY

by JOHN P. GILLIN

THE SOCIAL REVOLUTION which is under way in Latin America has explosive potentialities beside which the usual political and military revolutions pale into insignificance. Political instability is still evident, but political revolution has ceased to be simply a normal and expected way for the "outs" to take over from the "ins." "Outs" and "ins" alike are beginning to develop both ideologies and programs derived from them. Most important of all, a new and as yet unconsolidated middle class is emerging. Its members are developing effective leadership and power. They are receptive to new ideas which are now reaching them through modern means of communication, whether from within their area or from abroad, whether from free-world sources or the Soviet bloc.

The half-formed traditions of this new middle element in Latin America are not made of the stuff from which were forged modern Western democracy, free enterprise, social responsibility, and all the other values and institutions that are prized in the modern cultures of North America or of Northern and Western Europe. The new middle groups have a tradition of values peculiar to Latin

This essay is one result of a research grant made to Professor Gillin in 1951 by the Carnegie Corporation of New York. The Carnegie Corporation is, of course, not responsible for the facts or for the opinions presented.

America. Equipped with this set of mental or cultural furniture, they face the ideologies and ambitions of the competing forces of the outside world, now knocking loudly on their doors.

I shall attempt here to highlight some underlying values and some trends of change in the social and political situation of Latin America, and to indicate in a general way their significance for the United States' relations with Latin America now and in the next few years. Yet any such attempt runs many hazards of criticism, if only through being condensed into a few pages. After all, Latin America comprises twenty republics, eighteen of which speak Spanish officially, one Portuguese, and one French. Many national and regional details and differences have necessarily been omitted in this brief discussion, which is devoted to clarifying certain patterns characteristic of the Latin American area as a whole.

For the United States' relations with Latin America— whether public or private—the problem is, basically, to bring North American and Latin American points of view into common focus or to get them on a common wave length—to borrow these terms from another field. Those elements which are opposed to the strengthening of friendship and cooperation within the hemisphere try to persuade people everywhere that the positions and interests of the United States and Latin America are in basic opposition to each other. An objective analysis of the underlying values indicates, I believe, that this is not the case.

It is true, of course, that U.S. and Latin American traditions differ in many particulars, including not only superficialities but also some aspects that lie below the surface. It is all the more essential for North Americans to understand how the world looks when examined from the point of view of the emerging leadership in Latin America. An error common to most of us, especially when dealing with members of distant cultural groups, is to assume either that the other fellow sees things just the way we do or that, if he does not, there must be "something wrong with him." This

can produce serious difficulties if it governs the formation
of national policy or far-reaching private activities abroad.
This habit of mind tends to distort reliable predictions of
what the foreign peoples and nations will do and thus may
lead to the adoption of inappropriate and ineffective policies.

In recent years the U.S. Department of State has made a
notable effort to remove the "blinders" imposed by our
own culture and outlook. A good example is found in an
analysis of the situation in Guatemala which was prepared
by the Division of Intelligence Research after the situation there had reached a critical stage in 1954.[1] Ten years
before, in 1944, the thirteen-year-old dictatorship of Jorge
Ubico in Guatemala had been overthrown in a revolution
which U.S. policy-makers apparently interpreted as merely
another routine Latin American "changing of the guard."
As a matter of fact, it marked the beginning of an attempt
at a basic social and cultural revolution, though at first it
was not associated with Communist ideas or groups. However, in large part because of the United States' failure to
perceive and respond to the new situation, Communists
and fellow travelers had succeeded by 1952 in infiltrating
and practically taking over the government. The new challenge this posed was clearly stated in this study of 1954,
which put its finger on one very important aspect of the
awakening of Latin America, the source of much of its
leadership in pressing for change. In 1944, most of the
active leaders of the revolution were between nineteen and
thirty-seven years of age; three, in fact, were only nineteen
in 1944. "All of these young men had much the same background: they were of mixed Spanish-Indian blood; their
families were relatively poor, and they had attained an educational level higher than the average Guatemalan in these
circumstances." As the study points out: "The appeal of
communism to this group may be traced to its frustration
at the failure of the Guatemalan community to make sub-

---

[1] *Intervention of International Communism in Guatemala,* Department of State publication 5556 (Washington: GPO, 1954).

stantial progress for at least two generations prior to World
War II in adjusting its political, social, and economic
structure in harmony with the ideals of the modern
world." [2]

. . . Guatemala assimilated in the late nineteenth and first
part of the twentieth centuries some of the technological
advances of the outer world. . . . The middle class which
evolved to furnish the merchants, professional men, educators,
and technicians to service these assimilations had the most
contacts with the outside world and became the social stratum
most conscious of Guatemala's social backwardness. However,
this class eventually divided into one segment which was
drawn to the idea of progress by evolutionary means and another segment drawn to reform by revolutionary means. The
majority of the middle class obtained in the years 1871-1944
a sufficient stake in the economy to be content to hope for
modernization by evolutionary means. The minority, made up
of those "intellectual" elements such as schoolteachers, whose
resentment of Guatemala's backwardness was sharpened by
lack of ties to the existing structure, became something of an
insoluble lump in the Guatemalan social organism. . . . Frustrated in their desire to provide ideological orientation to an
evolutionary society, they lived traditionless on the periphery
of the national life, often with makeshift personal lives and
prey to the facile "isms" which seemed to provide a formula
for quick solution to the problems they perceived.[3]

If, in Guatemala, U.S. policy-makers had perceived the
new facts in 1944 rather than in 1954 and had adopted
a new policy based on them, international communism
would probably not have been able to establish a beach-
head there, and many headaches, as well as present difficulties in other parts of Latin America, could have been
avoided. In 1954 the late Colonel Carlos Castillo Armas
led a maneuver from the neighboring republic of Honduras which forcefully ejected the Communists and their
followers from positions of power in Guatemala. However,

---

2 Same, pp. 47, 41.
3 Same, p. 43.

it is still widely believed throughout Latin America that the U.S. government or its agents engineered and financed this "liberación," and this belief has been exploited so successfully by Communist and other antagonists of the United States that the "Yankee Colossus" has suffered a severe loss of prestige. Many Latin Americans, stimulated and abetted by propaganda hostile to the United States, have interpreted the "liberación" of 1954 as a reversion on the part of the United States to the use of force for removing a weak regime which is distasteful to it.

What was needed after the Guatemalan revolution of 1944 was a positive U.S. policy that would have recognized the seriousness of the shift in leadership and would have attempted to win the confidence of the idealistic but inexperienced architects of "the New Guatemala." The series of mistakes which resulted in the increasingly strained relations between the two countries between 1945 and 1954 have now largely been recognized and have produced a more realistic U.S. approach to the Latin American situation.

The modern world has learned that change is inevitable and also that it can be terribly upsetting when it arrives unforeseen. For this reason it is important for us to examine more closely some of the old traditions and new trends in Latin American societies that are bound to have an important influence on the United States' future relations with that crucial area.

Race and Society

The Iberian conquerors found in the New World a variety of native tribes and civilizations, to which they gave the name "Indian." In a few regions of Latin America, the natives were so few—and their cultures so weak—that the invaders, in effect, eliminated them, either by extermination or by shunting the survivors off to reservations or fringe areas. Native Indians, either by blood or culture, are today an insignificant element in the nations of Argentina, Uruguay, Costa Rica, and Chile, whose populations are predominantly "white" in racial type. Even in these countries there are, of course, some *mestizos* (people of mixed Indian and white heredity), and these countries, like all Latin America, have received certain cultural contributions from the Indians, such as domesticated plants, folk beliefs, and additions to the language. In several Latin American nations, including Mexico, Guatemala, Ecuador, Peru, Bolivia, and Paraguay, Indians constitute a large and recognizable segment of the population. In all other countries, except Cuba and the Dominican Republic, the Indian element, although smaller, is still visible.

According to accepted Latin American definitions and practices, "recognized Indians" are not considered members of the various national societies or cultures. The custom, in Spanish, of speaking of the Indians in terms of race *(raza)* is confusing to North Americans. In Spanish-American countries Indians are regarded as a separate race, not because of any distinguishable physical characteristics, but because they have a different culture and social status as compared with recognized or Europeanized members of the national society.

In most countries many prominent people are as "Indian" in their inherited physical traits as any recognized tribal member. Conversely, any member of an Indian tribe or community may be accepted into the national society, usually on the basis of three accomplishments. He must learn to speak the national language, Spanish or Portuguese, fluently. He must adopt European-type clothing. And he must move away from a recognized Indian tribe or community and settle in a city, town, or village considered to be national—i.e., Spanish or Portuguese—in its culture. If he adopts these new "European" ways while remaining on his home ground, everyone will say that he is "just an Indian trying to be a Peruvian" (or whatever the national adjective may be). Elsewhere he will be accepted, provided he takes on the symbols of the national culture. So long as they cling to their native language and costume and remain affiliated with their aboriginal tribe or community, Indians are usually not able to contract recognized marriages with the members of the national community or engage in other activities typical of full membership in the national society.

It is thus obvious that "recognized Indians," so long as they remain in that status, do not form a part of modern Latin American society. Not only do they lack social status within the national system, but also they are usually denied effective political or economic influence, with the one exception of Bolivia. The difference in racial definitions in Latin America compared with the southern region of the United States is obvious. A Negro in the South cannot change his individual social status, defined by a visible factor, color of skin. In Latin America, on the other hand, an Indian, provided he gives up his cultural identification with the aborigines, can be readily accepted into the national structure, although at first his position may place him in its lower classes.

Recognized tribal or community Indians thus form a part of the total population in most Latin American countries, yet they are not included in the national social structure. However, even while they remain in their self-contained tribal or community groups, Indians may be "swung" or influenced by middle-class leaders. For example, in 1951 I became acquainted in Ecuador with at least the leading elements of a group of 30,000 "Communist" Indians. Representative members affirmed emphatically, "Yes, we are Communists." When I sat down to talk with them, I discovered that they did not know who Stalin was, where or what Russia was, or what Marx had said. But they did want their own pieces of land and were against the large landowners who, they felt, had abused them. Responding to the Indians' known grievances, several avowed middle-class Communists from the capital city, Quito, had taught them that they were "Communists."

Perhaps ten million persons still live as recognized Indians, in a total Latin American population of about 180 million. As such, they are not effective members of their respective national societies and do not provide national leadership, except in Bolivia. Unless some radical changes occur in long-established patterns, they will continue to be absorbed gradually, contributing their genes and some of their culture traits to the nations where they live.

The other principal non-European element, important in parts of Latin America, is of Negro background. People of Negroid stock live in appreciable numbers in all the Caribbean republics and everywhere along the Caribbean littoral. They are also numerous in Brazil, parts of Colombia, and Ecuador. Because the Latin American definition of "race" is based on cultural traits rather than physical differences, Negroids, generally speaking, have been assimilated into the national societies.[4] Otherwise, race in the physical sense is of little social or cultural significance. To be sure, a few families in the "Indian countries" claim to be "pure" white descendants of the *Conquistadores*, but their pretensions are usually considered something of a joke, even by their social peers. In all Latin American countries one can point to persons of mixed racial inheritance who hold prominent positions in politics and economic life, although they are proportionately less numerous in the countries of predominantly European settlement. Racial purity in the genetic sense is not an important value in present-day Latin America as a whole.

Class and Society

Under colonial rule and for some fifty to seventy-five years following the achievement of independence, Latin America was dominated by a fairly rigid two-class system— a landowning aristocracy claiming descent from the *Conquistadores*, and a lower class composed mainly of peasants and domestic servants. From the first, however, there were

---

4 In Brazil, darker-colored Negroids tend to lower-class status in larger proportions than lighter-colored Negroids; see Charles Wagley, ed., *Race and Class in Rural Brazil* (Paris: UNESCO, 1952), p. 8, and elsewhere.

small numbers of petty merchants, scribes, artisans, apothe-
caries, and other persons who occupied a middle position.
As racial intermingling proceeded, large numbers of *mesti-*
zos, mulattoes, and other mixed types appeared, some of
whom likewise assumed middle status, which was also open
to "pure" Indians who acquired education and "civilized"
culture. Beginning in the latter half of the nineteenth
century many countries—notably Argentina, Brazil and
Chile—also received large numbers of European immigrants, most of whom found their way into the middle
layers of society. The middle category was recruited from
many sources, including members of the old upper class
who, having lost their landed fortunes, now entered business, the bureaucracy, or the liberal professions on a par
with their less blue-blooded associates.

Today, at least two lower classes can be identified: (1)
peasants and agricultural laborers, and (2) industrial
workers, including factory workers and labor employed in
extractive industries. The distinguishing features of the
lower class as a whole are that it earns its living by manual
labor and is less than completely literate. The agricultural
lower class falls generally into several subclasses: peasants
who own miniscule properties providing at least part of
their livelihood; workers on old-style family-owned plantations; and laborers on modern industrialized farms.[5]

In addition, in most countries two upper classes can be
distinguished. One of these comprises the members of
the old landowning aristocracy or its remnants. For it,
abolengo—descent based on antiquity and class purity
of hereditary lines—is of fundamental importance. The
other is what may be called the new upper class, composed
mainly of self-made men and their families and descendants, persons who, either in business or politics or a combination of both, have accumulated fortunes enabling
them to live on a luxurious scale of comfort and conspicuous consumption. More important is the fact that this new

---

[5] Charles Wagley and Marvin Harris, "Typology of Latin American
Subcultures," *American Anthropologist,* June 1955, pp. 428-451.

upper class runs or owns most of the larger business enterprises not controlled by foreign corporations. In some cases these people are also associated with foreign concerns and hence are identified with foreign business interests. In any event, their upper-class position rests on their extensive power, mainly economic. Most managers and smaller businessmen, lacking such obvious power, are rated in the middle segment, though often in its upper brackets.

Both old and new upper classes are distinguished from other segments of society in that both claim power and prestige, although of different types. Apart from these common characteristics, however, the landed and the moneyed upper classes are often opposed in many of their interests. The landed class, which can usually be entered only through birth or marriage, tends to conserve the semifeudalistic values of colonial times. While the moneyed upper class comprises a diversity of interests, it is in general open to all those who can achieve success within the structure of power and influence. Those segments of it which draw their profits from the internal consumer market are interested in promoting higher living standards and in developing new wants among the general population.

The new upper class usually has no close alliance with the church, which has been one of the bastions of the landed class. It exerts its power and influence through newly planned structures, such as business organizations, and it is inclined to regard these as flexible rather than rigid. In general, the new upper class is much more open to innovation from the outside world than is the landed upper class, especially in business methods, modern technology, and sophistication of manners and mores. Since most of the self-made men have risen from the middle segment of society, they also share many of the values and confusions of the much more numerous middle groups.

A Class in Search of a Future

Between the boundaries of the upper and lower classes there lies a large and growing middle segment. An unconsolidated and somewhat unstable layer of society, its members nevertheless hold a traditional ethos and have access to the press, radio, television, mails, and other media of mass communication. They have had sufficient education to be influenced by and to influence the larger outside world. Above all, they aspire to a better life and to progress, however vaguely these concepts may be defined. In the process of defining these aspirations more precisely and putting them into effect, the Latin American middle class is also a prime target for ideological propagandists of all shades from the outside world.

The middle groups embrace a wide social span, from the country schoolteacher, with two white shirts to his name, and the village storekeeper, barely able to tot up his accounts and scan his weekly newspaper, to regular army officers, managers of business concerns in the provincial and national capitals, university professors of international renown, and members of cabinets. Its emergence has been stimulated by the spread of education and by expanding opportunities in trade and industry, coupled with a constantly increasing need for literate and technically trained people in both government and private enterprises. Today, practically all prominent politicians, whether military or civilian, are of middle background.

Despite the wide differences in their economic standing and power, all members of the middle segments bear certain hallmarks. They are set off from the lower classes by their disdain for manual labor as a means of earning a living and by their literacy. In addition, they strive for a certain minimum of "decency" *(decencia, decoro)* in their standard of living, beyond what the lower classes consider necessary. This involves at least one outfit of European-style clothing in presentable condition, as distinguished from workmen's clothes, a dwelling with its floors made of something better than packed earth, and the possession and use of furniture and table service of "decent" (as distinguished from Indian and peasant) pattern. The value of material possessions as symbols is at least as important as their direct utility. For example, middle-group families will often spend money for proper furnishings and dinner services for the entertainment of guests before they consider buying household conveniences or automobiles.

The middle segments are distinguished from the upper strata of society by the absence of any claim to power based on either distinguished ancestry *(abolengo)* or great wealth. Formerly, most persons of middle status aspired to copy the way of life of the old aristocracy. During the past quarter-century, as their numbers have grown and their spokesmen have become more articulate, an awareness of their own importance has begun to appear.

Despite the absence of precise statistics, available data suggest that, for Latin America as a whole, the middle strata constitute just under 20 per cent of the national society (exclusive of Indians). The estimates of the Pan American Union Series range from 8 per cent for Venezuela to 50 per cent for Uruguay.[6]

Latin America is experiencing the decay of an old class system and the growing pains of a new one. In the middle groups the lack of class consciousness and of a sense of belonging has been remarked by almost all observers. The Latin middle segments as yet lack an explicit and self-conscious "ideology" which is "spelled out" and fairly well known to most members, as is the case with the Western European and North American *bourgeoisie* or middle class. Speaking of the "middle class" in Bolivia, Humberto Palza reports: "Psychologically, it does not feel itself a class nor

---

[6] Estimates of the middle class by twenty-nine experts from Latin America itself are available in Theo R. Crevenna, ed., *Materiales para el estudio de la clase media en la América latina,* 6 v. (Washington: Pan American Union, 1950-51); statistical studies of Mexico are available in José E. Iturriaga, *La estructura social y cultural de México* (Mexico City: Fondo de Cultura Económica, 1951); and of Argentina in Gino Germani, *Estructura social de la Argentina* (Buenos Aires: Editorial Raigal, 1955).

act as such; in other words, it has no consciousness of its condition." [7] In Chile, says Abarca, "Formed of such heterogeneous professional and economic elements, the middle class has no ideological homogeneity. Although the majority has a center position, its members evoke quarrels and [flaunt an] egotism, which, if but properly channeled, will give rise to a striving for excellence." [8]

The same "unconsolidated" condition is found in the embryonic "middle classes" in many underdeveloped regions. The London conference in 1955, of the Institut International des Civilisations Différentes, concluded that it did ". . . not find it possible to reach any completely satisfactory definition of the term 'middle classes'. . . . It is probable that the concept . . . has a different content in different parts of the tropical and subtropical world, and may vary from time to time in the evolution even of one country." [9]

Despite their apparent heterogeneity, the middle groups constitute beyond doubt the segment of society most in touch with the modern world, most susceptible to influences for change, and most potent in the internal and international affairs of their own nation. Not only are most professional politicians and army officers from the middle strata; so are practically all intellectuals—writers, painters, journalists, actors, radio and television performers and producers, professors, schoolteachers, doctors, lawyers, scientists, "pundits," and "thinkers." These articulate people speak to the outside world for Latin America, and the outside world must speak to Latin America through them. They supply most of the wordage that passes through the media of communication—books, newspapers, radio, television, domestically made motion pictures—and, not least, the formal educational systems.

Furthermore, all clerical and white-collar workers, as

---

7 Crevenna, cited, v. 3, p. 13.

8 Same, v. 6, p. 66.

9 Ivor Bulmer Thomas, "Conclusions de la 29e session de l'INCIDI," *Civilisations* (Brussels), no. 3, 1955, p. 481.

well as most technicians, mechanics, engineers, farm extension workers, social workers, nurses, hygienists, and government servants, regardless of administrative rank, are of this middle segment. Finally, labor leaders of national importance are middle-status people. They may start out in life as proletarians, but they must normally acquire the skills and symbols of at least lower middle-class status if they are to act effectively on the national scene.

Although middle-status groups are often riven by conflicts, ideological and economic, the members of one segment have in common the fact that they live from salaries or relatively fixed fees, rather than from income-producing property of their own. Another sector of the middle class comprises owners of small to medium-sized businesses, farm owners, and the upper level of salesmen (as distinct from plaza market sellers and peddlers). Businessmen may range from the owner of a small store or mine to the salaried manager of a large enterprise. They are sometimes at loggerheads, depending on whether they are primarily producers or distributors, on whether the goods they handle are mainly imported or produced within the country for local consumption or for export, and so on. As a group, however, they have more in common with each other than with the owners of medium-sized farms. The latter do not work their land, unlike lower-class landowning peasants. Neither do they operate large estates, unlike the landed aristocracy or the commercial companies producing for export. A white-collar salesman usually does not have an investment in his employer's business, but, being paid on commission, he has a financial interest in the success of the enterprise. All of these business-oriented people, in contrast to the professional and white-collar personnel, have in common an interest in private property and free enterprise.

Thus, there appear to be two large blocs within the middle strata—the salaried and professional people, and those with a direct stake in private property and free enterprise. At present the first far outnumbers the second.

The "blocs" are in most parts unorganized and only dimly aware of their own positions. In effect, each is a bundle of splinters, and many splinters of each bundle are entangled with those of the other. For example, a doctor may own a drugstore or a private hospital on the side. All of the "salaried and fee" conglomeration acquire land when they can. Within the business and farming bloc, there is little agreement on the proper role of private property and "free enterprise." Urban middle-group people tend to look down on those from the provinces and rural areas. Divisions within the middle strata are usually more obvious today than common points of view or a readiness for concerted action. Nevertheless, below the surface a certain common set of traditional cultural values tends to unite the members of the middle segments.

The Middle Segments and Their Values

The values which are held in common and "taken for granted" by most members of the middle sectors in Latin America determine how they decide among alternatives offered by competing cultural and political systems of the outside world. They also serve to define a set of attitudes that distinguishes the Latin American middle strata from the middle classes of the United States and Western Europe. These controlling values may be grouped, for convenience, under several rubrics: personalism, kinship, hierarchy or stratification, materialism of a special kind, transcendentalism or interest in "spiritual values," the high worth of inner states and emotional expression, and fatalism. Two other values of the middle class have already been mentioned—"decency" in mode of life, and disdain for manual labor.

The controlling values of a culture perform many functions in a society. They provide a way of looking at the world and at people. They furnish those who hold them with a set of beliefs which explain, as it were, the structures and functions of what is perceived. They set out one or more approved goals toward which human effort ought to be channeled within that part of life with which each value is concerned.

PERSONALISM, A CENTRAL VALUE

Both North Americans and Latin Americans place a high value on individuality and "the person." The use of similar words in English, Portuguese, and Spanish tends to conceal the profound differences between their actual meanings. To put the differences succinctly, the North American credo holds, at least ideally, to the notion of equality of opportunity. Each individual has inherently equal rights and supposedly each has an equal chance with every other. The culture places a heavy emphasis upon the external or social equality of persons. It implies that any claim to uniqueness must be proved by achievements of a socially approved type. In the United States the cultural definition of "the person" lays great emphasis upon the broad similarities among various social types. Individual differences, if disapproved, may lead to various types of social punishment; if approved, they may result in conferring "distinction" for greater than average achievement.

In Latin American culture the value emphases are quite different. Although most middle-status Latin Americans hold the Rights of Man in high verbal esteem, the underlying emphasis is upon the inherent uniqueness of each person. The individual is valued precisely because he is not exactly "like" anyone else. Each individual merits respect because of his unique inner worth, regardless of the social form it may take. This is the fundamental meaning of *respetar* (to respect), a word widely used in American Spanish to describe one's relations with others.

The inner essence of the person is usually spoken of as the "soul" or "spirit" *(alma, ánima, espíritu),* and Latin Americans are usually not at all loath to discuss this subject at length. This makes for misunderstanding on the part of North Americans, because in their current usage they usually feel uncomfortable in using words like "soul" or "spirit" when discussing living individuals, except perhaps in intimate discussions with priests or ministers of the Gospel.

The idea that each person merits respect for his inner worth and integrity does not hinder the complementary recognition of social position, of dignity of office, or of an established hierarchy of persons and "things." However, a Latin American, when first confronting an unfamiliar individual, typically "sees" in him a "soul" whose essence he must endeavor to understand and respect for what it is.

Each person has a certain endowment of dignity, honor, and valor which merits respect from others and which he must safeguard at all cost, even death. This is the value usually described as *dignidad de la persona,* literally, "dignity of the person." It refers, however, to inner dignity, rather than to social or other outward prestige. Originally, no doubt, the influence of the Catholic Church, with its strong emphasis upon the soul, contributed heavily to the definition of this value. As a part of the middle-strata culture, it has now lost any exclusively religious connotation and has become a secular guide to conduct.

The Ecuadorian writer, Benítes, explains in sociological terms the heavy emphasis upon the "soul." To the socially insecure Spaniards who conquered America, says Benítes, one's own person, one's soul, was the most tangible reality. "It was the *mystique* of a marginal class which wished to mark off its individuality. . . . *Dignidad* is the formulation of a marginal class insecure in its social position." [10] Another Ecuadorian writer, Pérez Guerrero, describes Latin Americans as "individualists," but in a manner different from North Americans. There is an "exaltation of the I, which does not perceive itself as a unit in the group, but as the whole group itself. Pride and *dignidad* are exaggerated, and the group serves as a pedestal for the self." [11] Essentially, the same is true of Mexicans, according to Itur-

---

10 Leopoldo Benítes Vinueza, *Ecuador: Drama y paradoja* (Mexico City: Fondo de Cultura Económica, 1950), pp. 52-54, 86.

11 Alfredo Pérez Guerrero, *Ecuador* (Quito: Casa de la Cultura Ecuatoriana, 1948), p. 74.

riaga. "The Mexican," he states, "is not gregarious, but individualistic, and, as a consequence, he often lacks the spirit of collaboration. His unsociability and asperity unfit him to live with others without friction or to work creatively as a member of a team." [12] These observations, quoted more or less at random among many statements by Latin Americans, carry a critical tone, but they reflect the awareness among middle-group writers of the value attached to the inner person.

The emphasis on personalism means that words or actions interpreted as insults to the individual's inner worth are highly explosive in their effects. They may evoke an intense emotional reaction, with verbal or physical violence, or else a sullen resentment, a refusal to cooperate, and a devious search for "revenge." For this reason perhaps, American Spanish and Portuguese idioms contain elaborately precautionary patterns of ceremonial politeness which are in constant use as a buffer between all but the closest of friends and kinsmen.

Various types of admired personalities are derived from the high value attached to "personalism." The *macho* (literally, "male") type is highly valued. The *macho* is expected to show sexual prowess, zest for action, including verbal "action," daring, and, above all, absolute self-confidence. He may express his inner convictions by resorting to physical force, as in the case of bandits and revolutionary military leaders, or he may do so verbally as a leading intellectual, lawyer, or politician. Not all *machos* are *caudillos* (leaders), but all *caudillos* must be *machos*. In politics, a man is not commonly elected or acclaimed to office because he represents the social, economic, and political positions of his followers, but because he embodies in his own personality those inner qualities that they feel in themselves and they would like to manifest, had they but the talent to do so, in their own actions.[13] Of course, some

---

[12] Cited, pp. 233-234.

[13] Cf. René de Visme Williamson, *Culture and Policy: The United States and the Hispanic World* (Knoxville: University of Tennessee Press, 1949).

of the same charismatic qualities attach to leaders elsewhere. Yet, over the long run, in contrast to Latin America, North American followers or constituents seem to be
more strongly motivated by rational or pragmatic judg-
ments in choosing their leaders, when considered in prospect or on the basis of performance.

Traditionally, for the middle-status individual, only
those with whom he feels an intimate, personal relationship are trustworthy. Personal friendship, plus a kinship
relationship of some kind, is essential for "getting something done." The impersonal confidence which, say, a
customer has toward a salesman of a large, established
corporation in the United States is not yet a general feature
of the middle-status pattern. This is one reason why the
forms of democracy which exist throughout Latin America, borrowed in the first instance from the United States
or the French Declaration of the Rights of Man, seem to
have little effect on actual political behavior. Similarly,
any "program," such as Point Four, requires the "personal
touch" if it is to succeed. North American administrators
and experts, regardless of their personal competence, will
have little success in their dealings with the middle segments unless they are able to develop personal confidence
and evoke *simpatía*.

It is notoriously difficult in Latin America to float large
issues of stocks and bonds, only in part because of the
scarcity of investment funds. Repeated studies have shown
that many individuals and families with funds available
for investment are loath to use them to buy "mere pieces of
paper." Unless they know personally and understand the
individuals involved, they lack confidence in them. The
same attitude accounts for much of the political instability
in Latin America. In the middle-status pattern of values,
it is only natural for political actions to be governed by
personalistic considerations, rather than by adherence to
"principles," party platforms, and similar abstractions.
The reliance on persons is, of course, open to exploitation
by politicians, who, by personalistic attacks upon the *digni-*

dad of their opponents, can block the kinds of compromise which in the United States and England are regarded as one of the mainstays of the democratic process.

THE STRENGTH OF FAMILY TIES

The personal intimacy that a middle-status Latin American requires in his social dealings with other individuals is bolstered by the persistent patterns of kinship. Generally speaking, he feels that members of his family or of a larger kin group understand his inner uniqueness and provide the sort of intimate contact that does not require him to "keep up his guard." Kin relationships traditionally include a wide range of persons related by blood or marriage. In addition, there are usually strong ties to the "ceremonial kin," through the *compadrazgo* (co-godparenthood). Even now, the middle-status family in Latin America tends to include a much wider circle of relatives than is at present common in the United States. The average person is often in fairly intimate contact with a large number of kinsmen of several generations and of various degrees of "remove" on "either side." The small immediate family, consisting only of husband, wife, and minor children, and isolated from most other kinsmen, is still an anomaly even in urban life.

Originally the family was patriarchal, with the father officially in absolute authority and with the mother and unmarried females restricted in their close contacts with males to their relatives and members of the clergy. During courtship, unmarried girls were always carefully chaperoned. Married men and boys carried on much of their social life outside the home, with groups of other men at bars or clubs, or with their mistresses or in houses of prostitution. Sons of the family were usually "spoiled" from a middle-class North American point of view. Married women, on the other hand, although restricted in their social and intellectual contacts, necessarily were trained to a role of responsibility, for they were the practical administrators of the household. This traditional pattern is breaking down among the more advanced and upward-mobile members of the middle segments, especially in the larger towns and cities.

One of the important trends is the emergence of women as significant figures in public life, a phenomenon so far confined almost entirely to the women of the middle groups. Yet, few "emancipated" women have cut themselves off from a large net of kinfolk, and kinship of all types is more highly valued by both sexes than among middle-class urbanites in the United States. Even in large cities, a person without kin, such as an abandoned orphan, is regarded as one of the most pitiable of human beings. And it is not mere politeness that customarily leads a Latin American to greet a friend, even on the street, with a stream of questions about the health and doings of wife, children, father, mother, and numerous other kindred. The inquirer is often genuinely interested in his friend's relatives as individuals. More important, he also sees his friend as part of a kin group and knows that his personal welfare and state of mind are influenced by those of his kinsmen.

THE IMPORTANCE OF HIERARCHY

For the Latin American, the universe, including human society, has traditionally been arranged in a series of strata, and the culture is still strongly influenced by the values which he attaches to hierarchy. The political, social, and religious structures of the colonial era were highly stratified. A rigid political structure, ultimately controlled from the Iberian peninsula, imposed upon the colonies a system of political ranks and powers. Most office-holders were sent out from the home country without consultation with the colonists. Although this system was more rigid in the Spanish domains than in Brazil, there also the local people had to "look upward" in the political sense. Even under the republics, political thinking and action were molded so strongly by this structure that some observers regard it even now as a controlling value.[14] The stratification of political power was reinforced by the traditional pattern of social class and caste. And while the church has always insisted upon the equality of all human souls before God, the heavenly scheme and the terrestrial ministry are alike arranged in explicitly hierarchical orders.

Under the weight of this tradition, it is not surprising that the typical middle-status individual sees most things on a scale ranging from "lower" to "higher." At first glance, this emphasis on hierarchy seems to contradict the value attached to personalism or inner uniqueness. But the distinctive worth of each individual has nothing to do with his social position or his recognized distinction; advancement in the hierarchy may come, although not necessarily so, as the result of fulfilling one's unique potentialities. In contrast with the United States' credo, Latin Americans do not believe that all men are born "equal." You cannot be equal to anyone else in your inner essence when, by definition, you and everyone else are "unique." It is also obvious that, from the point of view of social rank, everyone is not equal.

For at least the last hundred years the idea has been gaining ground that the ranks of the human hierarchies on this earth are "open," rather than preordained, and this is, of course, demonstrated above all by the emergence of the middle segments. The liberal revolutions and constitutions of the last quarter of the nineteenth century opened the doors of law and politics to increasing numbers of middle-status people and to the eventual appearance of the new upper class. And it is certainly true that the concept of equality of opportunity as a right of the citizen is spreading throughout Latin America.

Despite these trends, the controlling concept of hierarchy still explains much of the behavior of the middle

---

[14] Blanksten sees the political system of Ecuador, as late as 1948, as "monarchy in republican dress"; George I. Blanksten, *Ecuador: Constitutions and Caudillos* (Berkeley: University of California Press, 1951), p. 169, and elsewhere.

groups. It is reflected, for example, in the strong sense of social position, in the pattern of "decency" of living standard, valued as much or more for symbolic than utilitarian values. A very important role is still played by the *patrón* system, or its modern variants, as a substitute for a more general sense of social responsibility. In Latin America the old aristocracy did not cultivate the patterns of *noblesse oblige*, as was the case in England, and perhaps one consequence has been the continuing absence of any real feeling of community responsibility. Although Rotary International and similar "service clubs" have been organized among upper-level middle-status businessmen in the larger cities, the notion of the "more fortunate" elements of society actually getting down to a man-to-man basis with the "more unfortunate" in order to help them is virtually unknown.

The *patrón* relationship was originally a reciprocal arrangement tying members of various social strata together, in terms not of social or economic equality, but of reciprocal obligations of an unequal sort. On a typical *hacienda* (plantation) or ranch, the owner was, and usually still is, *patrón* to his workers or tenants. They owe him a certain amount of work, variously calculated, in return for his supplying them with housing, tools, and perhaps individual plots of land. They also owe him a certain loyalty in disputes and other difficulties. In return he acts as their "protector" in brushes with the law and with higher authority. The custom by which *patrones* serve as godfathers to the children of their more faithful retainers sets up a solemn tie of ceremonial kinship, which in a way defines the whole enterprise as "one big family," although social equality is by no means implied. The *patrón*, nonetheless, is expected to take a personal interest in the welfare of his workers or tenants and their families. He knows them by their first names, attends them or sends them aid when they are ill, and contributes to their *fiestas*. Essentially the same sort of relationship has been traditional in handicraft shops, mines, and small factories. The *patrón* or "protector" idea permeates most sectors of the middle category.

Small *patrones* usually have *patrones* of their own—"bigger" and more powerful men upon whom they can rely and who serve them as protectors and as contacts in communicating with the higher political, social, or economic powers. A distributor of merchandise is often in a *patrón*-like relationship with his retail tradesmen, a manufacturer with his suppliers of raw materials, an employer of seasonal workers with his labor recruiters *(enganchadores)*. In public service and political employment the system is especially strong. Every public employee tries to gain a "protector" in the higher levels of the administration simply as a form of job insurance, if not in the hope of promotion.

The armed forces, although organized hierarchically in Latin America as elsewhere, appear to constitute one of the few graded systems of social status in Latin American society in which the *patrón* relationship is relatively weak, possibly because the common soldiers are conscripted for a limited term of service and therefore are not in any continuing relationship with their superiors. However, career officers, whether commissioned or noncommissioned, usually try to develop *patrón* relationships with superiors.

Presidents of republics, whether dictatorial or democratic, are expected to play the *patrón* role toward their constituents. For this reason, they are usually available for several hours each week to any citizens, no matter how lowly their stations in life, who wish to see them in person.

Large business enterprises and large bureaucracies cannot preserve the personal relationship between the *patrón* and his clients. Nevertheless, the hierarchical outlook remains, and with it the expectation that someone or something "higher up" owes one certain obligations. As a consequence, the state has had to make some gestures toward filling this void, and it has moved to do so through developing labor codes, with appropriate machinery for supervising them, social security programs, free health and hospital services, public housing programs, and the like. Much of the leadership and all the administrative personnel for the development of the new "public *patrón*" system of welfare services have come from members of the middle groups.

In some quarters in the United States, there is a tendency to look upon these "welfare state" provisions in Latin American countries as dangerously "socialistic" innovations which may eventually lead to communism. On the contrary, I believe that they should be considered as responses to deep-seated values and as defenses against communism, provided they are honestly and efficiently administered. The danger of communism arises when a Latin American government merely pays lip service to the expectations of its people and fails to meet its need for protective services. It is noteworthy that much social legislation has been established under dictatorships that were opposed not only to communism, but also to democracy.

A VARIANT OF MATERIALISM

Many articulate Latin Americans like to say that their culture is essentially a spiritual one, and some of them derive an obvious satisfaction from contrasting this assumption with the "crassly materialistic" values they attribute to the United States. Yet even such critics, when in a frank and confidential mood, admit that they and their compatriots are not entirely uninterested in material things. The point is, I think, that materialism is seen and defined somewhat differently by them.

Perhaps the traditional Latin American variety can best be termed "tangible materialism." The pattern has been to trust and seek only those kinds of property "one can put one's hands on." Stocks and bonds, and other securities of corporations and companies not known "personally" to the investor, are mere pieces of paper; they are not tangible. Nor are copyrights, patents, royalty agreements, and similar "invisible" properties to be trusted. One apparent exception is lottery tickets, which many Latin Americans buy each week, but a lottery ticket is generally regarded not as "property" but as an investment in "fate."

Among all classes, land and buildings are regarded as the most tangible types of property. People of the middle class, however, do not work the land with their own hands. When one of them owns productive land, he has *peones* or tenants to do the labor. Furthermore, the ideal pattern is to have one or more servants to work about the house, as the wife and other members of the family are not supposed to stoop to domestic drudgery.

In some parts of society the controlling power of the values associated with tangible materialism is weakening. Still, its persistent strength explains some forms of behavior which differ widely from those now customary in the United States. It has usually been difficult, for example, to finance large undertakings by the widespread sale of securities. Savings and insurance plans are poorly developed, because of the distrust of smaller savers for impersonal pieces of paper and impersonal institutions. The disdain for manual work means that the market for labor-saving devices is proportionately much smaller among middle-class families than among similar groups in North America. It is usually cheaper and certainly more "respectable" to hire a maid, a cook, and a yard man than to buy the numerous gadgets that middle-class North American husbands and wives use in doing the household chores themselves. Credit is difficult to come by, and interest rates are high. A man who invests his money in a business enterprise may expect a return of 30 per cent or more a year and is reluctant to take risks.

This pattern has permitted foreigners or local people of foreign extraction to develop large areas of business more by default than by competition. Much of the alleged "Yankee economic imperialism," despite some mistakes and excesses, has simply represented a movement of outside enterprise into areas of economic vacuum. In almost every country some middle-status intellectuals have recognized the economic weaknesses of the present pattern and have sought to remedy them through governmental action and institutions. In the last twenty-five years many governments have endeavored to provide parts of the structural framework which have traditionally been provided by private enterprise in the United States: development corporations to encourage investment, with the government supplying much of the capital and taking most of the risk; government-financing of large industrial projects; small-loan banks of various types; government insurance plans; and so on. Again, some critics see these as moves toward "socialism" and the "welfare state," but until or unless basic patterns are changed they will probably continue to grow in importance.

Although middle-group people are sensitive about the degrading symbolic effects of "manual labor," it is a gross libel to call them lazy or indolent. They habitually expend enormous amounts of personal energy when engaged in something they consider valuable or interesting. On the other hand, working just for the sake of keeping busy is not regarded as necessarily a good thing, and temporary idleness is not regarded as in itself immoral.

Within the realm of materialistic values, the mere manipulation of things in order to explore their mechanical or functional potentialities is not an all-engrossing interest. Most Latin Americans of the middle class are not dominated by a "mechanistic world view," nor are they usually moved by an urge to undertake systematic, empirical investigations. There have been few outstanding contributions to science, either basic or applied, and little solving of everyday material problems to which industrially more advanced peoples have applied the common-sense ingenuity developed from their long familiarity with machines and physical forces. There is ample evidence that Latin Americans are able to achieve success in the mechanistic arts, but traditionally they have not been much interested in them.

THE WEIGHT OF TRANSCENDENTAL VALUES

Of far more importance to most middle-status Latin Americans are what they often call spiritual or transcendental values—"the something beyond" *(lo algo más allá)*. Just as, to them, an individual has an inner essence and a dignity that may not be immediately apparent, so the universe and human experience are believed to have a deeper, not always manifest, meaning. Not all people can express this pattern of values succinctly, but much of the cultural behavior does so obliquely. The cultural life of the middle groups has an aesthetic tone which middle-class North Americans of today do not often permit themselves. Northrop see this as "aesthetic intuition." [15] And Iturriaga says, ". . . of the great cultural values—truth, goodness, justice, beauty, saintliness—the Mexican does not hesitate in his preference; beauty constitutes a force of gravity that attracts him. . . ." [16] "Literary activity is of such vital importance to the lives of Latin Americans," writes Torres Ríoseco, "that it may be said to occupy a position similar to that of economic interest in the life of North America. . . ." [17] And in philosophy, says Sánchez Reulet, Latin Americans "have a deep humanistic sense. They recognize the value of science and technology, but doubt that man can fulfill his destiny only by the road of science and technology. And in all this there is an exaltation of human creative energies, a constant insistence on the values of action and liberty." [18]

Nor are these views confined to professional "long-hairs" and "egg heads." In contrast to the tendency in the United States to regard the arts and philosophy as the exclusive province of ivory-tower specialists, among Latin American middle groups no one hesitates to pursue and display these interests. There it is not regarded as effeminate or eccentric to exhibit whatever talent one has. Even a businessman, before getting down to mundane matters, may display a verse he has written the night before or boast about his

---

15 F. S. C. Northrop, *The Meeting of East and West* (New York: Macmillan, 1946), p. 23.

16 Cited, p. 237.

17 Arturo Torres Ríoseco, *The Epic of Latin American Literature* (New York: Oxford University Press, 1956), p. 168.

18 Aníbal Sánchez Reulet, ed., *La filosofía latinoamericana contemporánea* (Washington: Pan American Union, 1949), p. 19.

children's prowess in music. The middle-status reader expects his newspapers to inform him of philosophical questions and to offer him good literature and art criticism. Practically every large newspaper carries at least one page of literary material daily, whereas few of them have a financial page with complete stock quotations and other business news. Interest in the aesthetic aspects of architecture and city planning has always been strong in Latin America. Even small provincial towns take pride in beautifying at least the central plaza. Publicly supported band concerts, theaters, orchestras, opera and stage companies, and art museums are taken for granted as part of urban life.

Although undoubtedly there are psychological factors involved in this search for "the ultimate" and "something beyond," it is surely these values that in large measure make life worth living for many Latin Americans of middle status, and it is foolhardy for North Americans who wish to be friends with them to ignore or disparage this cultural strand. It must be kept in mind that in the field of practical politics and international relations prominent holders of political office, civil servants, and diplomatic representatives are often writers, philosophers, or poets of international renown. They receive such posts not only because of their prestige, but also because of a genuine belief that their success in aesthetic pursuits fits them for posts of national responsibility and leadership. It is obvious that for such men and women, and for the middle groups they usually represent, a purely pragmatic approach to problems does not necessarily constitute the most effective appeal.

The emphasis upon words, ideals, and elegance of expression has been condemned by some Latin American critics.[19] One of the causes of instability in political life, as they see it, is the tendency to feel that the job is finished when written expression has been given to ideals, through

19 For example, Carlos Octavio Bunge, *Nuestra América: Ensayo de psicología social* (6th ed.; Buenos Aires: Administración General, 1918). This author is still quoted frequently by Latin American writers on this and other matters.

the composing of constitutions, party declarations, and statutes, while systematic, determined efforts to translate the verbalized ideals into reality often are wanting. Yet we must recognize that cultural idealism, even though occasionally naïve and falling short in adequate implementation, offers better prospects for progress than indifference or crass cynicism. In addition, it must not be forgotten that, along with the value they place on words and concepts, Latin Americans demonstrate a high degree of aptitude for logical thinking and clear statement.

Their consuming interest in ideas and sentiments also makes Latin Americans responsive to outside ideologies and emotional appeals. It is no accident that the slogans of the Four Freedoms, set forth in the Atlantic Charter, were eagerly accepted in Latin America, or that Marxist ideology has received careful study in many Latin American circles. Because of their admiration for a certain elegance in argumentation, Latin Americans are not slow to identify and ridicule inconsistencies and confusions which they perceive in U.S. propaganda. Nor is their enthusiasm aroused by what they often consider to be an undue emphasis on utilitarianism and pragmatism.

EMOTION AS FULFILLMENT OF THE SELF

For Latin Americans, to be alive is to feel strongly, and when one feels an emotion one should express it. Such expression is one of the openly approved values of the traditional culture. This deeply held value apparently is derived in part from the Iberian mother countries. It is difficult to find any parallel to it among the aboriginal peoples. As a rule the Indians are schooled to patterns that in public give the impression of passivity and taciturnity. Not so the average middle-status Latin American. He will usually speak his mind or, more properly, his feelings on almost any subject, given the slightest occasion. "The Spaniard," as Schurz puts it in sketching the Iberian background, "is a man of passion. . . . he may not do things according to reason or logic or cold calculation . . . but according to the light of intuition and the urge of strong feeling. He may even do something for no good reason at all, but only by the prompting of caprice. Then he will act under the blind impulse of *gana,* or the moving of the spirit." [20]

In Latin America many ordinary, "undistinguished" persons are among the most interesting conversationalists and impromptu storytellers in the world. Any mundane incident, such as a day's trip to the market, is often "milked" of all possible emotional content in the telling. And serious matters must customarily be expressed emotionally if they are to receive a positive response and interest. In politics the appeal to the emotions is, of course, ever present and frequently obscures other interests.

If all this is the positive aspect of the value attached to feeling, the negative facet is ennui or routine, which must be avoided or broken whenever possible. The most frequent expression of this urge is through the *fiestas* which occur at regular intervals throughout the year. The community *fiesta* serves as an occasion for renewing personal contacts and symbolizing social solidarity with a pleasant emotional overtone, in addition to being an escape from ennui. Laughter and *alegría* (happiness) are as important as the expression of more "serious" emotions. Latin Americans of most regions are particularly adept at the *chiste,* or joke, the play on words *(juego de palabras),* and the aphorism or proverb. In the exercise of this skill, sympathetic laughter and admiration are the storyteller's sole rewards. Witticism is also used with devastating effect in politics and other public affairs. This can lead, however, to the emotionalizing of issues which in other cultures may be examined in their practical context. North Americans, in contrast, are often criticized for being dry and cold.

---

[20] William Lytle Schurz, *This New World: The Civilization of Latin America* (New York: Dutton, 1954), p. 82.

THE SENSE OF FATALISM

Running through the other values which shape the outlook of the average member of the middle segments of Latin American society is the sense of fatalism. Perhaps it is less pervasive in Brazil than in the Spanish-speaking countries, but it is nowhere absent as an underlying factor in determining modes of behavior and attitudes. Its two general forms are those of heroic defiance and passive resignation. The first appears as a heightened expression of the value of personalism. Each person owes it to himself to strive, to mobilize and exert his inner resources, to live and die with *dignidad*. Yet, fate must ever be reckoned with and, for reasons beyond the control of man, it may often be unjust. As Unamuno expressed it in his classic statement, paraphrasing Sénancour: "And if it is nothingness that awaits us, let us so act that it will be an unjust fate." [21] This point of view has been accepted by many authors in Portuguese and Spanish America.

In the Spanish countries the bull fight *(corrida de toros)* is a dramatization of Man facing Death. The matador pits all his skill against the bull, which is Death incarnate. But he does it with finesse, with imperturbability, and with grace. If he is successful, Man has once more defied and conquered Death—for the time being. But in the next bull fate may show its hand, and the matador may fly through the air with his body ripped open, to fall a bloody, quivering mass on the sand. And fate can always win if, at "the moment of truth" when Man and Death face each other for the kill, the man's courage falters and he cringes, even in spirit. While the *corrida* is a dramatization of this theme staged before a great crowd of spectators, many a Latin American thinks of less spectacular situations as a continuation of the same dramatic struggle with fate. He sees himself as "acting out" the heroic theme in his own small way.

---

21 Miguel de Unamuno, *The Tragic Sense of Life,* tr. by J. E. Crawford Fitch (New York: Dover Publications, 1954), p. 263. (Original title, *Del sentimiento trágico de la vida,* 1912.)

The sense of fatalism may be manifested in the seemingly fanatical defiance of danger by soldiers and revolutionary mobs, in an apparent willingness to endure hardships disproportionate to the goal at hand and to take risks beyond all rationality. The elaborate cult of death, funerals, and graveyards is a further expression of the value attached to fatalism.

The theme of resignation, within the deep-lying sense of fatalism, is expressed in both "happy" and "melancholy" customs. A cheerful aspect is shown in the universal hope for good luck, of which the lottery is perhaps the most ubiquitous form. Its less optimistic aspect is seen as the mood swings into *tristeza,* a sort of sweet sadness, to which people surrender with pleasure. A crowd will ask a brass band in the park to play *un triste.* Friends around the tables then start drinking earnestly in the hope of working into a mood of sadness, meanwhile having the time of their lives. Much popular music and the accompanying words are sad, and melancholy poems appear every day to please the public.

In public life, fatalistic resignation may lead to what Bunge, the Argentine sociologist and critic, called "creole indolence" *(la pereza criolla),* a tendency to shirk the seeking of constructive solutions to problems.[22] In politics it has induced a general paralysis of action. In public health, one of the principal problems has been the ingrained belief that a certain amount of sickness and death is inevitable. It is "the will of God" or "fate." [23] As social mobility and the rewards of pragmatic ingenuity, combined with group action and the workability of democratic procedures, are demonstrated, the fatalistic complex will probably decline in importance.

From the viewpoint of social psychiatry, however, one advantage of the value associated with fatalism should per-

---

22 Cited, p. 18, and elsewhere.
23 George Foster, *A Cross Cultural Anthropological Analysis of a Technical Aid Program* (Washington: Smithsonian Institution, 1951; mimeographed), discusses this theme in several situations.

haps be mentioned here. The sense of the blind power of fate is combined, for most members of the middle groups at least, with the theme of striving, one of the values of "the person." An individual must strive to fulfill his inner potentialities as a unique person. If he fails, after having made "a good try," he is not torn by feelings of guilt, conscience, or inadequacy, which play a large part in the psychological aftereffects of failure in North American culture. For a Latin American who has "done his best," failure is due to the inscrutable ways of "fate" (or "the will of God"). It is not his personal "fault."

The Changing Life of Latin America

These are some of the basic values, rapidly sketched, which shape the outlook of the restive middle groups. They suggest the background of traditional culture from which this rapidly growing segment of Latin American societies is facing the turbulent changes of the present. Working today largely within these familiar ways of looking at life and human nature, the nations of Latin America and their leaders face new forces of change and challenge. If they come to terms with the new values which these forces present, they may emerge with a new cultural integration which will enable them to act strongly and independently in the free world. Or the clash of values may result in prolonged confusion and disorganization, terminating in surrender to some outside ideological system, such as that proffered by communism. Dramatic changes are taking place in the areas of demography and population, social structure and economic life, religion, political life, and international relations. Even a brief glance at these turbulent zones of change will help us to see older patterns of value being reshaped and new ones emerging.

POPULATION AND SOCIAL STRUCTURE

The population of Latin America as a whole is increasing much faster than that of North America, even taking into account the latter's stepped-up growth since World War II. Reliable estimates indicate that the total population of Latin America has passed that of the United States in the early 1950's.[24] Most experts believe that if present rates of increase continue, Latin America will have twice as many people as the United States by the end of this century. The rise in population is in large part due to new medical and public health programs, which have, for example, resulted in a marked reduction in the infant death rate. Present life expectancy averages about forty years at birth. The result is that the population is predominantly a young one, with higher proportions in the lower age categories that are unproductive economically and place a heavy burden on educational facilities.

The population of Latin America, according to Halperin's analysis, has risen faster than food production, and since World War II the city population has grown three times faster than the rural population, creating political and social tensions among the uprooted peasants who have migrated to the cities.[25] Furthermore, population pressures in traditionally more heavily settled areas have resulted in large-scale displacement and resettlement in more empty regions, as exemplified in the government-sponsored colonization of highland people in the Pacific littoral of Ecuador and Colombia, in parts of Guatemala, in the interior Minas Geraes area of Brazil, and in the Amazon regions of Peru.

As the population has been increasing in total numbers and changing its patterns of settlement, new aspects of social structure have been emerging. Some of these have been mentioned: the gradual disappearance of Indians as a distinct caste and their absorption into the national societies; the emergence of various segments of the middle class; the

---

24 *Statistical Yearbook, 1957,* 1957.XVII.1 (New York: United Nations, 1957); see also American Academy of Political and Social Science, *A Crowding Hemisphere: Population Change in the Americas* (Philadelphia: Author, 1958; *The Annals,* v. 316).

25 Maurice Halperin, "Latin America in Transition," *Science and Society,* Fall 1956, pp. 290-319.

growth of a new urban proletariat; the development of a moneyed upper class. The growth of the urban working class has been accompanied by the development of trade-unions. And these, in turn, have spread among the rural proletariat, for example, on the fruit plantations in Central America and among workers employed in the extractive industries, such as oil and large-scale mining. The new proletariat, in contrast with the old *peón* and servant lower classes, has also begun to display independent political power, usually organized and led by middle-group politicians who have recognized its potential.

Although illiteracy remains high in most countries in comparison with North America and Western Europe, it has been declining with growing rapidity, stimulated by technical and financial aid to education from the U.S. Point Four Program, the Organization of American States, and the United Nations. The spread of education accounts in part for the emergence of expanding middle groups in society. And it will probably continue to produce a certain "leveling up" of social status and outlook by giving many previously isolated subgroups a common educational background.

Finally, we must not overlook the emancipation of women and the redefinition of their roles in society. At present this is largely a middle-status phenomenon. In conservative circles and in some provincial centers women are still expected to follow the older pattern, confining their activities mainly to the home and the church. In the middle groups, however, their emergence into business and public affairs has been spectacular. Middle-status women work in clerical positions, as teachers, as trained nurses and hygiene experts, as physicians and lawyers, and in a variety of other callings. And many middle-status housewives who are not gainfully employed take part in activities of women's clubs similar to those now customary in the United States.

From the traditional point of view, one of the most startling phenomena is the rise of prominent women politicians. The cities of San Juan, Puerto Rico, and Santiago, Chile, have recently had women mayors, and women are serving as senators or congressmen in several legislatures, even that of tradition-bound Peru. Women have the vote in all countries except Paraguay. As previously indicated, girls have traditionally been subject to a more disciplined training in the home than boys, and as women they have assumed roles of great responsibility and stability in the household. However, it would be premature to say more than that the influence of middle-class women appears likely to expand considerably in the national life of Latin American countries.

IMPACT OF ECONOMIC CHANGES

Although all the national economies rely mainly on exporting raw materials, livestock, and foodstuffs to earn the bulk of their foreign exchange, the economic patterns are becoming steadily less "semicolonial." For one thing, over recent years many new contracts and other arrangements with large foreign-owned corporations have been designed to make the host countries partners in these basic enterprises. The oil companies in Venezuela have set a new pattern under agreements whereby they turn over approximately one-half of their gross profits to the national treasury, in addition to providing their workers with numerous benefits in health care, training, and housing. Since 1954 the United Fruit Company has negotiated agreements with most of the countries where it operates, turning over a minimum of 30 per cent of gross profits to the national treasury as well as providing a long list of other benefits.[26] In these major enterprises, both the labor force and all but a small percentage of the administrative and supervisory personnel are native to the country. In most of them labor is organized in unions, and a continuing program of train-

---

[26] Wayne C. Taylor, John Lindeman, and Victor López, *The Creole Petroleum Corporation in Venezuela* (1955); and Stacy May and Galo Plaza, *The United Fruit Company in Latin America* (1958); both published by the National Planning Association, Washington, D.C.

ing provides a new corps of specialists and executives drawn from the local middle class.

These changes in pattern are not due entirely to the generosity of the foreign concerns. They reflect the growing power and competence of segments of the middle groups in politics and economic life. The new technology and new industries have opened hundreds of new types of jobs as well as calling for vastly increased numbers of workers and employees to staff some of the older ones. These changes in the working force have produced important new blocs of people whose opinions and attitudes carry great weight. One of the main problems arising out of the rapid growth of technology and industry is the pressing shortage of scientists, engineers, and technicians. Higher education, dominated by the lofty values of transcendentalism, has traditionally emphasized the humanities and slighted the sciences. At present, the gap is being filled in part by training younger experts abroad, but many additions to the local educational curricula are needed. As more young Latin Americans are trained in these fields, we may expect to see develop a new source of prestige based on the practical management of human and natural resources, probably with a peculiarly Latin American flavor, perhaps involving "spiritual" and "personalistic" seasoning.

So long as Latin American economies continue to operate mainly on a basis of nationalistic self-sufficiency, it is unlikely that heavy industry can develop sufficiently to meet the major needs of most countries. Imports will continue to be required from North America, Europe, Japan, and elsewhere. However, several groups of countries have already experimented with regional tariff arrangements, and it is not impossible that economic "blocs" may emerge and become an important and stabilizing factor. On the other hand, the uneven distribution of subsoil resources means that complete national economic autarchy is impossible at present in any of these nations, and total self-sufficiency of Latin America as a unit is improbable. Latin America will

continue to be dependent upon trade, a fact which makes
for continued close ties with the outside world.

The system inherited from the colonial era, of large
landed estates held exclusively by the old aristocracy, with
its virtual monopoly of the more productive terrain, is
under attack throughout Latin America, and land reform
of some sort is a prominent plank in the political platforms
of all parties appealing to the middle and lower groups of
society. In some areas the redistribution of land and the
resettlement of peasants on new lands result in establishing
large numbers of independent farmers, as well as cooperative plantations and *ejidos;* the same changes are creating
new patterns in the techniques of work, the organization
of labor, and the location of economic power. As more and
more farm workers are released from peonage, they tend to
develop a new interest and a new stake in national affairs.

The technological revolution is changing the face of
Latin America at an unprecedented speed. In agriculture,
machinery is steadily replacing the labor of men and animals on large commercial plantations and cooperative
farms. In manufacturing, the growth of factories, although
not sensational, is proceeding apace, especially in consumers' goods, pharmaceuticals, and building materials.
Expanding industries have drawn large numbers of country people into urban life, with many new problems of
adaptation. Even in rural communities, electric or gasoline
flour mills are replacing the old household handstones.
Electricity, which brings not only light but also movies
and radio, as well as piped water systems, autobus transportation—with necessary improvement in roads and streets
—and factory-made furnishings and fixtures are coming to
be a part of everyday life. Technology is producing a rising
standard of community services and family living.

Finally, these manifold changes are effecting a marked
shift in the distribution of incomes, with an expanding
share of the national income going to the middle-status
groups and, in varying degrees, to organized labor. This
redistribution of income is bringing about many changes

in consumption patterns. To satisfy the new demands, the U.S.-style supermarket and department store are rapidly displacing the older types of shops in some metropolitan centers.

THE RELIGIOUS FERMENT

Regardless of the varying legal relationships of the Roman Catholic Church to the state, certain significant changes are apparent even on the surface.[27] In most regions, the active participation of laymen in Roman Catholic activities has been on the decline over several decades, along with their active adherence to the teachings of the clergy on secular affairs. The notion that communism, for example, cannot make headway in Latin America because the people there are "safely Catholic" can no longer be complacently accepted. The power of the clergy to influence public opinion has by no means disappeared, but there are few if any countries where it any longer dominates public opinion or action completely. In some areas several varieties of Protestantism have made significant inroads, particularly among persons who are moving upward on the social ladder. Most of the Protestant missionary sects, it is worth noting, emphasize interpretations of the Bible which exalt the "bourgeois" values associated with the rise of capitalism. The "Protestant ethic," however, is not widely disseminated. In contrast, spiritualistic cults, a not infrequent reaction to the difficulties of social uprooting and adaptation, have undergone an amazing growth in some areas, particularly in Brazil. The many social and educational changes in Latin American life work, on balance, toward

---

27 In eleven of the nineteen countries, church and state are officially separated: Brazil, Chile, Cuba, Ecuador, El Salvador, Guatemala, Honduras, Mexico, Nicaragua, Panama, and Uruguay; W. W. Pierson and Federico Gil, *Governments of Latin America* (New York: McGraw-Hill, 1957), p. 445. Although all countries constitutionally permit freedom of worship, in those where the church is "established," "public worship" may be defined and regulated by law. On this basis, interference with non-Catholic public worship has occurred in recent years in Peru and Colombia, and under Juan Perón restrictions were imposed on Roman Catholic activities in Argentina.

secularizing the middle-status man and weakening the traditional authority of the church.

Roman Catholic movements to bring the appeal of the church more into line with present-day needs have appeared here and there and may be expected to increase. The Third Order of St. Francis, for example, preaches the puritanical virtues and endeavors to limit the cult of saints and the extravagances of religious fraternities. Catholic trade-unions have been organized to protect the interests of the laboring classes. Many of the liberal or reform Catholic movements base their action on Pope Leo XIII's encyclical *Rerum Novarum* (1893). But, as one Catholic critic puts it, "unhappily, the Church in Latin America is not fully aware of the present social upheaval." [28] In the minds of many of the middle-status people, the church, if not regarded as an antiquated and expensive relic of no modern significance, is actively resented for its alleged "reactionary" position and its traditional support for the hereditary aristocracy, with its landed monopoly. Today, Latin America is no longer monolithically Roman Catholic, in the traditional sense, and new religious ferments are at work.

THE MIDDLE SEGMENTS AND THE POLITICS OF CHANGE

In the area of national politics all other factors of change find their ultimate focus. For one thing, the great majority of practicing politicians are of middle status, and a minority among them have recently climbed into the new upper class. With very few exceptions, the older aristocracy lacks large blocs of votes or other sources of political power. Generally speaking, it no longer commands the armed services. The lower classes, on the whole, have not yet developed the techniques necessary for political action except when leadership is provided by middle-status people. Even in those instances where conservatives have taken over the government because of divisions in the ranks of the opposition, as happened in Colombia in 1950 and in

---

[28] François Houtart, "Silent Revolution," *Commonweal*, July 22, 1955, p. 391.

Ecuador in 1956, the president and major officials of the government are usually men of middle status. The middle strata, however, are not united in their goals. They tend to divide along personalistic and ideological lines. In the United States there are few basic disagreements between the two major political parties regarding ultimate goals; they differ on how to reach the same generally shared objectives. This is not true of Latin America. Still dominated by traditional values, middle-status politicians are often deeply divided over both goals and methods.

The new technologies are having a varying impact on the conduct of politics. The expansion of mass communication and travel has brought about an increased interest and participation in politics throughout far wider circles of the people than before, even though the group in power may attempt to monopolize the channels of communication. On the other hand, modern technologies of armed force tend to make it easier for those who control them to suppress opposition. Today, in order to carry out a successful revolution without foreign help, it is necessary, first of all, to infiltrate and secure the adherence of an important sector of the officer corps. The old pattern of "rebellion in the backlands" is almost always doomed to failure without cooperation from some parts of the armed forces.

The responsibility for welfare-state services and their supporting structures has been assumed, or at least been given lip service, by all national governments. This trend is going forward regardless of whether the government of the moment is democratic or dictatorial. Both this development and the great increase in numbers and administrative complexity of all branches of government—finance, public works, banking, education, public relations—require, in Latin America as elsewhere, more and more technical experts and trained administrators. The role of this segment grows even under military rule. The officers of the armed forces often rationalize their frequent intervention in politics by their alleged impartiality in matters of party politics and also by their claim to be the only organ-

ized element capable of keeping order. Army officers, however, are not usually trained administrators of government
bureaus, and military regimes are more dependent than
ever before on trained and experienced civilian personnel.

Practically everywhere the old division between liberal
and conservative political parties has broken down. In
countries where more than one party is permitted,[29] the
numerous parties that have filled the resulting void have
been notoriously unstable, personalistic, and irresponsible,
with one outstanding exception. This is the Communist
party, whether operating under that label or not, and
whether in the open or underground. This party offers a
plausible platform or program from which it rarely devi-
ates in principle. It displays cohesion and discipline among
its members. It has also shown itself adept at making surface compromises and expedient alliances, as in the days
of the "Popular Front" in Chile.

Although the number of hard-shell Communists is small
at present and the party is legal only in Mexico, Colombia,
Ecuador, Argentina, Venezuela (since the revolution of
1958), Cuba, and Uruguay, its influence is vastly greater
than its numbers.[30] The Communists have gained many
supporters among middle-group intellectuals. Describing
the Guatemalan situation under Jacobo Arbenz Guzmán
(1951-1954), the State Department's study said: "At first
the older administration parties tried to form alliances
omitting the new Communist groups, but they failed to
develop a non-Communist revolutionary ideology as
cement, and the alliances one by one fell of their internal
dissensions." [31] Arbenz himself, probably not a Communist
on taking office, apparently came increasingly under the
influence of party members, largely because they were the
most efficient political group for getting things done for

---

[29] In several countries only one "party" is at present permitted,
notably the Dominican Republic and Paraguay.

[30] Membership is estimated at about 200,000, or less than two-tenths
of one per cent of the population; Pierson and Gil, cited, p. 328.

[31] Intervention of International Communism in Guatemala, cited, p.
73.

the administration.[32] Whether the democratic parties will, in the face of Communist efficiency, improve their own organizations and operations remains to be seen. Unfortunately, financial and other forms of personal aggrandizement, rather than party solidarity behind programs and principles, are still a frequent motivation for many of their members and leaders.

In summary, it is doubtful that a democratic system closely resembling that of the United States will soon, if ever, develop in Latin America. The cultural and social backgrounds and forces within which democracy must develop in Latin America are very different from those of the United States. But there is no reason to think that truly democratic patterns adapted to the requirements of Latin American societies will not evolve in time, provided the people have the opportunity to perceive the rewards that democratic government can bring them. One purpose of U.S. foreign policy must be to foster in every way possible the demonstration of the lasting benefits of democratic freedom and institutions.

Perhaps the outstanding factor which molds Latin America's relations today with the United States is the attitude of extreme nationalism publicly assumed and fostered by the more articulate leaders in all countries. This is combined with frequent defensive reactions against suspected U.S. attempts to infringe upon their sovereignty in the political, economic, or cultural spheres. The fires of suspicion and sensitivity are constantly kindled and stoked by astute anti-American propaganda, chiefly but not exclusively Communist-inspired.

Yet, in every country there are growing cadres of people, chiefly in the middle strata, who have formed a sympathetic understanding of the North American way of life, without thereby feeling disloyal to their own basic cultural values. They are aware that a mutual give and take between the two great cultural areas of the Western Hemisphere does

---

[32] John Gillin and K. H. Silvert, "Ambiguities in Guatemala," *Foreign Affairs*, April 1956, pp. 469-482.

not inevitably mean the stamping out of the virtues of
either. There is no need for Latin Americans to assume that
the borrowing of certain pragmatic and scientific ap-
proaches to their problems entails the loss of their own
spiritual values in exchange for a "crass materialism."
There is no need for them to think so, unless our policies
and our actions in Latin America should leave them no
other visible alternative.

Some Suggestions for U.S. Policy

What do these social changes and the new social forces
mean for the United States' relations with Latin America?
The following suggestions are offered by a layman speaking to other laymen, in the belief that no policy can be
more effective than the force of public opinion makes it.

First, the ferments of the continuing revolution, the
ideological and social changes, in Latin America must be
closely followed by up-to-the-minute reporting, research,
and analysis. Policy made on the basis of old news frequently turns into bad news. From the point of view of
U.S. security, Latin America, because of its very proximity,
is one of the more important world areas. Although not
highly developed industrially, Latin America does not
belong in the same category of "underdeveloped areas"
as do certain parts of Africa, Asia, and Oceania, whose
cultures have hitherto been neither European nor modern.
For more than four and one-half centuries Latin America
has had a part in that style of life we call Western civilization, meanwhile developing its own version of it. Its
leaders are determined to guide it into full participation
in the modern world. Neither conditions nor the leaders'
reactions to U.S. policies can be taken for granted without
running great risks.

A practical need in this respect is the establishment of
a central research institute for Latin America somewhere
in the United States, preferably close enough to Washington to be accessible for consultation by policy-makers. Such

an institute should have access to a full range of information, in addition to carrying out investigations under its own auspices.

The full information required includes a close analysis of programs and propaganda emanating from the Soviet bloc. To many North Americans all Communist-inspired moves appear subversive, but it would be shortsighted to ignore the conditions and problems which make them appealing to many Latin Americans.

Second, while the United States is prepared to cooperate in the modernization of Latin America by financial credits, know-how, and moral support, all such projects should be planned and carried out with full attention and respect to the traditions, honor, and intelligence of the Latin Americans. A Good Neighbor does not patronize nor does he expect his friends to transform their ways into exact copies of his own.

Third, U.S. plans and programs must be drawn up and carried out in full coordination. In the recent past certain Latin American countries have received a variety of U.S. "missions" or field parties, each with a praiseworthy program of its own, but each working on its own. Public health, agricultural, educational, and military missions, for example, usually report separately to their respective Washington headquarters and maintain no more than friendly or bowing relations with each other in the country to which they are assigned. As Latin Americans have often pointed out to me, such a lack of over-all plan leaves many *grietas abiertas* (open cracks), into which the Communists and their friends do not hesitate to penetrate. Each nation is a complex whole. An economic policy must be judged not only in terms of its probable effects on national production and consumption, the balance of payments, the banking system, and other strictly economic aspects of the situation. Its influence must also be measured with respect to its effects on the various social segments of the nation, on ideological interpretations, political movements, and so on.

Likewise, a policy with respect to any one Latin American nation must be examined for its possible repercussions throughout the area.

Fourth, it is in the interests of both the United States and the new Latin American leadership that the former should prove to be not only a symbol of democracy and progress, but also a reliable partner in the practical achievement of these goals. Even when it is indirect or temporary, U.S. support of dictatorships undercuts its support among friends of democracy and provides local critics of the "Colossus of the North" with free opportunities to create confusion and sow distrust. Each situation, of course, presents a special case, and sweeping generalizations are dangerous. But it is certainly desirable for the United States to establish a general image of itself throughout Latin America as the friend of responsible democrats and liberals and an opponent of dictatorships of the right or the left. In this connection North Americans need to give closer attention to their military policy in Latin America. In respect to each country, it is important to know whether gifts or loans of arms and machines of war actually strengthen U.S. and hemisphere security or merely provide means for the consolidation of dictatorships.[33]

Fifth, much could be done to bring U.S. public and private foreign policies in Latin America into a common focus. In some Latin American regions the activities, installations and personnel of one or more large North American business corporations are more visible than the embassy or the official missions. Large business concerns have realized only recently that they are in effect representing the United States as well as their own private interests, and in recent years many of them have begun to devote more attention to their local public relations and to the public image they create in the minds of leaders and people. Coordination of policies does not mean domination by the Department of State, but it should mean a

---

[33] For a fuller discussion see Edwin Lieuwen, *Arms and Politics in Latin America* (New York: Praeger, for the Council on Foreign Relations, 1960).

friendly and cooperative relationship between official and private U.S. policies that could in turn win the friendship and the good will of representative official and private elements in Latin America.

Sixth, the United States must be prepared to support projects and movements that are needed for the development of Latin America, even though they are not always within the "free enterprise" context as understood in North America. For example, in some countries large economic development programs must be carried out by public bodies set up for the purpose, for want of local capital and private organizational experience. It is essential that their management and control be in the hands of persons committed to the values of the free world, and this can be encouraged more readily if U.S. policy is helpful and sympathetic. A tendency for American representatives to label as "socialistic" or "communistic" everything that does not strictly conform to U.S. patterns may have the effect of stimulating many idealistic Latin Americans to identify themselves with real Communist movements and groups.

Seventh, in view of the still persistent personalistic value in Latin American culture it is essential for U.S. representatives to develop sympathetic personal contacts with the leadership elements of the middle groups and learn to appreciate their sometimes hazy aspirations. In the past, North American diplomatic and business people have all too frequently confined their personal relations to the very rich, cosmopolitan, or Americanized segments of the national society, and consequently have had no firsthand comprehension of the subsurface trends of change. Latin Americans love to argue and to deal with general concepts, if this is done in a friendly atmosphere. They are quick to grasp new ideas and to appreciate sound logic. And the emotional aura of human relations in a common confrontation of "fate" possesses great value. On the other hand, American attempts to settle arguments or solve problems by resort to superior force, economic power, or snobbish prestige will often result in a fanatic and "heroic" opposition, regardless of its practical consequences.

It is entirely within the realm of possibility—provided the United States shows no comprehension of the values and urgencies of the social revolution now going forward in Latin America—that some or all of the nations to the south will choose the path of stubborn opposition to the "Colossus of the North" or even decide that they can best fulfill their aspirations by seeking the protection of the Communist bloc. This need not happen if both North Americans and Latin Americans learn to understand each other's cultures and needs.

Ultimately, it is the task of U.S. policy to lay a general groundwork for a better understanding of the common interests and shared aspirations of the two Americas, so that detailed policies of the nations may be spontaneously brought into harmony as new or unforeseen problems demand solutions. Once this is accomplished, such "explosions" as may occur will not be painfully surprising or unmanageable, and Latin America will be encouraged to move forward into full participation in the affairs of the modern world by developing its great human and material potential, without illusions concerning the mirages offered by Moscow, and without fears of its big neighbor to the north.[34]

---

[34] This chapter was written before the publication of Professor John J. Johnson's important book (*Political Change in Latin America: The Emergence of the Middle Sectors* [Stanford University Press, 1958]) and without knowledge of its preparation. It is significant that two students should independently focus upon the importance of the middle segments of Latin American society. My first treatment of these matters was published in Spanish in 1956. See John Gillin, "Cultura emergente," in Jorge Luis Arriola, ed., *Integración Social en Guatemala* (Guatemala City: Seminario de Integración Social Guatemalteca, 1956).

Two

CHANGING COMMUNITY ATTITUDES AND VALUES IN PERU: A CASE STUDY IN GUIDED CHANGE

by ALLAN R. HOLMBERG

IN OUR dealings with Latin Americans we North Americans often fail to realize that the ways of life of many of our southern neighbors are grounded in assumptions and imperatives which differ in many important respects from those of our own society. It is difficult for us to realize, for example, that the "American dream" of equal opportunity for everyone, of peace, prosperity, and happiness for all, does not have the same appeal everywhere. For a great many Latin Americans these goals have never been highly valued. Indeed, for many they are completely outside the range of their experience. A widespread ignorance of each other's cultures has led on both sides to many misunderstandings and has left behind many distorted images.

Whether we like it or not, both North Americans and Latin Americans have to learn to live together in the modern world. But getting along well together—establishing relations of mutual understanding, benefit, and respect—does not mean we have to conform to their standards of value or they to ours. To arrive at rational policies in our dealings with Latin America, and to implement them persuasively, we must have a better understanding of the basic institutional structures and the value systems of the

Latin American nations themselves. Only then can we appraise the potential effects of current influences from the outside, including those which come from the United States, and go on to formulate useful policies for the future. In this study I propose to touch on these problems as they relate to one single country, Peru.

Peru: The Historical Setting for Change

Few nations of Latin America can point to a more ancient and distinguished cultural heritage than Peru, where the beginnings of civilization go back many centuries. The earliest remains show that more than 5,000 years ago the irrigated valleys of the desert coast—the "fertile crescent" of the New World—already supported settled and industrious populations. Gradually, as these valleys came to support larger and larger populations through the development of irrigation and agriculture, distinctive civilizations and even empires grew strong. Indeed, long before the arrival of the Spaniards, there were large and thriving urban centers in most of the oases of the desert coast. The city of Chan Chan for example, the capital of the Chimu empire, whose vast remains lie well preserved just outside the modern city of Trujillo, is estimated by archaeologists to have had a population of some 200,000 inhabitants.

Parallel developments were also taking place in the intermontane valleys of the Andes, as evidenced by the massive ruins of Chavín de Huántar, which lie on the east slopes of the Cordillera Blanca, in north-central Peru. In the first half of the fifteenth century, however, the situation changed drastically. A relatively small and well-organized group, now known as the Incas, who had previously been confined to a small region of mountain valleys in southern Peru, began a period of warlike expansion which, in less than a hundred years, established their rule from Ecuador in the north to Chile in the south, and from coast to jungle. The Inca empire had from six to eight

million subjects within its domain, the richest and the
most populous state in pre-Columbian America. Its capital,
Cuzco, then a city of over 200,000 people, is a striking
monument to the Incas' power and wealth.

After overthrowing this great Indian empire, the Spaniards, bent on exploiting Peru for the crown and themselves, gradually wrought profound changes in the patterns
of life which they found there. Peru was stripped of much
of its manpower and wealth, and Spanish colonial institutions were implanted firmly throughout the realm. The
new rulers imposed a rigid class system, with a small
Spanish elite at the top and a great mass of Indians at the
bottom. The new landowners introduced a highly commercialized economic system based on the use of money
and on competition in the international market, where
no market had existed before, and they consolidated
their power through the *encomienda,* or entail, and later
through the *hacienda,* or plantation estate. By these
changes the original population was reduced to a state
of social and economic disrespect which persists to the
present day. Both the empire of the Incas and that of the
Spaniards were rigidly stratified along class lines. Thus,
the concept of a natural and hierarchical ordering of society, based on an aristocratic tradition, has been an all-
pervasive and dominant theme throughout the history of
Peru. The masses of the people, whether Indian or *mestizo,*
have been ruled by a small and dominant minority, often
with an iron hand. No change that has yet occurred, unless
it be the new technological revolution now taking place,
has done much to alter this basic fact.

In spite of recent changes, Peru as a whole represents
a fairly rigidly stratified social system. Out of a total population of over nine million people, more than three million are still classified as Indians. Most of them follow a
way of life derived from the pre-Spanish era, modified, of
course, by the aftereffects of colonial rule which assigned
the Indians to the lowest status within the caste-like social
structure. In this respect, the Andean countries, partic-

ularly Ecuador, Peru, and Bolivia, stand somewhat apart from the other nations of South America. Moreover, unlike Mexico and more recently Bolivia, Peru has undergone no sharp break with its traditional past in the form of a profound political and social revolution. In it, political power is still closely held and social changes are affecting the various segments of the people and the various regions of the country at widely differing rates of speed and impact.

The Geographical Setting and Social Change

As a habitat for man, Peru has been abundantly blessed and mightily cursed by nature. It contains majestic mountains and fertile valleys, interspersed with barren wastes and impenetrable jungles. On one point there is substantial agreement. Peru is a land of fantastic geographic and climatic contrasts among and within its three principal geographic areas—the coast, the mountains, and the jungle.[1]

The coastal plain is a vast desert. Because of cold offshore currents in the Pacific, the prevailing westerly winds lose their moisture before they reach the shore, and the trade winds from the east discharge theirs before crossing the maritime range of the Andes. Consequently, that part of Peru lying between the coast and the higher peaks of the coastal range, a strip of about 1,400 miles in length and from 20 to 80 miles in width, is rainless the year around.

Nevertheless, the coast is the most important part of Peru, economically, socially, and politically. The Pacific offers ready access to the outside world while the Andes provide the rich, silt-bearing rivers which irrigate large, fan-like valleys of the desert coast and make this region the most productive agricultural area of Peru. Some forty

---

[1] For a useful review of geographic and demographic factors, see Thomas R. Ford, *Man and Land in Peru* (Gainesville: University of Florida Press, 1955).

or more of these valleys, divided by barren wastes of twenty to fifty miles in width, crisscross the coastal plain. For lack of water, however, only about 5 per cent of the desert coast, which in turn constitutes only about 10 per cent of the total area of the country, is actually under cultivation.

From the coastal plain, and sometimes directly from the sea, rises the Andean mountain chain, covering about 40 per cent of the total area. By almost any standards the Andes constitute a formidable barrier to human habitation and economic development, for the arable part, or *sierra,* consists of a series of intermontane valleys, whose floors are at about 8,000 feet in altitude, overtowered by the high wall of the Andes. The even loftier *altiplanos,* or high plains, at 12,000 feet or more, are suitable for little except grazing.

A third geographical area, the *montaña,* or jungle, covering about 50 per cent of the total area, encompasses the eastern foothills of the Andes and some parts of the Amazon flood plain. Belonging to the Amazon drainage basin, the whole area, potentially rich in natural resources, lacks both the communications and population necessary for its further development. It is the home of aboriginal tribes of the Amazon basin. Historically, this has been the least significant geographical area of Peru.

Population Distribution and Social Structure

Peru is a nation of relatively unintegrated plural societies. The Quechua and Aymara Indians, for example, are but two instances of fragmented social communities, separated from each other and from the nation as a whole by geographic, linguistic, and cultural differences. More significant for our discussion are two major groupings, *mestizos* and Indians. The coast, which contains about 25 per cent of the total population, is almost exclusively a *mestizo* area; it is rapidly moving toward a commercial agricultural and industrial economy, with a mobile social structure founded on an essentially dynamic system of

values. In many respects, it is not unlike some parts of the
United States.

The inter-Andean valleys and the high plains of the
mountain areas, on the other hand, contain a high percentage of Indians, as well as lower-class *mestizos;* this
population lives by traditional subsistence farming, under
a fairly rigid social structure founded on an essentially
static and fixed system of values. Between these two
worlds, *mestizo* and Indian, a rather sharp division of culture and outlook, which grew up during colonial times,
persists down to the present day. In language, social and
political organization, and values, the two groups, although dependent on each other, represent quite distinct
modes of life. This fact constitutes one of the major dilemmas now faced by Peru in striving for national unity and
social and economic progress—goals which are given constant lip service, at least, by middle-class policy-makers.

In Peru the distinction between *mestizos* and Indians is
attributed in part to an imputed racial inferiority of the
Indian, derived from colonial times. However, over the
past four hundred years, the population has become pretty
thoroughly mixed biologically. In Peru today, as in other
"Indian" countries of Latin America, the assignment of
an individual to the subordinate group is not determined
primarily on the basis of physical characteristics such as
skin color, as in the case of the Negro in the United States.
It rests largely on a configuration of cultural characteristics, among which language, dress, and manners are most
important. A person who speaks an Indian language, wears
homespun dress, and chews coca will be classed as an Indian. If the same person speaks Spanish, wears Western
dress and does not chew coca he may be classed—depending on other characteristics such as family name, occupation, education, and wealth—as either *mestizo* or white.
In a biological sense, at least, Peru has no racial problem.
Its so-called "racial" problem is largely a cultural one.

The problem of achieving a homogeneous national culture is further complicated by the factor of geographical

and cultural regionalism. If there are sharp differences between coast and *sierra*, the same is also true of the inter-Andean valleys, which differ greatly in population and culture because of the barriers which the Andes pose to ready communication between them. Historically, this has resulted in a considerable proliferation of local differences in language and culture within both Indian and *mestizo* groups. Even within the two major Indian languages, Aymara and Quechua, the latter contains a number of mutually unintelligible dialects.

The wide span of cultural differences is reflected in and reinforced by the distribution of the *mestizo* and Indian populations. About 70 per cent of the total population of Peru is rural. On the other hand, Lima, with its port, Callao, is the only city of major commercial, industrial, and political importance. Other urban centers, with few exceptions, are little more than farming towns or mining centers. By and large, the *mestizos,* most of whom belong to the lower class, predominate in departmental, provincial, and district capitals of both the coast and the *sierra.* The Indian population, on the other hand, is concentrated on large *haciendas* or in so-called indigenous communities of the highlands, often isolated physically from the *mestizo* world. Of a total of about three million Indians in Peru, roughly one million live as landless *peones* on *haciendas,* one million as small but independent farmers in indigenous communities, and one million detached from the land as workers in mines and *mestizo* villages or as migrant laborers and servants. While most of the Indians live separated from the *mestizos* by caste barriers and physical isolation, the *hacienda* Indians probably occupy the lowest position, economically and socially, of all Indian groups. At the top of the status hierarchy, and centered on the coast, stands a very small upper-class elite which is considered white.

At least in part because of this hierarchical ordering of society, which has remained until recently in a kind of static equilibrium, the relations of the individual to the

community and of the community to the nation are very
different from those which are considered customary in the
United States and in some other Latin American nations.
Dependence and submission, rather than independence
and freedom, characterize social relations within the community and these same themes tend to govern relations between the community and the nation. In other words, at
one level the *mestizo* is *patrón* of the Indian; at another,
the government is *patrón* of the community. The close
holding of power, characteristic both of the *patrón-peón*
system and of dictatorial governments, has tended to forestall and discourage any local initiative for change. Moreover, since many governments in Peru—like many *patrones*
of *haciendas*—have often played far from beneficent roles,
community attitudes toward government like those of
peón toward *patrón,* have frequently been hostile and
aggressive.

Present Trends of Change

The traditional system is now being subjected to many
inroads. Today there are few communities but that have
been touched, however lightly, by the technological revolution. Coca Cola, the tin can, penicillin, and even the
wrist watch and radio have penetrated to the most remote
haciendas of the Andes. More important, there has been
going on a shift of political power from the landowning
aristocracy of the older type to a more commercially
minded *hacendado* and a new entrepreneurial class. This
has been matched by a shift in ideology, away from the
maintenance of the *status quo,* toward the demand for a
more mobile society, one which can eventually provide
sources of skilled labor and a solid market for manufactured goods. Industrialization, of course, has been responsible for most of these changes and demands.

For better or worse, however, the effects of these changes
have thus far been confined largely to the coastal region—
to the big-scale commercial *haciendas* and the urban
centers. In the *sierra* changes are much less apparent. The

coast has been and is the high-status area of Peru; Lima is the Mecca of prestige, power, and wealth. To gain stature in the social system, a Peruvian literally comes down from the heights of the Andes, he does not go up. Apart from a business venture or a week end in the mountain air, there is little movement of a permanent nature from coast to *sierra*. Such a shift can bring on not only physical *soroche* (mountain sickness), but "social *soroche*" as well. On the other hand, as a Peruvian comes down from the mountains and takes root in the coastal area, he not infrequently forgets all about the mountain valley where he grew up.

This raises what is perhaps Peru's most serious social issue. Frequently referred to as the "Indian problem," it might better be called the problem of the *sierra* or the mountain region as a whole, for it involves *mestizos* as well as Indians. The *sierra* is still the backbone of the Peruvian nation, almost as much as in Inca and colonial times. It contains Peru's major resources, natural and human.[2] Yet, by comparison with what the *sierra* has contributed and could contribute to the nation as a whole, it has received relatively little in return. Most of its wealth and its best manpower are siphoned off to the coast. In my opinion, until new attitudes toward the *sierra* are accepted both in the *sierra* and on the coast, particularly new attitudes toward the indigenous population, Peru is destined to remain a relatively "underdeveloped" nation.

Of course, many changes have recently been taking place in some types of *sierra* communities. Since the 1930's, and indeed even before that, an active program of road-building has greatly lessened the isolation of the highlands from the coast. It is possible now to go by car and truck to most *mestizo* towns and villages of the highlands, even though they are often cut off in the rainy season. Although trade has increased greatly between highlands and coast, most of

---

2 I have not considered the *montaña*, or jungle, region because it is still largely unpopulated, and mass migrations to it are not likely to take place in the immediate future. Much capital will be needed to develop this area.

the many changes that have followed have been technological, not social or ideological, in character. The one exception has been the tenure of the APRA party.[3] Although
APRA took important steps toward breaking the caste barriers, spreading power more widely, reforming the land
system, and promoting higher standards of living and education among Indians and lower-class *mestizos,* it was overthrown before it could consolidate these gains. Since the
failure to bring social change to the most numerous, isolated, and depressed groups, the processes of change have
reverted to the traditional social channels and therefore
are felt primarily in *mestizo* communities. The gap between social groups is widened in turn by the fact that
influences coming from the coast to the highlands are carried there largely by *mestizos* who subscribe to upper-class
values, among which "keeping the Indian in his place"
ranks high. Consequently, Indian communities, particularly *hacienda* communities, have remained much the
same.

One by-product of the growing contacts of *mestizo* highland villages with the coast deserves special mention.
Increased geographical mobility has led many young *mestizos,* both men and women, to leave their *sierra* villages for
greener pastures in urban centers and on the coast. In one
such *mestizo* village a community study found relatively
few people between sixteen and forty.[4] As no one is left
except the Indians to do the work, *mestizo* villages in the
sierra have come to depend more and more on the surrounding Indian population.

More and better roads have, of course, also had their
effects on Indian villages. Though in the highlands most
large *haciendas* and many Indian communities still lack
roads to connect them with the highway system, they all

---

3 Alianza Popular Revolucionaria Americana, the party headed by
Víctor Raúl Haya de la Torre; the latter has recently been in Peru
again after a long period of exile.

4 See Humberto Ghersi, *El indigena y el mestizo en la communidad
de Marcara,* Ph.D. thesis, University of San Marcos, Lima, 1954.

have access to some market town which is tied in with it. Yet, the greatly increased geographical mobility of the Indians has had little effect on their highland communities. The explanation is not far to seek. It is possible, though not easy, for an Indian to move to the coast and become assimilated in *mestizo* society. Within the *sierra,* however, it is much more difficult for him to lose his identity as an Indian. Strong pressures operate within and between both castes, Indian and *mestizo,* to keep him in his place.

Frequently an Indian who has lived on the coast as a worker or a soldier, has enjoyed a higher standard of living and a period of freedom from the rigid pattern of village custom, and has learned Spanish and adopted new values and attitudes, finds himself in a situation of considerable conflict when he returns to his highland village. He is no longer satisfied to conform to Indian standards, yet he is not accepted by *mestizo* society. Within his Indian community, where standing is based on age and wealth, he finds no channels through which to express his coast-acquired enlightenment and skills. By *mestizo* society, where prestige is based largely on descent, he is again assigned to the lower caste.

What can the "displaced" Indian do? He can go native again, sometimes under worse conditions than before because pressure on the land has been mounting. He can return to the coast. There, because of increased immigration and the lag in economic development, opportunities for employment better than he can find in the highlands have been steadily falling behind the growing demand. As a result, while individual Indians are being increasingly assimilated into the national society, the communities from which they come remain much the same. This situation is likely to prevail unaltered until some direct attack is made on the traditional caste structure. Only then will it be possible to foster social and cultural change among the Indian population in their own villages.

Perhaps the greatest barrier to any change in this social system is the persistence in the *sierra* of an outmoded but powerful institution, the haciendas or latifundia. In many respects this institution, which governs the lives of more than one million Indians, does not differ substantially from what it was in Spain of the Middle Ages. Yet, there is encouraging evidence that, where Indians live under conditions of greater independence and freedom as they do in indigenous non-hacienda communities, changes in attitudes, values, and behavior are occurring at a faster rate. In many non-hacienda villages, which have owned their own lands from pre-Columbian times and have enjoyed a large measure of local autonomy, the spirit of community solidarity and cooperation is fairly strong.

This does not hold true for the haciendas, in which the individual's sense of responsibility to' the group and the continuity of effective local leadership were largely destroyed under the colonial regime. In terms of fostering a modern and even democratic development, the non-landlord Indian communities do not present nearly as great or as many problems as do the haciendas or the mestizo villages, for their built-in traditions of responsible local leadership enable them to act as a group. When they feel threatened by the outside world, they can defend themselves jointly against it; when attracted by it, they have group mechanisms for adjusting to the desired change.[5]

---

[5] Perhaps a note of caution should be injected at this point. There exists in Peru and abroad a somewhat distorted image of the indigenous peoples of the Andes as fundamentally cooperative and among whom the group spirit runs high. In this view, some four hundred years of harsh and brutal exposure to the outside world have done little to upset the collectivistic patterns which were a heritage of pre-Columbian times. The evidence usually cited is that over one million Indians still live in "indigenous communities" where they share and share alike, and that even on haciendas cooperative patterns are the rule. Actually this is not so. Present research indicates that, while it is true that the indigenous populations are united to a man when it comes to defending the group against the outside world, for example against an encroachment upon their lands, internally they are little influenced by a spirit of group loyalty or altruism. Individualism runs high in most indigenous communities, particularly in haciendas. Social responsibilities seldom extend beyond immediate kinship groups. For this reason, it is likely that the differential distribution of such values as power and wealth is as marked in most Indian communities as in the population at large. This appears

This is in sharp contrast to the *hacienda* system where the *patrón* alone holds the reins of power and where his interests are strongly opposed to those of the group, or even to *mestizo* villages over which the national administration exerts a centralized control, sometimes with a very strong hand.

In order to catch up with the modern world, Peru must break the chain of dependency relationships that bind all levels of the present social structure. Both the caste structure of the society and the latifundia system of the *sierra* are destined to disappear. In fact, they are already doomed. The question is whether they will disappear in a fairly gradual and orderly manner, as has happened in many parts of the coast, or whether this change will take place suddenly and by more drastic means, as in Mexico and Bolivia.

Present trends indicate that Peru may succeed in gradually assimilating the Indian and other depressed populations into the wider national community by peaceful means if the government continues a policy of giving more and more active encouragement to the *sierra* in the fields of education, health, and economic development. If these policies are not continued and strengthened, there may well arise a pan-Indian or pan-peasant movement, as in Bolivia, which would usurp the power of government and initiate drastic reform. In this connection, it is significant that in Peru the strongest center of Communist activity is in Cuzco, the former capital of the Inca empire.

Peru's Indian Problem

Valiant efforts have been made and are being made by the national government, as well as by international and private agencies operating in Peru, to offset the dangers of the unbalanced development of some regions to the neglect of others. The *sierra* has long been recognized as

---

to be the case at least in most areas where modern research has been carried out.

a problem, and the *montaña* has been pictured, quite un-realistically, as a future paradise. Yet, both the financial resources available and the training of the people have been sadly inadequate to foster the industrial development of any but the coastal regions, with the exception of some mining areas, which, however, contain a relatively small part of the total population.

It has been relatively easy to modernize and industrial-ize the large *haciendas* of the coast. As a result of the im-proved standards of living and education, the people of this area have largely assimilated the values of a modern industrial society, at least to a point where they can now move ahead under their own steam as rapidly as economic factors will permit. The plain fact of the matter is, how-ever, that the coast does not have the immediate economic potential to absorb the accelerating migrations from the *sierra* that have been taking place in recent years. Both the push exerted by pressure on land in the *sierra* and the pull of the positive attractions of the coast, with its higher wages and better standards of living, have created an un-balanced type of development within Peru as a whole, a situation that gives rise to great concern. So grave has this problem become, in fact, that a few years ago the national congress gave serious thought to prohibiting further mi-grations from the highlands to the coast. However unreal-istic this attempt at a solution would be, policy-makers have come increasingly to recognize that, if Peru is to achieve any kind of integrated development as a nation, more attention must be paid to the neglected areas, the highlands and the jungle.

Peru's basic problems in developing its vast jungle areas are going to be technical and economic in character. What they need above all is more people and more capital. Given the economic situation of Peru, these are not likely to be supplied in the directly foreseeable future. The *sierra* also suffers from overpopulation, as well as from a lack of capi-tal, but in addition its people are poorly equipped to face the stresses of adjusting rapidly to the industrial influences exerted by the coast. Herein lie difficulties of the greatest magnitude. Recent governments, it is true, have recognized that the maldistribution of population cannot be solved solely through migration to the coast. Through encouraging private investment in the overpopulated *sierra,* backed by the state-owned Santa Corporation, the Peruvian government is trying to create many new jobs in the valleys of the *sierra,* especially in processing locally produced commodities and in small-scale industries.

Nevertheless, the success of new developments in industry and agriculture in the mountain areas will depend primarily on the ability of the Indian and *mestizo* subsistence farmers, often landless, to make a reasonably satisfactory adjustment to a new way of life based on commercial agriculture and industry. Now living under the domination of whites and *mestizos,* the Indians are too poor to buy land, even when it comes on the market, and the land on which they live has been steadily declining in fertility. In many instances, they are obliged to work off tenant obligations without pay. They are badly undernourished and are without health and educational facilities. Many are victims of coca and alcohol.

These and other frustrating conditions have combined to produce in the Indian communities deep-seated attitudes of distrust, fear, suspicion, and even hate toward the outside world. Precisely because of these attitudes, they have so far resisted and are likely to go on resisting the halfhearted, piecemeal, unintegrated attempts at modernization which have been initiated thus far by more "enlightened" *hacendados* and industrialists or by the Peruvian government. The plain fact is that social and economic conditions among the highland populations, especially the Indians, have reached such an alarming state that only a large-scale and well-coordinated effort to promote change can enable them to find a place in the modern world, by making them a productive force in an emerging democratic society.

Studies that have been made of highland communities

in Peru clearly support the logic of undertaking a broad and integrated approach to change among the Indians. In fact, this is the only approach with much promise of winning enthusiastic acceptance among the Indians. Beneath a profoundly pessimistic outlook on life, derived from long experience, they feel strongly the need for, and desire, drastic changes in many aspects of their present mode of life. Fortunately, they are not completely apathetic to the broader outside world, nor to the hope that they may soon be given an opportunity to improve their lot within the nation. This hope is clearly reflected in the vigor with which they occasionally defend what few rights they now possess and by the diligence, dignity, and pride with which they assume obligations of leadership and responsibility in their own society. It is likely that, if given opportunities to develop a more progressive and optimistic outlook on the world, the Indians will adjust fairly rapidly to modern conditions and will assume a productive and responsible place in Peruvian national life. Actually, the hope of the Andean countries, not only Peru but Bolivia and Ecuador as well, lies in the mountain regions with their masses of hard-working peasants. It is no less true, however, that, unless the Indian populations are increasingly provided with opportunities and assistance in changing their way of life and improving their lot markedly, present conditions of unrest and dissatisfaction can lead to more and bloodier revolutions, as has happened in Bolivia, or, at the least, to extreme and continuing conflicts in the process of their adjustment to modern life.

A Pilot Attempt at Social Change [6]

To document the problems and potentials of social change among the Indians of Peru, it may be helpful to

---

[6] Some of the findings have been treated elsewhere. See Allan R. Holmberg, "Participant Intervention in the Field," *Human Organization,* Spring 1955, pp. 23-26; and William Foote Whyte and Allan R. Holmberg, "Human Problems of U.S. Enterprise in Latin America," same, Fall 1956, pp. 15-18.

review one current attempt to incorporate a community of
hacienda Indians into a more modern way of life, one
which will also be in keeping with the *sierra* environment.
In 1952, in collaboration with the Indigenous Institute of
Peru and with the support of the Peruvian government,
Cornell University undertook a systematic program of research and development in order to determine how an
Indian population would respond to a concerted effort to
introduce it to a more modern way of life. The community
selected was Vicos, a *hacienda* situated in an inter-Andean
valley, Callejón de Huaylas, about 250 miles northeast of
Lima. Known for its conservatism and its hostility to the
outside world until 1952, this *hacienda* had undergone
little change since it was first established in the colonial
period, over four hundred years ago.

Surrounded by snow-capped peaks, some of which rise
to over 20,000 feet, the *hacienda* of Vicos has a land area
of about 35,000 acres, of which some 7,000 are now under
cultivation or are used for grazing. It is rocky and hilly,
with elevations of about 9,000 to 14,000 feet. The lower
slopes of the *hacienda* are used principally for farming,
the most important crops being maize, potatoes, barley,
wheat, beans, and quinoa. The higher slopes are utilized
solely for pasturing animals, particularly cattle and sheep.

Like some two or three hundred similar properties,
Vicos belongs to the state and until recently was leased out
to the highest bidder at public auctions held every ten
years. Attached to the land, but owning none of it, were
some 1,850 Quechua-speaking Indians, in over three hundred families, most of whom live on small and scattered
subsistence farmsteads on the lower slopes of the *hacienda,*
constituting roughly 90 per cent of the arable land. The
remaining 10 per cent of the land, or about five hundred
acres, was formerly farmed for commercial purposes by the
lessee of the *hacienda.* The necessary Indian labor was supplied without charge, except for a small gratuity to buy
coca. By custom one adult member of each household was
obligated to pay a labor tax of three days each week to the

hacienda in return for the right to occupy a small plot of land supposedly sufficient to support his family. In addition to the labor tax, which also involved the unpaid use of the Indians' domestic animals, the *peones* were obligated by turn to supply the *hacienda* and its employees with certain free services as cooks, grooms, watchmen, shepherds, and servants. For failing to fulfill these obligations a *peón* could be dispossessed of his tools, his animals, or his plot of land.

Until the Cornell group assumed responsibility for the administration and development of Vicos, power—economic, political, and judicial—was completely concentrated in the hands of a single individual, the *patrón*. Thus the fate of each *peón* depended almost completely upon him. Theoretically, he held control of all the lands of the *hacienda* and of all of the people living within its boundaries. In this respect the *patrón* was not unlike a feudal baron. Actually, about the only area of life on which his authority did not impinge was that of religion, for which the parish priest and Indian officials were responsible. This does not mean that the Indian community had no organization of its own. A local mayor, who also appointed a number of assistants, was selected annually by a process which may be loosely termed an election. But the responsibility and authority of these village officials did not go much beyond the conduct of religious life within the community. They had little or nothing to say in matters of secular concern, which remained exclusively the province of the *patrón*.

As a result, positions of responsibility in public affairs were lacking in the life of Vicos, adequate leadership did not develop, almost no public services were maintained, and the community was in a highly disorganized state. Apart from alliances with immediate kinship groups and a common devotion to religious practices, particularly the *fiesta* of the local saint, there were almost no values that were widely shared among the members of the Vicos community. At the same time standards of living were at a bare minimum.[7] Health and nutritional levels were extremely low.[8] Educational facilities and consequently skills were almost completely lacking. Cooperation within the community was the exception rather than the rule, and resistance to the outside world was high. Attitudes toward life were static and pessimistic. Such, in fact, were the conditions prevailing among the Indian population of Vicos when the Cornell group assumed control. Similar conditions are found on many *haciendas* and in many Indian communities of the highlands.[9]

Changing this state of affairs, without a large investment of resources or without a revolution, would seem at first glance to be an almost insoluble problem. To be sure, it was and still is no easy task. Yet it is not as hopeless as it might seem. In the case of Vicos, at any rate, it has been possible, on the basis of careful studies carried out in advance of initiating any action, to design a modest program

---

[7] Surveys indicate that the differential distribution of the lands among the Indian population at Vicos was very great. Many families held less than an acre while others farmed as much as thirty or forty acres. The per capita distribution of crop land among the Indian population is about an acre, at least one-half of which is on rocky and upland soil. Cited from an unpublished manuscript by Robert Stevens of Cornell University on agricultural production on the Hacienda Vicos, 1954.

[8] Recent studies by Dr. Carlos Collazos and collaborators (*Journal of the American Dietetic Association,* v. 30 [1953], pp. 1222-1230) indicate that the Indians of Vicos have a per capita consumption of about 1,500 calories per day. This is only about 70 per cent of the recommended minimum for reasonably good health. In addition to caloric deficiency, nutrition surveys indicate that the Indians have an extremely low intake of calcium and vitamin A. All families at Vicos consumed less than 75 per cent of the recommended amounts.

On some aspects of health in the highlands of Peru, see E. H. Payne, L. Gonzáles-Mugaburu, and E. M. Schleicher, "An Intestinal Parasite Survey in the High Cordilleras of Peru," *American Journal of Tropical Medicine and Hygiene,* July 1956, pp. 696-698. These investigators found a very high rate of such parasites as pinworm, roundworm, and amoebic dysentery on the Hacienda Vicos and in other communities of Callejón de Huaylas. Recent investigations at Vicos by Dr. Marshall Newman of the Smithsonian Institution indicate, however, that Indians have a very low rate of heart disease and high blood pressure, characteristic of modern civilization (personal communication).

[9] See, for example, William W. Stein, *Hualcan: An Andean Indian Estancia,* Ph.D. thesis, Cornell University, Ithaca, N.Y., 1955.

of technical assistance and education which has gained fairly wide acceptance and has helped to awaken most members of the community to new opportunities for improving their lot through their own efforts. I must again stress, however, that only a broad and integrated approach to problems of development made it possible to reach the desired goals of higher standards of living, social respect, and a self-reliant and enlightened community which can eventually take responsibility for the direction of its own affairs as a functioning part of the nation. Under this approach, every effort was made to tackle each problem in terms of understanding and respecting the local culture, the only basis on which lasting changes can be understood by the community as desirable and can be accepted by it.

From the beginning the Vicos project has been conducted with a minimum of outside personnel and funds.[10] Except for graduate students engaged exclusively in research, and agencies of the Peruvian government normally operating in the area, not more than two North Americans and two Peruvians have at any time been concerned directly with the administrative and developmental aspects of the Vicos program.

On the basis of preliminary anthropological and technical studies and after consultation with the residents of the *hacienda* concerning their needs and hopes, it was possible to initiate a unified program of change centered on three major areas of development: economics and technology, nutrition and health, and education. To these

10 Most of the funds for research and development at Vicos have been provided by grants from the Carnegie Corporation of New York to Cornell University. In addition, the author has received special research funds from the Wenner-Gren Foundation for Anthropological Research, Inc., and the Social Science Research Council. The Peruvian government has also been most generous in its support of the project and in supplying technical and scientific personnel. Particular thanks are due to the following people, all of whom at one time or another have been associated with the Cornell-Peru project: Dr. Carlos Monge M., president of the Indigenous Institute of Peru and co-director of the project; Dr. William C. Blanchard, Dr. Humberto Ghersi, Sr. Enrique Luna, Dr. William Mangin, Miss Joan Snyder, and Dr. Mario Vázquez.

should be added a fourth area, that of social organization, although, because of the deeply ingrained nature of the *hacienda* system, it was neither desirable nor feasible to move rapidly in this area at the outset. In all these areas of activity some people in Vicos felt the need for improvement; hence, they were responsive to suggestions for innovation. In fact, these were also areas in which change was absolutely necessary if the research and development program was to reach its two fundamental goals: changing the initial and predicted image of the project members from one of hostile *patrones* to that of friendly consultants and observers; and developing within the community independent and dynamic problem-solving and decision-making organizations which could gradually assume the responsibilities of leadership in public affairs in a rational and humane manner and along democratic lines.

To promote movement toward these general ends, the project leaders designed a great many specific steps. In the first place, many of the abuses under the traditional *hacienda* system could be eliminated from the very start. Interviews with a large sample of villagers showed, for example, that the obligations which were most irksome to the Indians were not, as might be expected, the three-day labor service which they rendered for the right to use their plots of land. They were, rather, the additional unrecompensed services they had to provide to the *hacienda* and its employees. Under previous administrations, for example, a man might suddenly be called out for a tour of duty as a shepherd for the *hacienda,* or a woman as a cook, just when their services were most urgently needed at home. In such matters abuses had apparently been frequent in the past and feelings in the community ran high. Under a more enlightened approach it proved possible to abolish these free services and to hire paid employees, training them to assume a genuine responsibility for their new jobs. One example will illustrate the kind of change that was introduced.

On the upper part of the *hacienda* is a large grazing area

known as the Quebrada Honda. This is a glaciated canyon which provides the only route to other valleys across the mountains from Vicos. Here both the *patrón* and the Indians traditionally grazed their cattle. The canyon served also as a public trail, and since distances were great it was customary for pack trains coming to and from a mining area over the passes (a three-day journey) to spend at least one night in the Quebrada Honda. For the right to pasture their animals there, muleteers were required to pay a small fee to the *hacienda,* and the collection point was at the narrow mouth of the canyon, which also served as a check point to prevent the theft of cattle. Traditionally, *peones* had to perform a period of free duty at this post, but, since this gave them no rewards, abuses were rife. "Deals" were made with muleteers; cattle were stolen; and animals were allowed to despoil fields. All this caused considerable loss to the *hacienda* and to the Indians themselves, much more than was gained by the tax. Simply by placing at the check point an Indian employee who then received the toll as his income, it was possible to reduce this loss to a minimum. Actually it resulted in a saving for the *hacienda* and for the Indians as well.

In addition to eliminating the worse direct abuses of the *hacienda* system, it was necessary to take positive steps toward solving other problems, first of all in the sphere of economic life. Unless the output of the Indian households and the *hacienda* fields could be raised substantially, it would not be possible to support the institutions necessary for the adjustment of Vicos to modern life except on a welfare or gift basis, and this is not a likely prospect in Peru, considering the state of its economy and the nature of its power structure. Nor would a welfare approach lead to a solid type of development, rooted in the desires and responsibilities of the community itself.

In the area of economic activity positive steps could be and were taken, for the desire to improve the community's livelihood existed, at least in a dormant state. Wealth is held in high esteem in the Indian community. Unlike *mestizo* communities, in it the genealogical factor is of little or no significance in assigning positions of prestige in the social structure. To accumulate wealth in an agrarian society like Vicos, however, the peasant must work hard and also be frugal. It is through physical labor that he gains dignity and it is through frugality that he accumulates wealth. These values, too, contrast sharply with those of *mestizo* society, in which people go to extreme limits to avoid the indignity of physical labor and attach a high value to conspicuous consumption.

This does not mean that an Indian is willing to labor long and well under all conditions. In most instances he will do so only when he is working for himself or within his own culture. When working outside this framework, under conditions in which he is held in disrespect and generally receives little in the way of reward, he usually tries to get by with as little effort as he can. This was true under the traditional *hacienda* system at Vicos, and labor productivity was much lower on *hacienda* fields than on the Indians' individual plots. As economic rewards to the Indians have increased, as well as their self-respect, the improved productivity has more than offset the cost of the additional investments required.

Today, the "miracles" of modern science make it possible to increase agricultural output sharply, even in the steep and rock-strewn fields of the Andes, as has been proved at Vicos. Poor soil was not the only factor responsible. Seed had degenerated; inherited techniques, such as row spacing, were outmoded; adequate fertilizers were unavailable; the use of insecticides against plant diseases was unheard of. The motto at Vicos was, as it still is in most of the mountain areas of Peru, "plant and pray"—a formula that has not always produced very good crops.

At just about the time the Cornell-Peru project was being launched at Vicos, the potato crop, the Indians' mainstay, had failed because of a blight which affected the entire region. On the basis of good technical advice,[11] it was found not only that this blight could readily be controlled but that the potato crop could be greatly increased by following a few simple rules: adequate preparation and fertilizing of the soil; healthy and disinfected seed; proper weeding and cultivation; and periodic spraying with insecticides. Presented with this formula for increasing their potato yields, the Indians did not immediately scramble to adopt the practices suggested. Many were too poor to purchase the necessary supplies. Others had no land to plant. Still others—in fact, most of the people, including local Indian leaders—were suspicious of any advice or aid that came from the outside.

In the end, the Cornell project worked out a plan by which the Indians could buy the necessary supplies on credit, paying it off at the end of the season with a share of the crop. This arrangement was sufficiently attractive to a small group of Indian families so that some new agricultural practices were at least initiated within the community. Actually, yields of healthy potatoes more than doubled the first year, with the dramatic result that the new practices were adopted by almost all Indian families within the next two years. Today it is almost impossible to find anyone who plants by the old traditional methods. Since then, it should be added, Vicos has become the largest producer of potatoes in the region; yields have increased, in some instances as much as 400 per cent. In short, potatoes, in addition to serving as a main subsistence item, have also become a commercial crop, providing Indian families with much-needed cash to buy other necessities.[12]

---

11 Supplied by the Servicio Cooperativo Interamericano de Producción de Alimentos, a branch of the Institute of Inter-American Affairs.

12 A full account of this experiment can be found in Mario Vázquez, *A Study of Technological Change in Vicos, Peru*, M.A. thesis, Cornell University, Ithaca, N.Y., 1955. In 1958, the community of Vicos sold 262,000 kilograms of potatoes on the Lima market and with the profits made a substantial down payment on the purchase of the *hacienda* lands. In addition, it is now conducting its own Point Four program in several other communities, to pass on the improved techniques to its neighbors.

This is simply one example of what can be done through a bootstrap operation to raise both the economic level of the Indian household and the production of food. When we examine the important increases in food production which can be brought about in Peru and elsewhere through the patient and careful introduction of more modern methods, the *sierra* of Peru no longer stands out as the area of poor resources that it has always been considered. The Vicos experience indicates so far that dramatic results can be achieved at a relatively small cost. They can be attained, however, only if careful attention is given, not only to the problem of modern techniques, but also to the people and their culture. For this reason, from the very start the Cornell-Peru project has given careful thought to the problem of developing a spirit of independence, responsibility, and leadership in community affairs—a spirit that had never existed before except in the sphere of religious life.

Toward New Community Leadership

When the Cornell-Peru project first assumed control at Vicos, the making of decisions in most matters of secular concern was almost wholly vested in one individual, the *patrón,* who was not a member of the Indian community. On the *hacienda* the direct supervision of work was in the hands of six Indian leaders or foremen, called *mayorales,* traditionally appointed by the *patrón.* Although selected to represent the *patrón's* interest, they were also people of status in the community at large, particularly in those districts from which they came and in which they had direct supervision of the labor force. Most of them had previously occupied important positions in the politico-religious hierarchy of the Indian community through which prestige and power are gained. All of them were old men, hence highly respected in the traditional community.

The project was concerned with transferring power to the community, not with retaining it, as in the traditional *hacienda* system. As a first step, it was necessary to establish some local group, as representative as possible, with which it could share the power of making decisions. Because of their knowledge, experience, and prestige, the body of *mayorales* was selected to assist the project in directing the economic and social affairs of the *hacienda,* for example, in settling conflicts over land and cattle. As this group developed greater skill, more and more responsibility was delegated to it. The project leaders met in weekly session with these six men; with friendly guidance and encouragement, they soon began to take a perspective somewhat broader than their original vested-interest or "dog-eat-dog" outlook on *hacienda* and community affairs. In addition to these sessions, all decisions made by this group were discussed with the labor force as a whole so that necessary modifications could be made in the interests of the community at large.

Through the use of these and similar methods, together with positive advice and assistance in matters of economic development and social respect, of health and education for all members of the community, the way was cleared to promote better understanding and greater self-reliance and to seek out reasonable solutions to community problems. Over several years a number of groups have been organized and trained to assume creative leadership in various aspects of life, including economic development, nutrition and health, education, and political affairs. These groups gradually learned to assume more and more responsibility for community affairs and developed a growing ability to work together without serious frictions. Finally, in 1957, when the project had prepared the ground for giving up its control of the *hacienda,* that control could then be transferred completely to an elected body of proven leaders. The Vicosinos had come of age, not without turmoil and strain.

New Goals in Education and Health

Perhaps the most significant change that has occurred at Vicos is that education for the children and for the villagers has now become both a possibility and a goal. In the whole process of changing practices and perspectives within this peasant community, education and enlightenment have played the key role. It was assumed from the very beginning of the project that, without a carefully designed program of education, both formal and informal, it would be impossible either to establish or perpetuate whatever changes were proposed, in ways of work or of thinking. For this reason a basic rule in the Vicos experiment has been to find out first what the community aspired to achieve and then, through the formation or strengthening of local groups, as in the case of the *mayorales,* to place these goals in a broader setting, so that in achieving them the community would also be building a body of knowledge, skills, and attitudes which would in turn foster in it a solid and self-reliant growth. In the long run this kind of growth can only take place through education in the broad sense of the word.

Something of the educational problem in the *sierra,* as well as the significance of education for the future development of the Indians of Peru, can be gleaned from a brief review of the Vicos experience. When a member of the Cornell-Peru project first came to study Vicos in 1949, he found that a primary school had already been in operation for the past nine years. Yet he was unable to find a single child of primary-school age who could read or write, either in Spanish or in his own tongue. A little Spanish was spoken by a mere handful of young men, most of it learned during their army service.

On investigation, the reasons for this situation soon became apparent. For one thing, under the traditional *hacienda* system, no support was given by the owner to education. *Hacienda patrones* were concerned not with developing an enlightened population but with maintaining the *status quo*. For them, children were a source of unskilled labor which might be lost once they were given the opportunity to learn new skills and acquire new values.

In the second place, the parents of the children resisted the idea of providing an education for their children. To a certain extent this was attributable to defects in the national educational system as well as to the conditions in which it functioned under the traditional *hacienda* system. In Peru, Indian villages such as Vicos are frequently supplied with unprepared and ineffective teachers who are not qualified for a teaching post in an urban center. Conversely, such teachers often seek appointments to Indian areas in order to retain their professional status as teachers. Even if the teachers are conscientious in their efforts, they frequently come into conflict with *patrones* and are not given any facilities to live and work. More often, perhaps, being *mestizos,* they share the prejudices of the outside world and thus tend to treat Indian children as inferior and put them to work as servants and gardeners instead of teaching them badly needed skills. An Indian parent who observes these abuses—and they occur frequently—sees no reason to send his children to school, particularly when their labor is badly needed at home.

At Vicos, the teaching post and facilities were so inadequate that only the poorest teachers accepted an appointment there. The children who actually attended school had to sit on the ground in an outside and drafty corridor of a crumbling adobe building where the teacher herself lived in poverty and misery. In any single year the total school population had never exceeded fifteen to twenty pupils out of a possible 350, and none of them had ever had more than a year or two of the poorest possible training. Moreover, it was almost unheard of to send a girl to school. No wonder the process of learning was not highly valued! In the traditional *hacienda* system there was simply no place or need for education, as can be clearly seen by the following figures on the state of education at Vicos in the latter part of 1951:

Had not gone to school	1,576
Were going at the time	36
Could read and write (very poorly)	5

It may be added that of the 36 pupils then at school many had been encouraged in this by the influence of the Cornell-Peru project, which had only recently been initiated.

The first efforts at education, in any formal sense, were directed toward improving the facilities and training available for children as well as for younger adults. First, the leaders of the project had to win some measure of confidence within the community, largely through the visible rewards of economic progress and through the spirit of mutual respect fostered by sharing the making of decisions. Only then did they begin holding numerous meetings with parents, Indian leaders, and teachers to discuss the building of a school which would be adequate to provide at least a primary education for all children of the community. At the same time, abuses in the old system, such as absenteeism of teachers and the use of pupils as servants, were abolished. New rewards for good attendance were provided. Since many children had to come from as far away as a half-hour on foot, a school lunch program was initiated to provide better nutrition. Since many of the Indian families were desperately poor, this in itself may have provided the primary stimulus for more than tripling the school population after the first year of the lunch program.

Other means of support for schooling were found gradually. The Ministry of Education sent more and better teachers. The community set about building a new schoolhouse. By the end of the second year, the first wing of a modern school had been finished. By the end of the third year, a second wing was being built, including a spacious auditorium which is now used also for community functions.

All labor for this development, and a large part of the material, much of it made locally, were provided by members of the Indian community, organized, supervised, and trained by project personnel. Many new building skills were thus added to the occupational inventory of the community. One assumption that we made in planning the project was that, unless most members of the community made some contribution to the construction of the new school, few of them would have any interest in putting it to use. The more members who pitched in to help build it, the more who would feel entitled to a return on their investment in the form of sending their children to school. This assumption was borne out, as shown in the records of school attendance from 1951 to 1957:

Year	School Attendance	Number of Teachers
1951	14-18	1
1952	30-35	2
1953	35-60	2
1954	85-90	3
1955	110-120	5
1956	180-190	7
1957	200-250	7

By 1958 over 250 pupils were registered in the school, and the number of teachers had increased to eight.

In Vicos there are actually two schools in operation, one for girls and one for boys. Although the ratio of boys to girls is still about three to one, nevertheless a large proportion of both boys and girls have had several years of continuity in their education, a thing which was previously almost unheard of. The classification of the school has also been changed. Starting at a primary level, it has been raised to a pre-industrial category. This means that technical training is provided in agriculture and the industrial arts, in addition to the regular curriculum of Peruvian primary schools. An adult education program has also been initiated through which younger adults are rapidly becoming literate and acquiring useful skills needed for providing a more enlightened leadership in the direction of community affairs. In 1957, a *núcleo escolar*, a kind of central school, was formed at Vicos, which also provides educational services to nearby communities.

In terms of the future, one of the most important results of the program at Vicos is that the educational process is becoming a fully accepted value within the community. One index of this is the change which has been taking place in the parents' own behavior and attitudes. Not only are they sending their children to school increasingly, in some instances at a considerable sacrifice, but they are growing prouder of their children's attainments. I remember well one father who pointed with great pride to a letter he had just received in the handwriting of his own son, who had been to school at Vicos and was then on a vacation visit to another part of the country. Previously all such letters had been written by scribes.

The parents have shown in still other ways their changed attitude toward education. They are attending school events in steadily increasing numbers, until the graduation exercises have become a kind of secular *fiesta*. A few parents have taken responsibility for helping the teachers stimulate a wider interest in education throughout the community. There has been some success in forming a committee of parents and teachers for maintaining and improving school facilities. While the school has been transferred to the jurisdiction of the Ministry of Education, the responsibility for running and improving it is entirely in the hands of the community.

The acceptance of education as a value is also reflected in the behavior of the school children at Vicos. In many instances the acquiring of skills has enabled them to enjoy new prestige at home and to compete successfully in the outside world. This in turn has led to an increasingly optimistic outlook on life and on their prospects for the future. Perhaps more than any other aspect of the Vicos program, the school has become a symbol of progress and of hope for the future. As it happens, no other community of the region, and few rural communities anywhere in Peru, can boast of comparable educational facilities. These accomplishments—and they have for the most part been self-made—have rightly become a source of pride to the Vicosinos and of envy and respect by their neighbors. The Peruvian government has done much (even though it has only made a start) to encourage these developments. If they are continued on a much larger scale in the *sierra*, Peru will soon obtain its reward in the form of enlightened and responsible citizens who will make positive contributions to the national life.

One further area of development to which our pilot project gave special attention is that of health. Some indication has been given (footnote 8, p. 81) of the low levels of health and nutrition that prevailed in Vicos when the project began; and the age-old habit of coca chewing presented special problems.[13] At least in the field of health, substantial changes have taken place. In collaboration with the United Nations and the Peruvian Ministry of Health, a twice-weekly clinic was inaugurated at Vicos; it has raised standards of well-being considerably and has almost eliminated the most infectious diseases. Contrary to early expectations, there has been little resistance to the acceptance of modern medical practices or even to the purchase of modern drugs. As an outgrowth of this program, the Vicosinos, in collaboration with a neighboring Indian community, Recuayhuanca, have constructed a "sanitary post" or clinic at which basic medical services are now available.

---

13 See, for example, UN Economic and Social Council (12th sess.), *Official Records: Special Supplement 1, Report of the Commission of Enquiry on the Coca Leaf*, E/1666 (New York: Author, 1950). In my opinion the conclusions of this report are not based on the best scientific evidence. For one thing, preliminary field studies of Vicos indicate that the social aspects of coca chewing are more important than had been previously believed. Moreover, the habit is not as vicious as has been thought. It is likely that, as health and nutritional levels rise, the chewing of coca will pretty much cease to be a problem.

The End of the "Hacienda" System at Vicos

Perhaps the most significant development that has occurred at Vicos since the research program was begun in 1949 is that, after four hundred years of peonage under the *hacienda* system, the Vicosinos have now become the masters of their own destiny and of their own land. Helped along the road by an integrated program of change, one based on the felt needs of the people, the community is now approaching a level of social maturity at which its further development would be held back by a continuation of the *hacienda* system. When this had come to be clearly recognized by both the community and the government, plans were elaborated to enable the Vicosinos to purchase the lands on which they had lived as serfs ever since the Spanish conquest. Their new-found stature in freedom was symbolized by an event of great significance. In October 1956, democratically, by a direct vote of all its adult citizens, the people of Vicos elected their own delegates to assume the direction and management of community and *hacienda* affairs. Since that time, the *peón* system of obligatory labor has been abolished and the Vicosinos now pay taxes on their land. At least one community of the *sierra* has thus taken a new lease on life.

With the transfer, in October 1957, of the *hacienda* lease from the Cornell-Peru project to the community of Vicos, the leaders of the project withdrew from direct control or even supervision of its affairs. After centuries of serfdom the Vicosinos are now masters of their lands and their affairs. The former leaders of the project are available to offer advice when it is requested, for its field director, Mario Vázquez, is continuing his researches into the processes of change and I have also visited Vicos almost every summer. Now, as prior to 1951, the project is concerned with studying the process of social change, not directly with engineering it.

The results of self-rule and self-reliance have been strikingly demonstrated at Vicos since 1957. In the first year after "independence," production doubled, with a substantially smaller labor force. The year 1959 saw a further rapid improvement. With the increased resources now available to them, the Vicosinos are taking up many new projects, this time completely on their own. They are improving access roads to get their produce to market, working out better marketing and transportation arrangements and developing a better water supply. They are better fed, clothed, shod, and housed. It is truly hard to recognize in the new Vicos the bedraggled and hopeless village where our project first began its studies in 1949.

This does not mean that all the problems of Vicos have been solved. Obviously, much remains to be done there and in other parts of the *sierra* where poverty and disease, illiteracy and injustice, are still rife. But the experience of the Cornell-Peru project clearly indicates that the people of the *sierra*, once given proper encouragement, advice, and respect, can do much by themselves to better their lot. Certainly the Vicosinos, given the baseline from which they began, have made great strides toward shaping and sharing positive human values—freedom, respect, enlightenment, and well-being. Given the opportunity, other peoples of the *sierra* can do the same.

Peru's policy-makers have, as I reported above, given their encouragement and support to the Vicos experiment from its inception in 1951, and they have followed its progress with keen interest. Now they are working to multiply its benefits. In the past three years, convinced that the integrated or multifacet approach to social and economic development and self-respect offers the most effective means of arousing the *sierra* people, with their excellent human potential, to develop the spirit and the habits of community self-improvement, the Peruvian government has been engaged in launching five similar pilot projects in key areas of the country. In this expanding effort to crack the crust of centuries and release human energies and hopes, the Indigenous Institute of Peru and the Ministries of Education, Health and Agriculture, as well as United Nations and inter-American agencies, are playing an active part. Some of the leaders of the new projects first studied *sierra* life at Vicos and first learned there how to work with an Indian community to meet its great needs. As at Vicos, each project is based, first, on a careful field study of the community and, second, on the nurturing of responsibility and initiative within the community itself, rather than importing some alien and transitory institutions from without.

A Positive Approach for the Future [14]

What generalizations can be drawn from the experience of Vicos, and what are some of its policy implications? One basic conclusion is that, contrary to a widely held opinion in Peru and elsewhere, the indigenous populations of the *sierra* have a great potential for development and for becoming a progressive and dynamic part of the Peruvian nation. Moreover, the process of modernization within this long-isolated population can take place without the loss of certain fundamental and positive values that are deeply ingrained in Indian society: respect for work, frugality, cooperation.

Our experience at Vicos indicates that, if granted respect, the Indian will give respect. If allowed to share in the making of decisions, he will take responsibility and pride in making and carrying them out. The fundamental problem of the *sierra* is largely a problem in human relations: that of improving social relations between *mestizos* and Indians and incorporating both groups into a modern way of life. This calls for a policy not simply of technological and economic intervention, as has largely been the approach in the past, but also of cultural or educational intervention. Only this approach can open the way to a

---

[14] The writer wishes to acknowledge the collaboration on this section of Miss Joan Snyder, formerly a research associate of the Cornell-Peru project.

broadening of horizons in both groups and ultimately to
a basic change in the present caste structure and in social
values. An approach to the *sierra* people along these lines
can lead them into a dynamic and progressive society, more
like that of the coast, and ultimately will foster a more
balanced development of Peru as a nation.

Interdependence of Economic and Social Change

In the past it has been the assumption of technical aid
programs, such as those of the U.S. International Cooperation Administration, that the introduction of technological
changes will by itself bring about a broader outlook on
the part of the people aided, thus helping to incorporate
the community into the larger nation. Experience shows
that this is not always the case. It has become increasingly
apparent that the acceptance of new technology does not
foretell its later use; it does not necessarily promote the
broader development of the community or lead to a change
in values on the part of its members.

More often than not, increased economic benefits are
channeled through traditional value and social systems,
intensifying old imbalances. In the *sierra* of Peru, this
means, for example, that additional income derived from
economic development may be spent in gaining prestige
through staging more elaborate religious *fiestas* rather than
be put to productive uses. The offering of technical aid
alone has, in fact, often resulted in arousing the expectations of more technical help to come and in developing
highly opportunistic attitudes on the part of the recipients.
Certainly this has been the case in many communities of
Peru where the older, paternalistic type of social structure
still prevails.

Although there are evident trends toward a wider sharing of power, as attested by the increasing control of the
government by the middle segments of society, older and
hostile images of national government, derived from the
concentrated holding and misuse of power by the privi-

leged few, still persist in most *mestizo* and Indian villages of Peru. Consequently, many sincere attempts, even on the part of the present government, to initiate change at the local level meet with little cooperation or success. At the same time, most of the underdeveloped communities of Peru hold what are, by our standards at least, unreal images of what the government can and should do for them. Particularly among the *mestizos,* community expectations of what a government can and will do for them in the fields of education and health, economic and social development, and public services, are far in excess of what even the most benevolent *patrón* (except perhaps in oil-rich Venezuela) could possibly provide. Yet there is little willingness on the part of local communities to assume responsibilities for reaching these strongly desired goals.

The gap between aspiration and action cannot be explained by poverty alone. It is due as much to the failure of the ambition to achieve desired changes, despite much lip service given to it, to take firm root in community feeling and action. How best to bring this about still constitutes a major question for both research and policy. One thing is certain. The traditional paternalistic type of social and political structure must be overcome if the *sierra* communities are to be incorporated into the nation, but this alone will not assure their developing along democratic lines or for the best interest of the nation.

For the kind of development that calls upon the local community to help itself, rather than wait passively for help from above, the absolutely essential conditions, in addition to programs of technical and economic assistance, are: an improved standard of living, the effective functioning of the community within the larger environment, and a program of cultural or educational intervention. There must also be a deliberate attempt to develop local leaders who will remain identified with the future of their own village and who will find their deepest satisfaction in promoting its progress. Otherwise, potential leaders of the *sierra* will continue to be siphoned off to the coastal area, as they become aware of the opportunities for upward social mobility that exist outside their mountain valleys.

The experience at Vicos shows that much can be done to strengthen the economic life of the *sierra*. By introducing more modern methods and techniques, agricultural production can probably be doubled or tripled in most of its regions. So far, except for the state-owned Santa Corporation, little or nothing has been done to develop small local industries in the *sierra*, although they could absorb much of the population that now migrates year by year to the coast. Just one example. On even the poorer lands of the *sierra* it is possible to grow fiber crops for the production of rope and bagging; in many areas, in fact, there are enough fiber plants growing wild to support a small industrial operation. Yet Peru does not have a single factory for these products and actually imports them at high cost from abroad. The *sierra* holds a similar potential for the industrial processing of fruit, meat, and dairy products.

Much good work along this line has been and is being done outside the *sierra* by the Institute of Inter-American Affairs, under its bilateral agreements with the Peruvian government, as well as by the Pan American Union and the United Nations and its subsidiaries. Unfortunately, too little work has been done with the smaller farmers or the Indians. Most of these efforts have been concentrated on the large *haciendas* and on commercial farmers, who are easier to reach but who constitute only a small part of the total population.

Development of Local Leadership

In the promotion of social rather than merely economic change, the problems are more complex but far from insoluble. Indeed, at a number of key points in *sierra* society even a relatively modest amount of progress may stimulate a self-propelling and dynamic series of further changes. One of these key points is the development of community solidarity and community leadership. In most rural communities there is a growing body of people who have had contact with the outside world—particularly the younger men who have worked in the coastal regions or done their military service there—and these people are highly critical of the traditional village authorities. Through their experience with life outside their narrow valleys, these young men have taken on many of the values of a national society, and they cannot find fulfillment for them within the traditional village hierarchy.

Probably the only means by which this can be done is to find ways of identifying the prestige of the individual with his role in improving the welfare of the village as a whole. To achieve this, several other changes will be required. At present, neighborhood and kinship ties are far stronger than any feeling of internal unity within the Peruvian village. To overcome this, an essential first step is to promote a sense of loyalty to the community, thus cutting across the lines of neighborhood and kinship groups and stimulating an awareness that the welfare of the individual depends in some measure on that of the entire community. One way to do this is to foster the development of local organizations to deal with issues that affect all families, regardless of local affiliation or status, such as schools and health care. Another way lies in promoting recreational and athletic events that attract a wide participation. Many of these occasions, for example, the staging of dramas or chorales, can perhaps be linked to the major religious *fiestas,* which now draw a large though decreasing attendance.

To understand its own problems and opportunities, the *sierra* village needs to know much more about the towns and villages of its own area so as to copy useful changes more rapidly and to develop a spirit of emulation. The isolated village will then see that its problems are not unique and will understand better which things it can do for itself and in which it can reasonably expect aid from the central government.

In order to develop a greater degree of community
solidarity, it is essential to strengthen the role of local
leadership so as to make it representative of the community
as a whole. In the traditional *hacienda* or Indian community the range of activities of the village authorities
should be broadened to include all functions which are of
importance to all members of the community. To the
traditional ritual activities, with their stress on age and
the dignity of office, must be added an enlarged responsibility for new activities carried on for the active benefit of
the entire community. To promote cohesion and avoid the
paralysis of dissension, it is important, among people of
the *sierra,* to build up the prestige of holding office.
Placing new responsibilities on local authorities for a growing variety of activities will enhance their stature both
in their dealings with the outside world and in their
leadership within the community.

It is also important to broaden the number and functions of positions of leadership in the villages, in order to
provide active roles to a larger proportion of their members. This can help the people to see that authority is the
responsibility and the right of all, not the privilege of a
small group representing particular interests. This change
can be used to give active roles of leadership to the large
number of individuals who have had wide experience outside their valleys. As the *sierra* villages enter the path of
modernization, the functions of their leaders are also altering, and this requires a change in the qualities of experience and outlook expected of them.

Relations between "Mestizos" and Indians

The barriers to communication between Indians and
mestizos are a major factor isolating the Indian villages
from the influences of the outside world. The dominant
mestizo group, standing between the Indians and the nation, has served to block communication, not to facilitate
it. Even a partial lowering of this barrier would lead to

an increased involvement and participation by the Indian communities in the national society. Furthermore, no effort to develop the well-being of the indigenous villages and to retain potential leaders within their *sierra* villages can work if by staying there they must also remain forever at the bottom of the social ladder.

One approach to improving intergroup relations stresses the need for changing the behavior of the minority or depressed group, with the expectation that this will gradually modify the attitudes of the majority or dominant group. The assumption made is that present attitudes stem from the behavior of the minority and that altering this behavior will result in removing the prejudices of the majority group. It can, however, be argued on strong grounds that the unfavorable attitudes of the dominant group are often transmitted from one generation to the next without reference to the actual situation and that the "improvement" of the minority group will not necessarily create a more favorable attitude toward it. Indeed, the emphasis placed upon improving the status of the minority may actually cause the dominant group to feel that its superior position is being threatened and it may react even more negatively to evidences of that improvement.

An alternative approach is to tackle the problem of changing the attitudes of the majority group. The variety of techniques which have been studied range from formal programs of education to the creation of situations in which contact takes place between members of the two groups either voluntarily or under some degree of compulsion. Many of these methods have created more favorable attitudes toward the minority group. In such an approach, however, too little attention is paid to effecting changes within the minority. In the *sierra* of Peru, for example, it will be necessary to bring about changes in the behavior of both *mestizos* and Indians.

Still a third approach is to create new situations for which there is no set pattern of behavior, and in which each person must decide for himself how to act. In making his decision, the individual takes into account a number of new factors present, apart from his general attitude toward the minority group. These new factors may include the appropriateness or inappropriateness of discrimination as applied in other situations, the need for securing the co-operation of the other person, the relevance of laws or strongly held values forbidding discriminatory behavior, or the presence of other people who would disapprove of such conduct.

Whatever approach is stressed, it is clear that, as the process of modernization gets under way, a great improvement can be brought about in relations between *mestizos* and Indians in the *sierra*. This can be hastened, however, if new situations are arranged so as to bring members of both groups together in a way that will minimize discriminatory behavior. This is possible in schools, in developmental projects, in recreational events, and so forth, provided they are based on real needs of both Indians and *mestizos* and therefore elicit the cooperation of both groups in order to achieve shared ends.

Opening New Channels of Communication

A third broad area, highly significant for the future development of the *sierra,* is that of establishing better channels of communication with the outside world. This is essential if the Indian villages are to learn to deal effectively with the wider community, to utilize its resources for their own development, and to develop self-reliance and local initiative in support of desired changes.

Physical access of the mountain villages to the outside world is improving rapidly through the construction of roads and the increasing use of trucks and buses, but the channels of information are still very circumscribed. Orders and communications of various sorts are delivered to the local communities from district and provincial offices, without producing much effect, and the officials almost never visit the villages or explain the administration's purposes to the peasants. While the villagers have frequent contacts with nearby towns for purposes of trade or *fiestas,* the effects of this are slight because of the social distance separating Indians and *mestizos.* In these contacts, the Indians, being kept in an inferior position, can seldom learn anything new.

Channels of information can be broadened in a variety of ways. The improving of communications media involves more than simply teaching people to read and write, or imparting information through the written word. Many isolated villagers of the *sierra* have not learned to look at photographs in such a way as to grasp their full meaning. For example, the showing of a public health film at Vicos revealed that the picture had failed to convey its intended message, for each scene was understood as a separate incident. The audience was wholly unable to see any connection between the film and its own life, and it misunderstood any features that were not completely realistic. When lice were depicted as larger than life, the conclusion was that they were an entirely different sort of animal. Except for religious *fiestas,* few rural villagers have seen any variety of drama, and the functioning and purpose of radios are known only to a few individuals. While radio, newspapers, and films may play a leading role in the process of accelerated modernization—and the establishing of regional newspapers and radio stations would be a major step forward—in the early stages only patient face-to-face explanation and demonstration can provide effective channels of communication.

While there are many other aspects of community development that can be tackled in any program of induced social change, giving special attention to the three key areas—economic life, leadership, and communications—has the advantage of bringing about other changes. Increased economic contacts between the village and the outside world will lead to a growth of knowledge about outside markets, more effective techniques, use of available resources, and opportunities for putting special skills to work. Widening the channels of communication with the outside will make the rural villagers better aware of the governmental services that are available to them and will encourage them to play a more active role in their dealings with local, provincial, and national governments. Similar gains can be expected in other areas of *sierra* life, in health and nutrition, in recreation and artistic expression.

The Role of U.S. Policy

In the effort to help the depressed strata of Peru's population achieve their new aspirations, the United States has a key role to play. Economic cooperation between it and Peru has, to be sure, contributed to awakening the peasant and Indian populations to the idea of change. But this in itself is not enough, if Peru is soon to attain political stability, a broadening democracy, and a balanced development of the entire nation. Too much of U.S. economic aid and technical assistance—and, in my opinion, Peru has been helped far too little—has been channeled into the traditional social structure from the top. Too large a share of it has been directed to the large *haciendas* and urban centers of the coast, where the aristocratic tradition and paternalistic system are still strong, and too little to the people of the *sierra*. Because it has been easier to work with the dominant and educated groups, U.S. and other outside aid has not had the desired effect, that of enhancing the capacities of large numbers of the Peruvian people to produce more wealth and thus to share broadly in the benefits of economic and cultural development.

Any sound policy of economic aid, as Chester Bowles has written, in addition to "creating more wealth . . . must place heavy emphasis on the development among the workers and peasants of a healthy, cooperative attitude toward their national governments and their communities." [15] The counterpart of this is that strong emphasis

---

[15] "A New Approach to Foreign Aid," *Bulletin of the Atomic Scientists,* February 1957, p. 45.

must also be placed on developing among policy-makers healthy and cooperative attitudes toward the workers and peasants. For Peru, this means that these large groups must be allowed and encouraged to take increasing responsibility for the direction of their own affairs and to enjoy the benefits of modern development.

Any sound program of economic aid, as Bowles goes on to point out, "requires steady progress toward three essential objectives without which political stability . . . will almost certainly fail to develop: (1) a recognizable increase in economic output; (2) a sense of widespread personal participation in the creation of this increase; (3) a public conviction that the fruits of the increase are being fairly shared, with injustices steadily lessening." [16]

Toward the first of these objectives, Peru has recently made great strides. To reach the other two, it still has a long way to go. These are the neglected areas of development to which policy-makers must direct more attention. A broad program of exchange of ideas and of education is needed to aid in filling the gap. Such a program can help the people of Peru, and many other countries—for Peru merely provides a case study in the potentialities for social development—to achieve a wider sharing of power and wealth, of enlightenment and social respect. At the same time, a program of this integrated type, supplementing the now traditional contributions to economic development, can do more than any other to promote genuine understanding and enduring friendship between the two peoples.

---

[16] Same.

Three

BOLIVIA: U.S. ASSISTANCE IN A REVOLUTIONARY SETTING

by RICHARD W. PATCH

LATIN AMERICA has seen many kinds of political change that go by the name of "revolution," from trading offices between "outs" and "ins" to profound upheavals which remake permanently the political, economic, and social structure. Most "revolutions" are usurpations of power, conducted according to a well-understood and carefully observed set of rules. Often they have little popular support or opposition, are precipitated by a shift in the allegiance of key groups in the armed forces, and have little effect on the structure of the government or the condition of the governed.

Occasionally a revolution, in the sense of a sudden and radical change, does take place. For many years Mexico was unique in Latin America; it alone had undergone a revolution which struck at the roots of the previous order. The change that occurred after 1911 was in many ways more fundamental than that brought about by the wars for Mexico's independence from Spain. Then in 1952 Mexico was joined by Bolivia—the first South American republic with a large Indian population to undergo the upheaval of a revolution from which there was no return. The revolt was directed not only against a previous government but against the institutions that had made that government possible and even inevitable.

The revolution was a political success. The tin mines were nationalized, and the large estates were divided among the peasants who cultivated them. The Indians threw off their depressed status, and the entire class of wealthy landowners disappeared as a social power. The suddenness of the reforms, coupled with a sharp drop in tin prices and a devastating drought, brought economic disaster.

The United States recognized the new government and expanded substantially a modest program of assistance designed to help Bolivia achieve a measure of stability. But neither government nor economy achieved that goal, and U.S. assistance to Bolivia grew until it has now become the largest program of its kind in Latin America.

What is the present situation of Bolivia and how has it come about? And what are the purposes and the effects of the U.S. assistance programs? Only a careful, if brief, review of what the Bolivian government and the U.S. aid programs have done, have not done, and could not have done, can provide the basis for a realistic appraisal of U.S. policy in a revolutionary setting.

Divergent Approaches to the Bolivian Revolution

Until recently Bolivia was an almost unknown country, isolated in the center of a continent which has commanded less attention in the United States than its relative proximity and economic importance would lead us to expect. Yet from 1953 through 1959 economic aid and technical assistance to Bolivia by the United States amounted to $124 million. This total is exclusive of Export-Import Bank loans of $11 million disbursed during this period, authorized credits of $4 million from the Development Loan Fund, and a $15 million stabilization loan from the International Monetary Fund and the U.S. Treasury. It also does not include assistance from the United Nations, which has one of its largest missions in Bolivia.

The increase in U.S. aid to Bolivia—from $1.5 million in 1953 to $22.7 million in 1959, exclusive of loans—provides a rough yardstick for measuring the growing interest of the United States in Bolivia's future. This interest also is apparent in a growing volume of comment, some hostile to the new leadership, but most of it sympathetic.

The difficulty is that North Americans have known little of the deep-seated problems and wrenching social changes that are at the root of Bolivia's grave economic distress. Without a knowledge of the country's basic conditions it is impossible to estimate the wisdom of the aid program. U.S. policy must be appraised in the light of a new Bolivian nationalism, the Indians' struggle for emancipation, and other forces which very largely make the government a creature of the governed.

One major strand of these new processes can be examined only in the countryside, where the peasants have become a power to reckon with, and where agrarian reform has become the symbol and tool of social reform. The agencies to which we would normally turn for information do not have the experience or personnel necessary for gathering firsthand material on the village population, which is both different from and antagonistic to the city dwellers who alone meet and inform most foreign visitors.

A comprehensive United Nations report on Bolivia foreshadowed the revolutionary changes that have occurred since 1952.[1] Among analyses made by trained observers since the revolution of 1952, the most interesting is a brief study by Carter Goodrich, professor of economics at Columbia University, who headed the United Nations mission before and after the overturn.[2] Going beyond its

---

[1] UN Technical Assistance Administration, *Report of the United Nations Missions of Technical Assistance to Bolivia*, ST/TAA/K/Bolivia/1 (New York: Author, 1951), the report of the "Keenleyside Mission." Also, UN Economic Commission for Latin America, *Development of Agriculture in Bolivia*, E/CN.12/218/Add. 2 (New York: Author, 1951).

[2] Carter Goodrich, *The Economic Transformation of Bolivia*, Bulletin 34 (Ithaca: New York State School of Industrial and Labor Relations, 1955).

title, his booklet throws much light on the social as well
as economic transformation of the country. Because of
the nature of Dr. Goodrich's work in Bolivia, his study is
chiefly concerned with the population of the western
plateau (the *altiplano*) and with the mines and tin miners.

Alberto Ostria Gutiérrez, a former foreign minister of
Bolivia now in exile in Chile, has written a dramatic and
reasonably sober indictment of the present government of
Bolivia and its policies.[3] Written with an emphasis upon
the injustices suffered by the Spanish-speaking middle and
upper classes, it leaves out of consideration, as do many
books by Bolivians, the positive benefits which the government's reforms have brought the Indians.

Lilo Linke, a German journalist, has written an informal history of the revolutionary changes which have
taken place since the Movimiento Nacionalista Revolucionario (MNR) came to power.[4] It gives a number of
interesting sketches of the personalities of the government.
But if Ostria can see no good in the MNR party and
government, Linke can see no evil. Her book is often an
uncritical eulogy of Víctor Paz Estenssoro, re-elected president in June 1960 for a new four-year term.

My own approach to the study of Bolivia has been
through the methods of anthropology. When an anthropologist undertakes to interpret a total national culture,
he encounters certain limitations, chiefly imposed by his
usual preoccupation with preliterate or "primitive" groups
who remain largely below the horizon of the national state.
When he studies Bolivia, however, this avenue of approach
offers certain advantages because the preliterate population, comprising some 60 per cent of the nation, is the
principal object of the government's reforms and, in
addition, it now wields much of the power which has been
taken from the army and police.

The Indian populations of Bolivia have been studied

---

3 *Un pueblo en la cruz* (Santiago de Chile: Editorial del Pacífico, 1956).
4 *Viaje por una revolución* (Quito: Editorial Casa de la Cultura Ecuatoriana, 1956).

by several anthropologists, notably Allan R. Holmberg, Weston La Barre, and the late Harry Tschopik. In addition to benefiting from these studies which were carried out before the revolution of 1952, I have been able to study the Spanish-speaking and Indian peoples of Bolivia in three periods—in 1954-1955, in 1956, when the full impact of the changed status of the Indian was making itself felt, and again in 1958-1959. My studies were concentrated in the major area of the Indian upheaval, the Cochabamba valleys, but I have also made less intensive studies of the Aymaras of the *altiplano,* the transitional population of the eastern boundary of the Andes around Comarapa and Valle Grande, and the people of the eastern lowlands of Santa Cruz and the Beni.[5]

Land and People

Compared with other Latin American republics, Bolivia is a large country, with a total area of 412,800 square miles, roughly equal to that of Spain and France combined. Its situation as the only American republic without access to the sea has contributed greatly to a sense of isolation from the outside world. The Dirección General de Estadística estimates that Bolivia had a population of 3,161,503 in 1954. According to the criteria employed by the census bureau, in 1950 it had 1,703,371 "Indians." With Indians making up some 54 per cent of the total, Bolivia has by far the largest proportion of Indian population of any country in Latin America.

The distinction between "Indian" and "white" (or *blanco*) is crucial to an understanding of Andean social life. Both the Spanish-speaking *blancos* and many of the Quechua- and Aymara-speaking Indians believe that the terms denote a real difference in race as well as an important difference in the cultures of the two groups. In fact, however, in the four hundred years since the Spanish

---

5 My studies were made possible by grants from the Institute of Current World Affairs and the Grace and Henry L. Doherty Foundation.

conquest the two originally distinct races have so far intermingled that the racial difference has largely disappeared except in the most isolated Indian villages and in the largest cities, where many of the *blancos* are recent immigrants. Nevertheless, the fiction of the racial apartness and inferiority of the Indians has strengthened and preserved their very real distinctiveness of culture. Most writers, recognizing the inappropriateness of the word "whites," have adopted the substitute term *"mestizos,"* which, in fact, is sparingly used by "whites" and "Indians" of the Andes.

Thirty-eight per cent of "Indians" speak only Aymara. They are concentrated on the large *altiplano*, the level plateau of western Bolivia, which extends for hundreds of miles at an elevation of slightly over 12,000 feet. The Aymaras, living mainly in the heavily overpopulated areas near Lake Titicaca and also in the valleys of the Yungas, are surrounded by Quechua-speaking peoples, both to the west, where the Peruvian Indians also speak Quechua, and to the east, where the invading Quechua-speaking Incas settled in the richer agricultural valleys beyond the *altiplano*. Fifty-four per cent of the Indians speak only Quechua. Both Quechua and to a lesser extent the Aymara language are divided among numerous dialects, which limit the Indians' ability to communicate effectively with other Indians outside their immediate localities. And while Quechua and Aymara have many points of similarity in vocabulary and syntax, they are separate languages, mutully unintelligible. A few other independent languages, such as Uru are spoken by a very few individuals, most of whom also speak Quechua or Aymara. The diversity of languages and dialects creates a serious problem of communication within the population of Bolivia, for few of the Indians speak Spanish as a second language. The 6 per cent of "Indians" who also speak some Spanish are found in predominantly *mestizo* areas near the cities of La Paz, Cochabamba, Potosí, and Sucre.

The majority of the total population, and practically all

the Indians, live in the highlands. East of the plateau and
the mountains and valleys lies the subtropical lowland,
which makes up fully three-fifths of the national territory.
The eastern lowlands shade gradually from the arid pampa
of the southeast through the subtropical savanna and forest
of Santa Cruz to the jungle and flood plains of the Beni
and Pando in the northeast. Much of this lowland has a
rich potential for agriculture and grazing, but is little exploited by the few Spanish-speaking inhabitants and the
sparse and nomadic forest tribes, estimated at only 2 per
cent of the total Indian population.

The region of the Yungas, which encompasses the pre-
cipitous valleys of northwestern Bolivia, is also sparsely
populated. As the valleys of the Yungas fall off abruptly to
the lower altitudes of the eastern slopes of the Cordillera
Real, moisture-laden clouds moving west from the Amazon
basin deposit a heavy rainfall in the subtropical gorges.
In addition to coffee and bananas, the main product of the
Yungas is the coca leaf, from which cocaine is derived; the
coca leaf has been chewed by the Indians of the Andes
since before the time of the Incas.

From the Chaco War to Social Revolution

During the colonial period and under the republic,
Bolivia's economy has had a dual character. One part,
oriented to the world market, has been concerned with
exploiting resources which were not only exported but
largely processed beyond its borders. The rest of the economy, mainly agricultural and centered around local markets, was traditionally organized in small subsistence farms
or large estates—latifundia—whose produce flowed to local
markets little affected by world prices. Land-tenure patterns, modeled after Spanish manorial customs, served to
immobilize the agricultural workers in an unchanging way
of life. The religious structure likewise placed a high value
on acceptance of the traditional patterns and emphasized
the rewards of a future rather than a present life. The

social stratification of the society into caste-like categories fixed the tenure patterns and the economic and social behavior of different classes in a rigid system, in a traditional equilibrium which remained basically undisturbed down to the impact of the Chaco war which was waged against Paraguay from 1932 to 1935.

From this war the Bolivian government hoped to win a quick victory and to re-establish its prestige shaken by its previous losses of territory to Chile and Brazil. Bolivia's defeat was due largely to a weak government and an incompetent military leader, whose strategy proved disastrous in the unfamiliar terrain of the Chaco. Paraguay had the advantages of an able government, a shrewd military leader, and short supply lines into an area with which the Paraguayan soldiers were thoroughly familiar. Bolivia continued the fight with increasing desperation until, with both countries exhausted, the war was ended by a truce in 1935. Some 60,000 Bolivian and some 40,000 Paraguayan soldiers had lost their lives in the struggle.

During the war all classes of Bolivians volunteered or were conscripted into the army. For many of the Bolivians who called themselves "whites" or *gente decente,* it was an unparalleled experience to serve in an army with "Indians." The white and *mestizo* officers suddenly found themselves dependent upon the infantry of the once despised *indios.* For the Indians it was an equally strange experience to see unfamiliar areas of their country, to conceive of Bolivia as a nation, and to become the object of propaganda designed to persuade them that they were citizens of a single nation, no longer Indians, a people apart, but *gente,* or "persons," in the same sense as the "whites."

Bolivia was defeated, but it was neither the loss of lives nor the war itself which finally upset the country's social and economic equilibrium. It was rather the rise of a liberal image of the prospective role of the Indian within the nation, and a new sense of participation, real or frustrated, by the Indian population in the national life. In

Bolivia, as elsewhere in Latin America, the universities often provide the wellsprings of new political movements, and in the early 1930's a new political ferment was introduced by the rise in the Bolivian universities of a group imbued with Socialist and Marxist ideologies. At that time, a related movement, called "liberal" in Bolivia, was becoming fiercely nationalistic and anti-imperialist.

The long-maintained equilibrium, which had depended on preserving the role of the Indians as serfs in a feudalistic society, had been disturbed. To pacify the new unrest, liberal governments enacted new laws from time to time, thereby encouraging the Indian to seek a new status for himself, only to be forgotten by later, tradition-dominated governments as they attempted to restore the old regime. With each swing of the political pendulum the disequilibrium became steadily more pronounced, until the revolution of 1952 crushed the mainstays of the traditional society.

A new political party, the Movimiento Nacionalista Revolucionario had been formed in 1940 by a group of intellectuals headed by Víctor Paz Estenssoro, at one time a professor of economics in the University of San Andrés at La Paz. The MNR favored the nationalization of the tin mines and called itself "anti-imperialist." At first it represented an uneasy alliance between upper-class "liberal intellectuals," products of the universities, and the right-wing Vanguardia, composed of young army officers dissatisfied with their seniors' conduct of the Chaco war.[6] As the new party gained influence, it absorbed the political activities of the tin miners and the remnants of a much divided Marxist party, the "Party of the Revolutionary Left."

After having declared war on the Axis powers in December 1943, the government of Enrique Peñaranda was overthrown almost immediately in a coup organized by a secret lodge of army officers who then installed Major Gualberto

---

6 The Vanguardia should not be confused with the Vanguardia Obrera Movimientista, a group of the left.

Villarroel as president. Villarroel took several leaders of
the MNR into his cabinet and repressed both the traditional and the Marxist parties; Paz Estenssoro became
Villarroel's minister of finance. When the U.S. government denounced the coup as having been instigated and
financed by Nazis and by Argentine nationals, its example
in refusing to recognize Villarroel's government was followed by all Latin American republics except Argentina.
Unable to withstand the pressure of continued isolation,
the Villarroel government dropped the MNR members
from the cabinet, and six months later it was recognized by
the United States and other American republics. In July
1946, after the defeat of the Axis, discontent with the government exploded in La Paz. After several days of armed
conflict in the capital, the presidential palace was stormed
and Villarroel was hanged from a lamp post. Paz Estenssoro went into exile in Argentina, where he remained until he returned as president in April 1952. Throughout his
exile Paz Estenssoro remained the symbol of the aspirations of the MNR and "The Revolution." In the meantime Bolivia was governed by a succession of weak cabinets
of the right.

In the elections which were scheduled by the cabinet
of Mamerto Urriolagoitia for May 1951, the government
was expected to control the outcome by legal means, since
the franchise was restricted to literate males, largely urban
dwellers, who, it was thought, would split their votes
among several competing candidates. Under the constitution, if no candidate received an absolute majority, the
Congress could choose the president from among the three
candidates receiving the most votes. Since the Congress
was dominated by the government party, it would, it was
assumed, proceed to choose the government's candidate,
Gabriel Gosálvez.

The government party was more surprised than anyone
when the voters gave Víctor Paz Estenssoro 45 per cent of
the 120,000 ballots cast, and the MNR also elected six out
of nine senators and ten out of fifty-five deputies. How-

ever, in spite of the MNR's impressive showing in a restricted electorate which was not generally regarded as favorable to it, Paz Estenssoro had not received an absolute majority. Although he had a five-to-three plurality over Gosálvez, there was no assurance that the Congress would not choose the government's own candidate as president.

Then, suddenly, on May 16 Urriolagoitia resigned, handed over the reins of government to a military junta, and fled to Chile. The reason given by the junta for the coup was the necessity of keeping the MNR from power. The MNR, they proclaimed, was "an unholy alliance" of Nazi, Fascist and Communist elements which would establish a dictatorial type of government, nationalize the mines and industry, and institute a campaign of terror such as had prevailed in 1943-1946.[7] The junta lacked both positive leadership and popular support. It accomplished little, and its unity steadily deteriorated until in April 1952 a member of the junta, General Seleme, defected to the MNR.

From April 8 to April 11 a struggle was joined in La Paz to determine what forces would control the government and the country. In it, according to some estimates, as many as 3,000 persons were killed. Irregular forces led by Vice-President-elect Hernán Siles and labor leader Juan Lechín, both partisans of the MNR, finally overcame the opposition. The provisional government which Siles set up was turned over to Paz Estenssoro as soon as he returned to La Paz from Argentina.

Juan Lechín, recognized leader of the tin miners and guiding spirit of the Trotskyite Revolutionary Workers party (POR), became a nominal member of the MNR and was made minister of mines and petroleum. One of the government's first acts was to nationalize the tin mines, taking over the three large corporations belonging to the Patiño, Hochschild, and Aramayo interests.

Despite the present pride of the government in its

---

7 *The New York Times,* May 17, 1951.

agrarian reform decree of August 2, 1953, there was at first
little talk and less action about agrarian reform in the
period following the success of the revolution of 1952.
President Paz Estenssoro and Vice-President Siles were
essentially moderates. If agrarian reform was a part of their
political ideology, they apparently conceived of it as a
gradual turning over of inefficiently cultivated latifundia
to landless Indians. However, the Indians or *campesinos*
(farmers), as they now came to be called, finding themselves for the first time in a position of power, embarked
on a program of total land redistribution from below. It
was their demands and their power which soon forced the
government to recognize the serious nature of the problem
and to appoint an Agrarian Reform Council. One reason
why the MNR avoided making any pronouncement on
agrarian reform as long as it could was that its rightist
Vanguardia wing, which formed the main strength of the
party until it broke away in 1956, was opposed to land
reform.

In the later months of 1952 the situation in rural areas
had become unmanageable. The specter of a civil war of
extermination between *campesinos* and "whites" rose to
haunt the new government. A sweeping program of
agrarian reform was now indispensable, both to put some
order into the land redistribution which the *campesinos*
were carrying out by direct action, and to prove by a convincing gesture that the MNR was indeed the friend of
the *campesinos,* as it had so often proclaimed.

The Indians and Agrarian Revolt

The most striking and unexpected consequence of the
revolution of 1952 was the rapid and organized emergence
of the "Indian" *campesinos* as a decisive force on the national scene. The policy-makers, city-dwellers to a man,
still thought of the *campesinos* as unorganized, leaderless,
and susceptible to coercion. But this was no longer everywhere the case.

In the large interior valley of Cochabamba, located in
west central Bolivia, with the highest ratio of Indian
population to arable land, the campesinos had long been
in close contact with the town-dwelling mestizos. They had
become familiar with the norms of mestizo culture. As
early as 1936, almost immediately after the close of the
Chaco war, campesinos of one province, Cliza, in the department of Cochabamba, had established an agrarian
"syndicate" (sindicato) with the aim of freeing themselves
from the feudal obligations of service to the latifundium
owners and advancing their status toward that of the
mestizo. The first step was to arrange to lease their holdings
from the landlords, thus escaping from the traditional
obligations of rendering unpaid services to the patrón.

Very soon the campesino syndicate suffered a setback
which, however, in the long run only served to weld its
members more closely into a purposeful and determined
group. A number of large landowners of the area banded
together to destroy the nascent syndicate and remove this
direct threat to the customary pattern of landlord rule.
As a first step, in 1939 five landlords purchased those
latifundia which the syndicate members had succeeded
in renting from the previous owners, took back the lands
from the campesinos, and cleared large areas by destroying
the houses of the campesinos. They then proceeded to
"rationalize" the cultivation of the latifundia, retaining
the services of those campesinos who were willing to become pegujaleros (a type of share-cropper serf whose
obligations differed in minor ways from the older type
of colonos). Those campesinos who refused to submit were
driven from the lands which they and their families had
occupied in usufruct all their lives, and often from father
to son. This attack upon the syndicate members did more
than any other one act to unify the Indian population and
awaken it to political life. Treatment which had hitherto
been endured as acts against individual peasants was now
recognized for what it was, a concentrated attack by landowners upon the whole group of campesinos.

After this first defeat, the syndicate, now centered in the *campesino* community of Ucureña in the province of Cliza, turned from the direct attempt to secure the land for the peasants to a program of school-building and other improvements designed to organize and prepare the *campesinos* for what they now saw as an inevitable struggle with the landowners. Suppressed for several years, the syndicate re-emerged in 1947 when a PIR (Party of the Revolutionary Left) member was elected deputy for the province of Cliza, and a young man, José Rojas, took over the leadership of the syndicate. A native of Ucureña, who had been driven from the latifundium on which his father had been a *colono*, Rojas escaped to Argentina, only to return secretly to Ucureña later in the 1940's. There he worked as a laborer while he assisted in organizing the *campesinos*. Rojas affected to speak no Spanish but was an eloquent orator in Quechua. Deeply impressed by the platform of the Marxist PIR, he soon became a forceful and determined leader of the *campesinos*.

In 1949 members of the MNR began a new campaign in the rural areas, attempting to identify themselves with the *campesinos* and to enlist their support against the vested-power groups. They assumed correctly that, if they could win broad support among the *campesinos*, no government could resist their right to rule. During those years José Rojas held the syndicate of Ucureña at arm's length from the MNR, possibly because of the gap between his own PIR leanings and the MNR's more moderate objectives. The syndicate, as it happened, took no part in the revolution of April 9, 1952.

After the MNR had assumed power in La Paz, the syndicate of Ucureña emerged, after a short interval, as the organized spokesman of the *campesinos*. At first its influence was challenged by the new regime. The regional command of the MNR in Cochabamba attempted to place another *campesino* leader, Simón Aguilar, at the head of a "Syndicate of the Valley." Aguilar belonged to another *campesino* community, closer than Ucureña to the city of

Cochabamba, and was more sympathetic than Rojas to the MNR. The issue came to a head at the first meeting of the new syndicate, which was to unite all the *campesinos* of the Cochabamba valley. At the meeting, held in the provincial capital, Cliza, the delegates had to decide where the headquarters of the syndicate should be located. By a narrow margin they voted to remove it to Ucureña, and José Rojas thereby became the undisputed leader of the valley's hundreds of thousands of *campesinos*. In turn Rojas became resigned, at least outwardly, to cooperating with the MNR.

The early meetings of the Sindicato Campesino de Ucureña del Valle organized task forces of *campesinos* and young MNR students from Cochabamba, dispatching them to the farthest reaches of Bolivia. Often these teams of organizers were the first to bring news of the revolution to Indian villages of remote valleys and lofty plateaus. The syndicate groups showed the *campesinos* how to organize new syndicates of their own. Most of these later syndicates remain personally loyal today to Rojas, for they believe that he and no one else was responsible for their being established in the first place. As the wild fire of revolt and hope raced through the villages, the entire *campesino* movement was completely outside the control of the national government or the MNR party leaders. The only center it recognized was Ucureña.

In the early months after the revolution the national government in La Paz paid little attention to the rising tide of peasant unrest. It announced that the innocuous reforms decreed ten years before by the Villarroel government, which had placed certain restrictions on the exploitation of *pegujaleros* by latifundium owners, were again to be put into effect. The landowners were not much concerned over this mild gesture, and for a time the traditional landlord-peasant pattern seemed likely to remain unchanged by this as by so many previous revolts.

Then, on November 9, 1952, the syndicate of Ucureña demanded the return of eleven parcels of land to *peguja-*

leros who had been driven from one of the latifundia a
few years before. The landowner refused. Thereupon the
syndicate called for a general uprising of the *campesinos*
in the provinces of Cliza, Punata, and Tarata. It threatened
to pillage the town of Cliza and burn the houses of the
nearby landowners. This threat of direct action, reported
to Cochabamba, the departmental capital, found the governor and his officials, with their limited forces, understandably reluctant to interfere. Only prompt action by
the sub-prefect of Cliza finally succeeded in pacifying the
campesinos and in preventing a general assault upon the
latifundia and the smaller towns. The *campesinos* had
now come to realize their strength, and acts of violence
became more and more frequent.

The uprising of the *campesinos* could not but arouse
the national government to the necessity for drastic action.
If far-reaching concessions could no longer control but
only channel the emergence of the *campesinos,* they would
at least demonstrate that the sympathies of the government
were on the side of the now irresistible movement. Fortunately, the *campesinos* also had a direct channel to the
national leaders of the MNR in La Paz. The minister of
campesino affairs, Ñuflo Chávez, was acutely aware of the
government's dependence on the good will of the village
population, and was in close contact with José Rojas and
other *campesino* leaders. Ñuflo Chávez became an early
and insistent advocate of an extreme type of agrarian reform. His concept, if carried out, would have divided all
the land in areas of predominantly Indian population into
minifundios (small parcels). A reform of this type would
have converted the country's entire system of agriculture
to subsistence farming, leaving little or no marketable surplus to feed the cities. Had the *campesinos* been left to
their own devices this would assuredly have been the final
upshot.

As it was, the syndicates rapidly took over the most
accessible latifundia or *haciendas,* divided up the land
among their members, and expropriated the vehicles,

machinery, and houses of the former *patrones*. For example, at Ucureña the *casa hacienda,* or manor house, of one *patrón* was seized by the syndicate, which renamed it the "General Barracks" or village headquarters of Ucureña. Other houses were converted to serve as hospitals, schools or syndicate headquarters. By this time those landowners who had so far remained in the rural areas finally realized the full sweep of the revolution and fled for safety to the cities, especially to Cochabamba and La Paz. Since then most of them have not been able so much as to go near their former *haciendas*. Large areas of Bolivia have remained inaccessible for this class of *blancos,* often called *"la rosca,"* a bitter term applied to persons popularly believed to have used their wealth and power to exploit the Indians.

The Government and Agrarian Reform

The *campesino* uprising with its demand for agrarian reform posed several difficult questions to the MNR. As a political party, the MNR had risen to power as a congeries of groups each of which had its own purposes, and their amalgamation was not accompanied by a genuine unity of views or goals. The original inspirers of the MNR, leaders such as Víctor Paz Estenssoro and Wálter Guevara Arze, minister of foreign affairs until February 1956, were supporters of moderate, evolutionary "socialism." As such, they attempted to keep the use of force to a minimum. Hernán Siles, then vice-president and president of the republic from 1956 to 1960, also belonged to the moderates.

In the 1940's the moderate intellectuals had been joined by a group which called itself the Vanguardia of the MNR. The Vanguardia in turn was, in its origins, close to the RADEPA, an organization of younger army officers, veterans of the Chaco war, who had turned against the higher officers, holding them responsible for Bolivia's defeat.[8]

---

8 RADEPA stands for Razón de Patria.

However vague the political platform of the Vanguardia, its leaders were more conservative in social outlook than the Paz Estenssoro group, and also more willing to resort to force.

The universities had been another source of recruits and ideas for the MNR. While some professors and students were close to the moderate views of the MNR, many other students, no longer attracted to the older MNR intellectuals, had formed their own groups. The Avanzadas Universitarias (Avant-Garde University Students), as they were called, were young enough to be strongly influenced by the Marxist thinking that had flourished at the universities in the 1930's and 1940's. These groups were far to the left of the rightist Vanguardia wing of the MNR, whose adherents were barely lukewarm toward agrarian reform. Other influential leaders within the MNR took strong positions for or against the peasants' demands. Among them, the very influential Juan Lechín was an advocate of extreme land reform.

As the pressure of the *campesinos* and their syndicates was rising explosively, President Paz Estenssoro decided to put the government and the MNR at the head of the movement. On January 20, 1953, he proclaimed Supreme Decree No. 3301, creating an agrarian reform commission to study the "agrarian-*campesino* problem" and suggest the best ways in which the reform could be carried out. The commission, headed by Vice-President Siles, was given 120 days in which to prepare a report and draft a decree dealing with all interrelated aspects of the reform. These included property and tenure patterns of agricultural and grazing lands; "an adequate redistribution of this land, in order to raise the standard of living of the *campesinos*, intensify agricultural and livestock production, and develop the national economy"; procedures for liquidating the latifundia and suppressing "semifeudal" exploitive practices in rural areas; the effect of these reforms on agricultural production, work patterns, and the payment and protection of the *campesinos*; *campesino* housing; technical assistance and credit for agricultural producers; conservation of natural resources. While Paz Estenssoro assigned responsibility for carrying out the decree jointly to the ministers of *campesino* affairs, agriculture, and finance, the primary responsibility, significantly enough, was assigned to the minister of *campesino* affairs, Ñuflo Chávez, an intimate of the Indian leader, José Rojas, rather than to the minister of agriculture, Germán Vera Tapia, one of the stronger leaders of the MNR's Vanguardia wing.

Within the stipulated period of four months the commission completed a series of reports and prepared a draft decree which Paz Estenssoro enacted into law by Supreme Decree No. 3464. On August 2, 1953, the decree was signed with much pomp and ceremony by the president and the entire cabinet before a huge convocation of *campesinos* held in the village of Ucureña. Eduardo Arze Loureiro, who had aided in establishing the syndicate of Ucureña in the difficult years of the 1930's and 1940's, was named president of the Agrarian Reform Council.

The decree represented a compromise between two conflicting forces: the partisans of preserving productive and efficient agricultural units, whatever their size, and the advocates of distributing the maximum amount of land to the largest possible number of *campesinos,* regardless of the effect on production. On balance, the compromise favored the former. In addition, the decree recognized the overwhelming desire of the *campesinos* for individual private ownership, and had little to say of communal production cooperatives patterned after the Mexican *ejidos.* The decree, covering some thirty pages, may be summarized briefly:

The Nation maintains the original right of the Nation over the soil, the subsoil and the waters of the territory of the Republic. The State recognizes and guarantees agrarian private property when it fulfills a useful function for society. The State recognizes only the following forms of agrarian private property: the peasant homesite, the small holding operated by the farmer and his family for subsistence purposes, the medium-sized holding operated with the help of hired labor or with agricultural machinery for the purpose of marketing most of the produce, the Indian communities, the agrarian cooperative holding, and finally, the agricultural enterprise.

Specifically the State does not recognize the legality of the latifundium—the rural property of large size which may vary according to its geographical location, that remains idle or is exploited inefficiently by the extensive system (low capital inputs relative to other factors), with obsolete tools and with practices which serve to perpetuate the serfdom and submission of the peasant. The semifeudal estates are subject to expropriation in their entirety.[9]

The newly outlawed latifundium is distinguished in the decree from the approved agricultural enterprise. The latter is defined as an intensive farm, operated with large capital investments per unit of land, producing for the market, with labor paid in cash wages and enjoying the right to organize and participate in collective bargaining, regardless of the amount of land held by the enterprise.

The decree fixes the maximum sizes of holdings, which vary according to whether the holdings are on the *altiplano*, on the *puna* (high areas mainly used for grazing), in the interior valleys, or in the eastern subtropical region; in fixing them, only the cultivable area is taken into account. The size of maximum holdings for different regions, based on studies and reports by agronomists and land-use specialists, was defined as the area necessary to satisfy the needs of a rural family. The decree established the rights of the Indian communities to recover lands which had been usurped from them. From the date of the decree, communities which claimed restitution rights could occupy the land on which they had claims. This article, in practice, recognized the *de facto* occupations of land which had already been carried out by the *campesinos*.

---

9 "Texto del Decreto Ley No. 3464 que dispone la reforma agraria en Bolivia," *Revista Jurídica* (Universidad de Cochabamba), nos. 63-66, 1953, pp. 460-462.

All Bolivian citizens, 18 years of age or over, of both sexes, who intend to work on the land will receive grants wherever there may be available lands, on condition that they cultivate it within a period of two years. Peasants who have been subject to a feudal regime of work and exploitation are declared the owners of the land they now occupy or work until the National Agrarian Reform Service has granted them the lands to which they have rights in accordance with the definition of a small holding. The preferential right of one individual to receive a land grant in a given area rests upon his permanent residence in the area and upon his being a farmer.

In those areas where there is enough land the grants per family will be made by allocating one unit [the "small holding" as defined for the particular region] to each family. If the lands [available] do not suffice to grant a unit to each family, the size of the grant will be reduced in the proportion necessary to accommodate all those who legally have preferential rights to the land. The peasants insufficiently provided for reserve their rights to receive new grants in other regions where there are available lands.[10]

It was these provisions of the decree that opened the way for multiplying the small subsistence plots or *minifundios*. As the framers of the decree foresaw clearly, in those densely populated areas which stood in greatest need of land redistribution, there was simply not enough land to give each family an allotment even approaching the prescribed "small holding." By reducing the defined minimum holding in order to satisfy all *campesinos* legally entitled to receive land, the decree made a gesture toward appeasing the greatest possible number of *campesinos*. But it thereby made the sub-subsistence *minifundio* the dominant pattern in the more densely populated regions. Agricultural production and marketing have not recovered from this drastic change. That is the root of many of Bolivia's economic straits today.

---

[10] Same, pp. 473-475.

Bolivia's Seven Plagues

The continuing march of the Bolivian *campesinos* to power was symbolized by the election, in July 1956, of the syndicate leader, José Rojas, to the Senate. Since then, for the first time in Bolivia's history, the business of the Senate has been conducted in a native language when the speaker is unable to express himself in Spanish. In the same election the political figure most closely identified with the *campesinos*, Ñuflo Chávez, was elected vice-president.

After coming to power in 1952, the government had discovered, somewhat to its surprise, that it had no choice but to enact a drastic program of land reform. The same political realities compelled it to nationalize the tin mines in accordance with the MNR's electoral promises. The large vote cast for the MNR in 1951 showed how strongly the Bolivian people favored the nationalization, and the new government could not have survived if it had reneged on its promise. Meanwhile, tin mining, almost wholly dependent on world-wide economic factors outside Bolivia's control, was already encountering stormy weather.

For one thing, the Korean conflict had inflated the price of tin, and the price and cost of Bolivian tin were swept to abnormal heights. Suddenly, the turn came. On March 6, 1951, the U.S. General Services Administration announced that it would not pay the price Bolivia demanded for its tin, and suspended its purchases for stockpiling. On May 31, 1951, the U.S. Reconstruction Finance Corporation contract for the purchase of Bolivian tin also expired and was not renewed. Meanwhile, the quality of the Bolivian tin concentrate had been declining as the higher-grade deposits were exhausted. At the same time, the numbers of the tin miners, who enjoyed a privileged position during the Korean war boom and under the protection of Juan Lechín, had expanded out of all reason. The situation became so unfavorable that, before his retirement from the presidency in 1956, Paz Estenssoro reported that the production costs per pound of Bolivian tin averaged

$1.25. In early 1959, in contrast, the world price was about
$0.90 per pound. The full impact of this gap becomes
apparent when it is noted that over 95 per cent by value of
all exports from Bolivia is accounted for by metals, of
which tin is by far the largest part.[11]

Apart from tin, the other main pillar of the Bolivian
economy is agriculture. Yet Bolivia has been transformed
into a country mainly of subsistence farmers who are unable to feed the cities. The resulting serious food shortage
has been relieved only through U.S. aid which has been
granted for both political and humanitarian motives. In
1955 the U.S. hopes were expressed in a Senate document:

> The Department of State, which constantly appraises politi-
> cal, social, and economic developments, has concluded that
> the Bolivian Government is now Marxist rather than Com-
> munist and has advocated United States support of this re-
> gime on the same premise that it advocated support of the
> preceding military junta—to prevent displacement by more
> radical elements.
>
> The administration has accepted the appraisal and the rec-
> ommended policy of the State Department and is extending
> technical, financial, and material aid to support the Bolivian
> Government, at least until 1956. By then it is hoped by the
> State Department that political entrenchment and social and
> economic progress will have reached a point at which such sup-
> port can be sharply tapered off and ultimately no longer re-
> quired.[12]

The continuing instability of the moderate wing of the
MNR was amply illustrated in 1956, when Hernán Siles
publicly declared his reluctance, and at one point his
refusal, to be put forward as a candidate to succeed Paz

---

11 Bolivia, Ministry of Foreign Affairs, *Economic Development of the
Republic of Bolivia*, Memorandum II (La Paz: Author, December 1954;
mimeographed).

12 *Critical Materials*, Report of the Senate Economic Subcommittee on
Minerals, Materials, and Fuels of the Committee on Interior and In-
sular Affairs, Doc. no. 83, 84th Cong., 1st sess. (Washington: GPO, 1956),
pp. 116-117.

Estenssoro as president.[13] In turn, Foreign Minister Guevara Arze was forced by Juan Lechín to resign from the government. Finally, a series of riots in La Paz led President Siles to put an end to his policy of "pacification" and declare a state of siege.

Bolivia's failure to come anywhere near the economic goals which were envisaged in the U.S. aid program has been examined in detail in a report by the economic adviser to the American Embassy in La Paz and a member of the U.S. Economic Operations Mission. They placed the blame for the failure, not so much on the dubious wisdom of the economic policies, but rather on the circumstance that the policies had been framed in terms of a society and an economy which had existed prior to 1952, and which have since then been changed even more drastically than most people realize.[14]

The crux of the matter is that Bolivia's political and economic difficulties have been intensified, not reduced, by the basic social changes of 1952. By 1956, the life of a majority of Bolivians had been transformed in a mere two or three years to an extent which is paralleled in Latin America only by the transformation of the life of the Mexican peasants. But the transformation has taken place in Mexico over a period of thirty to forty years.

The election of 1956 installed Hernán Siles as president. In April 1952 he, with Juan Lechín, had led the fighting in La Paz that brought the MNR to power. But it was Paz Estenssoro, who had waited hopefully at the Argentine border until the fighting was over, who became the first MNR president, while Siles, as vice-president, remained out of the public eye. As a result, little was known of Siles' administrative abilities or personal convictions when he became president in 1956. However, he soon demonstrated a rare courage and unswerving belief in orderly processes.

---

[13] Paz Estenssoro was barred by the constitution from standing for a second term.

[14] Cornelius H. Zondag, *Problems in the Economic Development of Bolivia* (La Paz: U.S. Operations Mission to Bolivia, 1956; mimeographed).

The best example is his defense of the currency and exchange stabilization plan drawn up by U.S. experts, which was put into effect on January 1, 1957. A major difficulty in securing the adoption of the new plan was that many government officials were directly interested in continuing the old system, under which favored individuals could buy dollars at low "official" rates for importing scarce goods. Stabilization also brought a wage freeze, while prices continued to rise. Since this bore with special hardship on the tin miners, Siles soon earned the bitter opposition of both Lechín, with his fanatic following among the mine workers, and Vice-President Ñuflo Chávez, with his backers in the *campesino* organizations. Facing an uphill fight, Siles took up the struggle against inflation, large-scale graft, and the near-nihilism of the left wing of the MNR with remarkable determination.

Among the first to oppose Siles' campaign for economic reconstruction was Vice-President Chávez. When Chávez miscalculated his strength and backed an ultimatum to Congress with a threat to resign, Congress rejected the ultimatum and accepted his resignation. In December 1956 Lechín, a constant opponent of Siles, organized a miners' walkout at Llallagua as a demonstration against the proposed stabilization plan. By declaring a hunger strike, Siles rallied support and broke the demonstration. Again, in March 1958, Siles' harassment by Lechín, apparently seconded by Paz Estenssoro, who was threatening to return to Bolivia from his ambassadorship in London, was temporarily halted when Siles submitted his resignation and left the government palace. After six labor unions had struck in his support and a huge popular demonstration in the Plaza Murillo had urged him to withdraw his resignation, Siles consented to return. Speaking from the back of a small truck, he called for austerity and order, and warned his countrymen of the chaos that would follow any attempt to carry out Lechín's promises. Siles was carried back to the Palacio Quemado on the shoulders of the crowd. Shortly thereafter, a series of strikes which Lechín and his lieutenant, Mario Torres, attempted in the tin mines, ended in failure.

In 1956, a U.S. Senate committee described Juan Lechín as "Marxist-minded," and said of his former party:

The POR (Partido Obrero Revolucionario) became the Bolivian Trotskyist Party, closely linked with the Peruvian and Argentine POR and with the Bolivian Central Obrero Boliviano, the principal labor union headed by Juan Lechín, who, in May 1951, denounced as unconstitutional the law outlawing the Communist Party in Bolivia. . . .[15]

In 1955, when the U.S. Congress was considering continuing aid to Bolivia, Lechín resigned as minister of mines. The sentiment has been expressed frequently in Bolivia that this step was a condition for the extension of further aid by the United States.

Meanwhile the stabilization program had begun to have a dampening effect on the inflation. The boliviano, which had fallen to about 12,000 to the dollar under Paz Estenssoro, recovered to around 8,500. By the end of 1957 the cost of living had begun to decline slightly, thus interrupting a steep rise which had gone on since 1952. In January 1958, in the face of ineffective opposition, Siles again froze salaries and wages for another year. But by December 1958 the cost of living had resumed its upward climb, and at the end of the year the exchange rate was again 12,000 bolivianos to the dollar.

Meanwhile, Siles' political problems were growing worse. Before the congressional elections of July 1958, Paz Estenssoro returned briefly from London to participate in the campaign. In this instance, his role was not decisive, and Siles rode through the election without substantial gains or losses. In Bolivian politics it is now difficult, however, to distinguish who supports whom or who is elected to Congress because he may be less dangerous inside than out.

In August 1958, Siles issued a new ultimatum—his

---

15 *Critical Materials*, cited p. 115.

eighth—to Congress to maintain his "hold-the-line" policy, and for the eighth time he accompanied it by his resignation from the presidency in case the ultimatum was not accepted. For the eighth time Congress voted to support Siles, and for the eighth time he withdrew his resignation.

The opposition's reply to Siles' precarious success was strikes and more strikes. A transportation strike called by Lechín closed down the railroads for several weeks. By early 1959 it had become increasingly clear that Siles could not convince miners, workers, and farmers of the need of indefinitely prolonged sacrifices for the sake of stabilization. The white-collar workers, formerly a strong support for the moderate wing of the MNR, were losing faith as they attempted to live on $20 to $60 a month.

The right also opposed Siles' stabilization program. In mid-September 1958, Siles' half brother, Luis Adolfo Siles, representing the rightist PSD (Social Democratic party), signed a pact with Oscar Unzaga de la Vega, the leader of the Falange, the bulwark of the opposition, for closer cooperation between their parties, emphasizing their opposition to the stabilization and *status quo* policies of the Siles faction within the MNR. In it they declared: "The nation finds itself under a government which survives by inertia, without faith in its men or methods and without hope in its ideas."

In late September 1958, the economy and the MNR received a harsh blow from a new quarter. During the previous year, Russia had been selling substantial quantities of tin in free world markets, at prevailing prices. Most of it was purchased by the International Tin Council, which was attempting to maintain a price of 91 cents a pound. When the Council's funds were exhausted, the price of this plunged for a time below 80 cents, while Bolivia protested in the United Nations against Russia's economic aggression. The imposition by the United States of lead and zinc import quotas also weakened Bolivia's economic position. The combination of unfavorable factors caused the boliviano to slip from about 9,000 to the dollar, at which level it had been held for nearly two years, to about 11,220 in September 1958.

In the presidential election scheduled for May, and then postponed until June 1960, Hernán Siles was debarred from succeeding himself. A comparatively young man, he will continue to be a force on the political scene. In 1959 Víctor Paz Estenssoro returned to Bolivia to campaign for the presidency. In 1960 Paz again demonstrated his control of the MNR, was elected to a new four-year term in an election marred by scattered violence and by many charges of stuffing and stealing ballots. The popularity of the Paz candidacy was undoubtedly bolstered by Juan Lechín standing with him for the vice-presidency. The main opponent to Paz was Wálter Guevara Arze, who had done yeoman service in the MNR since its founding, serving almost continuously in high office. Guevara had apparently concluded that 1960 was his year for the presidency, and several MNR moderates supported him, even tentatively organizing a new splinter party, the Authentic MNR, to oppose Paz Estenssoro's candidacy. For a time Guevara attempted to dissociate himself from this faction and from open opposition to Paz, but strong support from "political control posts" (a kind of urban militia) and urban residents of Cochabamba forced his hat into the ring.

Retiring President Siles was as usual in a difficult position. When Paz apparently forced Guevara's resignation as minister of interior in October 1959, Siles appointed him minister of foreign affairs, a position he had previously held under Paz. The moderates' support of Guevara, and Siles' initial refusal to remove him from the cabinet, inevitably drove Paz closer to the left, headed by Lechín, although Lechín has never enjoyed Paz's full confidence. Immediately after the election of June 1960 it was far from clear how great Lechín's influence would be in the new Paz administration. Ñuflo Chávez's fall in 1956 demonstrated that MNR vice-presidents are expendable, and Paz had once before struck down Lechín from cabinet rank.

Paz's actions quite obviously will be subject to the pressures brought to bear upon him, and now it matters little that many of those pressures were of his own making.

In 1959 *campesino* leader José Rojas was named minister of *campesino* affairs, technically a step up, but in reality removing him from direct leadership. He remained in the cabinet only a few months before his resignation in November, thereupon returning to the Ucureña area to participate in virtually open warfare over the future leadership of the *campesino* movement. New patterns of peasant leadership had not emerged clearly by early 1960. Federico Alvarez Plata, one-time vice-president and president of the Senate, and Lechín's opponent in 1960 for the vice-presidency, has made little headway in his attempt to organize the Aymara-speaking *campesinos* of the *altiplano* to counterbalance the Rojas organization, which is strongest among Quechua speakers.

The Falange, the strongest adversary of the MNR, had meanwhile suffered a severe setback in April 1959, when, taking advantage of the economic discontent, it staged another of its abortive revolts against the MNR. In La Paz some two hundred persons were killed in street fighting, many of them the younger and more fanatic Falangists. This Sunday morning coup, in which much of the fighting centered around the Cathedral and the Church of San Francisco, further discredited the Falange. Party leader Oscar Unzaga de la Vega was killed, or accomplished the difficult feat of suicide by two mortal gun shots to the head. In the 1960 elections the Falange, as usual, gathered substantial support only in the cities.

In the early months of 1960 newspapers reported the Bolivian government as contemplating the establishment of diplomatic relations with the Soviet Union and the United Arab Republic. Simultaneously the Soviet government was reported to be offering a loan of $70 million to finance Soviet or Soviet-bloc exports, to help the state-owned Yacimientos Petrolíferos Fiscales Bolivianos build up the extraction and refining of Bolivia's promising but underdeveloped oil reserves. There were also reports of plans to withdraw Bolivia's diplomatic representatives from Panama and Costa Rica and to handle affairs with these countries through its ambassador to Cuba. Responsible newspapers in La Paz were critical of the rumored moves. But it was significant that the government found it necessary to plant the ominous rumors, if indeed the moves were not seriously contemplated, in order to dissociate itself from the accusation of slavish adherence to U.S. policy as epitomized in the stabilization plan. Unable for several years to secure U.S. government funds to develop its potential oil resources, in June 1960 Bolivia received its first U.S. government loan, in the amount of $2.7 million, supplementing private loans by U.S. business, to develop oil production.

Personal loyalties and ideological abstractions play major roles in Bolivian politics, but a central factor in the political struggle today is the persistent economic dilemma of the country. For the miners and white-collar workers a new round of inflation threatens their already meager livelihood, and political forces on the left and the right are awaiting the moment when economic despair may further erode the power of the moderate wing of the MNR. How have the *campesinos* fared in these turbulent years? Always insulated to a high degree against the fluctuations of the market economy, yet able to expand their subsistence farms after the land reforms, will their support offset the discontent of many urban groups, hard hit as they have been by the continuing crisis and perilously close to the seat of power? While much has changed since 1952 in the political power of the *campesinos,* they are, after all, only at the beginning of a complex process of social and cultural change.

"Campesino" Attitudes and Cultural Change

Before the Chaco war, the Indian *campesinos* had preserved many ancient patterns under the crust of a caste society. When people spoke of "the Bolivians" they meant the Spanish-speaking inhabitants of cities and towns. By merely stating this former basic distinction in Bolivian life, we can understand better the degree to which it has already lost its meaning. First, however, we must take a closer look at the two cultural worlds of the Indians and the whites, as they have persisted with but little change from colonial times until recent years.

One factor which has long contributed to the stability of the Indian-*mestizo* relationship has been a rigid class stratification, one so rigid as to approximate a system of closed castes. Social stratification both supported and was supported by the habit of viewing the world in terms of an unchanging hierarchy, of "lower" who were always lower, and "higher" who were born to be higher. Marriage within each class, the great obstacles to individual mobility, and the mutual imperviousness of the classes were reinforced by ascribing to each social class certain qualities which an individual could possess only through being born into that class. The caste-like rigidity of the society was strongly reinforced by the continued ascription of an ethnic or racial distinctiveness to "Indians," "*mestizos*," and "white" long after the physiological basis of the distinction had disappeared. This traditional force of immobility justified the continuing payment by "Indians" of many obligations—in money, in kind, in service, and in humble deference—to the benefit of that class which claimed the mantle of aristocratic status. But the price of immobility was stagnation.

The social immobility typical of the Bolivian class structure was further intensified by the absence of educational facilities for the *campesinos* living on the latifundia. While the traditional social stratification operated to restrict their social mobility, their economic and geographical mobility was also severely hampered by lack of education, widespread illiteracy, a general inability to speak Spanish, and their ignorance of other opportunities and other regions.

The religious values taught by the Roman Catholic Church, as it functioned in Bolivian society, and also the secular nonstriving values held in various classes, tended likewise to maintain the *status quo.* The general effect of these attitudes was to transfer to a future life the aspiration for rewards and to encourage a fatalistic acceptance of present conditions. In some regions of Latin America the church has developed an active concern for the social and cultural advancement of underpriviliged autochthonous groups and classes. No such autochthonous movement has yet appeared in Bolivia, and therefore secular leaders, drawn from the universities and trade-unions, and more recently from the peasant class, have supplied the impetus to break the enchanted circle of immobility.

Under these conditions, the *campesinos,* living from their subsistence plots on the latifundia, were barely able to maintain themselves at this poverty-stricken level, and even the assurance of a minimum livelihood depended on the will of the landowners or their agents. The life of the overpopulated and underdeveloped Andean villages has been shaped by what may be called the "conservatism of subsistence," with its suspicion and rejection of change, particularly as it affects the production of food. Andean agriculture has remained highly traditional, the *campesinos* reasoning that the methods they use have afforded a livelihood to past generations and are likely to do so for future ones. In a society which is close to a starvation level, experimentation with what may be better techniques involves a perilous range of risks. In a society which produces even a slight surplus, experimentation with new crops, new farming practices, and potentially better seed is practicable, for the penalty for error is to put up with a temporarily lower return. In the absence of any surplus, and with even day-to-day maintenance problematical, experimentation runs the danger of reducing agricultural output below the requirements for subsistence.

The institutions and customs of rural Bolivia placed political and economic power in the hands of small groups

who were primarily interested in preserving the static
social system. Cultural barriers between classes barred
those persons with an interest in changing the *status quo*
from reaching positions from which they could do so. The
teachings of the church, and widespread attitudes of fatalism, dependency, and conservatism, discouraged those
persons who had the most to gain from a disruption of
the equilibrium from interfering with its continued
preservation.

On another level, Bolivian society was strongly influenced by what can most conveniently be called "paternalism." The *patrón* of the latifundium was visualized as a
patriarch regulating the life of the *hacienda*. Within the
traditional pattern, the *patrón* functioned not only as an
administrator but also, ideally, as a benefactor who would
provide medicines for the sick, gifts when he stood as god-
father in baptisms, confirmations, or weddings, and perhaps succor for the family in the event of death. In return
the *patrón* expected from his peasants not only the prompt
fulfillment of their labor obligations, but also personal
loyalty, obedience, and faithfulness in all situations.

It must be emphasized that in practice this ideal pattern
was fulfilled only rarely. More often the *patrón* resided in
cities most of the time, visiting the latifundium only on
special occasions. *Haciendas* of absentee owners, and the
estates owned by the church or various monastic orders,
were supervised by salaried or commissioned administrators who, although they enjoyed the privileges of paternalism, felt little sense of reciprocal obligation.

But the theme of paternalism was not restricted to the
relation between *patrón* and peasant. It was fostered by
the church, through which the *padre* served ideally as the
benevolent father of his community and expected unques-
tioning obedience. Even the government encouraged the
pattern of paternalism by "giving" roads, public works,
and tax dispensations to communities in exchange for un-
reserved loyalty to the government, which, in turn, was

often personified in a single individual, a *caudillo,* a leader of absolute power.

Even today the pattern of paternalism persists in the relations between the *campesinos* and the government. The *campesinos* believe their problems will be resolved promptly if they can only set them personally before "Don Hernán" (Siles) or "Don Víctor" (Paz Estenssoro). They believe that special personal consideration is their due, and they feel that a complete personal loyalty may be legitimately expected of them by any leader in a position to benefit them. This is one factor behind the personal power exercised by such leaders as José Rojas or Juan Lechín.

The persistence of paternalistic attitudes has created many difficulties in the new setting of individual land holdings and the new climate of individual initiative. With the disappearance of the *patrón,* even as a symbol, the only substitutes which have arisen are the leaders of the *campesino* syndicates. In often inexperienced hands the resulting power has had some unfortunate consequences.

Although the effects of the Chaco war in disrupting the balance of the traditional society should not be overemphasized, it did, in fact, serve as a catalytic agent in a period of new thinking which accompanied the introduction of Socialist, Marxist, and "liberal" doctrines into Bolivia. This new stream of thought worked through the universities in the late 1920's and early 1930's, establishing the philosophic basis of an ardent nationalism, which found its expression in the disastrous war with Paraguay. Whatever the logic of the position, the effect of the reiterated slogans, the sudden physical equality of combatants of all classes, the new knowledge of opportunities, all operated to break or weaken those barriers upon which the former system had rested.

In the uneasy atmosphere which followed the Chaco war, troubled further by the vacillations and false starts of the national government in its promises to help the *campesinos,* the more alert and informed peasants of the

Cochabamba valleys took matters, as we have seen, into their own hands. With some help from *mestizo* leaders, the syndicate of Ucureña emerged as a prototype peasant organization, with a platform and leaders of its own. Officially, the new government is the strongest supporter of *campesino* hopes and actions. At a deeper psychological level, however, even the present government seems somewhat ambivalent toward that very part of the population which it has done much to set free. Otherwise, it is difficult to understand the official proclamation of the second of August as the annual "Day of the Indian" *(el Día del Indio),* for this assumes that the *campesinos* will be pleased by this annual reminder of past contempt for them as a distinct ethnic group. The purpose of the government is presumably to honor the folkways of its people. But the spectacle of a national celebration of "Indian Day," centered in Ucureña around a colossal statue of an idealized Indian, is a strange sight in a community which has done more than any other to eradicate from social consciousness the stereotype of "the Indian."

The Process of Cultural Change

When I first attempted to understand the changes that are taking place among the Indians of Bolivia, I found no really satisfactory analysis of these complex processes, nor any studies of the ways in which these changes in Bolivia may differ from similar processes in other parts of the Andes. In 1955, as a start toward gathering firsthand data on social change among the *campesinos,* I conducted a survey of seven widely scattered communities in the department of Cochabamba, based on an eight-page questionnaire administered to five hundred heads of families. Among the communities selected there were isolated settlements in the higher altitudes of the *puna,* villages located among the *mestizo* towns in the lower altitudes of the agricultural valleys, a community in the subtropical southern part of the department, some villages which had been parts of latifundia, and other villages of *campesinos* who had owned their individual small-holdings even before the agrarian reform.

The Indians of the Andes, even those who speak Quechua, are not a homogeneous people, nor are their communities made up of like-minded individuals. They cannot be accurately classed simply as "conservative" or "progressive," or assigned along a continuous spectrum between folkways and urban ways. There are great differences between individual communities, as well as in their images of themselves and in their attitudes toward that part of the outside world which they know.

The communities which I studied showed many differences in the process of cultural change, when compared with the Peruvian highland villages which I had investigated in 1951-1952 and again in 1953. The differences explain in part why the Bolivian *campesinos* have shown so strong a spirit of cohesion in their mass movement. The Peruvian Indians of the Callejón de Huaylas, in contrast, have not developed this potential for coordinated action, except after receiving the type of guidance described in this volume by Allan R. Holmberg.

In planning my survey I prepared a set of questions designed to measure change from a generalized Indian type to a generalized *mestizo* type of culture. It consisted of many of the common cultural indices: language spoken, type of clothing worn, attendance at Mass, church or civil marriage, sponsorship of *fiestas,* school attendance, use of coca, type of eating utensils, type of bed, diet, use of native curers or educated physicians, travel, and army experience. The questionnaire was administered by a Quechua-speaking interviewer to between fifty and a hundred male heads of family in each of the seven communities.

The survey brought to light one unexpected conclusion. Each community as a whole could be ranked, by the proportion of Indian or *mestizo* characteristics, somewhere on a spectrum between a purely Indian and a purely *mestizo* culture. But, strikingly enough, within each community the individual members could not be ranked meaningfully on any similar scale. Why this holds true of Bolivian communities is of great importance in understanding the way in which the society is developing.

Most theories of cultural change have assumed that when two cultures exist side by side and one is the "donor" and the other the recipient of cultural traits, there is a more or less continuous adoption of one set of characteristics by the recipient culture. By borrowing more and more traits and attitudes, the recipient culture moves along the scale until it becomes indistinguishable from the "donor" culture. Or else two cultures may borrow from each other until a third culture, distinct in many ways from both of them, has taken their place. In the process of cultural change, according to commonly held theories, individuals within the culture display differing attitudes and behaviors. Some are innovators of change, some are advocates. Others are acceptors, and still others are rejectors, of each change along the scale. Within individuals the sources of these different attitudes and roles toward change have been sought in psychological factors. Some individuals are more or less dependent upon authorities. Others favor changes because of a desire for prestige or because of their competition with rivals.

The assumption behind most theories of cultural change is that in any community there are certain individuals with a psychological or economic motivation to accept or resist innovation, to borrow or reject cultural traits which they observe in the other culture. In the process of cultural borrowing some individuals gradually accumulate more and more characteristics of the "donor" culture. In turn these innovators exercise an influence upon other members of their group and, in the end, the receiving culture comes to conform more and more closely to the characteristics of the donor culture.

What I found especially striking in the Bolivian villages I studied is that the individual villagers do not simply borrow one *mestizo* characteristic after another, in a continuous movement from Indian to *mestizo* status. On the contrary, in the Bolivian communities the adoption of a *mestizo* trait does not usually displace or destroy a corresponding Indian trait. The *campesinos* continue to exhibit both Indian and *mestizo* traits, treating each as an alternative rather than a mutually exclusive choice. One or two illustrations may help to show how the two cultures coexist within the same individual, as well as in the community to which he belongs.

In a Bolivian village an individual who suffers twice from the same symptoms of illness may on the first occasion go to an educated doctor for assistance, while on the second he consults a native curer. The same villager will wear *mestizo* clothing when living in a *mestizo* town, but he wears traditional Indian clothing while cultivating his fields. He may normally wear shoes, but he dons native *abarcas,* or sandals, while irrigating his crops. The same individual attends Mass and also publicly lights a candle before a representation, made of ears of maize, of the *Pachamama,* the native goddess of fertility.

Apparently the persistence of Indian traits as socially acceptable alternatives to *mestizo* ways is due to the way the Bolivian *campesino* looks upon each of these two sets of traits. Each of the two patterns of characteristics is recognized by him as defining Indian status or *mestizo* status. However, for him the images of Indian and *mestizo* are not images of two opposite and exclusive categories. An Indian who accepts more and more *mestizo* traits is still a *campesino*. But the *campesino* class is a transitional one; it partakes of both Indian and *mestizo* cultures although, taken as a whole, it is moving toward amalgamation with the *mestizo* population. Since the *campesinos* form an entire class which is becoming upwardly mobile, the Indian traits are not looked down upon, and individuals are not subject to disapproval if they continue to display them. Conversely, since there is no positive reward to the individual peasants for adopting *mestizo* characteristics for their own sake, few feel any urge to assume more of the *mestizo* characteristics than is justified by their immediate utility. The Bolivian *campesino* living in his own community attaches neither prestige nor condemnation to borrowing this or that *mestizo* trait.

In the *campesino* communities surveyed, certain *mestizo* characteristics have, of course, become norms of the village as a whole, and to that extent older, Indian traits have been displaced. The range of traits that have been generally adopted varies from community to community, but the same process has been going on, often in very recent years. For example, when church marriage, or civil marriage, or the wearing of European-style felt hats has come to be the norm for a community, social sanctions, such as ridicule or failure in courtship, are applied to those who deviate from the new norm, until adherence to it rapidly becomes universal within the community.

My survey likewise did not demonstrate a steady accretion of *mestizo* characteristics from one generation to the next. If individuals were the vehicles of acculturation, we would expect to observe a constant accumulation of borrowed traits. If individuals were the agents of change, these innovating individuals should at least be able to transmit to their children the *mestizo* traits which they themselves had adopted. It is true that in most cases individuals of each generation showed a greater frequency of *mestizo* characteristics than their parents. Yet, the surprising fact is that frequently individuals have not retained the specific *mestizo* traits of their own fathers. In some cases, while the father had also spoken Spanish the son spoke only Quechua. In many cases the father had attended school, the son had not. The son might sleep on skins laid on the floor, whereas the father had slept in a bed. Some fathers were married in civil ceremonies while their sons sometimes were not. Some sons had resumed coca chewing after their fathers had abandoned it.

What is the source of these apparent contradictions? The main factor is that in the Bolivian communities studied the attainment of *mestizo* status is not in itself a

highly valued individual goal which may be reached by
acquiring and displaying *mestizo* characteristics. Rather,
the process of acculturation is based on a generalized shifting of preferences within the entire community, a shifting
which is expressed in the gradual accumulation of *mestizo*
characteristics, over time, by the community as a whole.
In this situation, individuals seem to feel that they will
attain new status no sooner and no later than their fellow
villagers.

In these villages there is little or no conception of upward social mobility to be achieved by the individual
through his acquiring *mestizo* characteristics. Accordingly,
those individuals are rare indeed who, because of a personal aspiration for higher status, attempt to assume all
possible *mestizo* characteristics in order to reach a status
defined either by them or by the community as a desirable
one. Instead, social mobility within the Bolivian village
has continued to be defined by traditional *campesino*
norms or concepts, and these include leadership ability in
village affairs, oratorical and persuasive powers, and the
wealth needed to sponsor *fiestas*.

The process of cultural change which I observed in the
Quechua-speaking communities of Peru was a very different one. There two main processes of change stood out.

The first of these was typical of the *sierra* communities
of the Callejón de Huaylas. There the individual Indians
value *mestizo* status highly. But they can attain it only by
moving away from the Indian community, settling in a
mestizo environment, and there taking on the whole set
of *mestizo* traits and abjuring everything Indian. This
means changing completely their dress and their diet, giving up coca chewing, and even denying that they have come
from Indian communities. This type of change involves
first moving physically out of the Indian environment and
then moving socially upward. Actually, this process is not
one of "acculturation," properly speaking; it is better described as a combined pattern of geographical and social
mobility. Many of these individual migrants do not return

to their original communities. Those who do go back
revert completely to Indian norms and are reintegrated in
their original status within the community. Thus, neither
the *mestizo* culture nor the Indian culture is affected importantly either by those individuals who are absorbed
into the *mestizo* milieu or by those who eventually return
to their Indian communities.

A second type of cultural change can be observed in the
transitional communities of Peru, usually made up of free-
holders who are not attached to latifundia. There, social
mobility within the community is directly related to the
predominance of *mestizo* over Indian traits. It is to this
limited case that traditional theories of cultural change
apply. In these villages *mestizo* traits constitute a set of
both outward and psychological characteristics which are
adopted one after another in a fairly well-defined sequence.
Usually the learning of the Spanish language comes first,
then the adoption of Western non-Indian clothing, and
finally a borrowing of more general *mestizo* behavior and
attitudes. In this situation individuals seeking personal advantage or prestige serve as agents of change within their
own setting, and their examples influence others to emu-
late them.

In these transitional communities in Peru, there is a
high correlation between travel outside the community,
the learning of *mestizo* traits, particularly the Spanish
language, and upward social mobility. At any given time
a significant number of adult males are absent from the
communities, working on coastal *haciendas* or engaged in
commercial transactions with *mestizos*. These individuals
return periodically to their native communities, and there
they retain their newly acquired *mestizo* characteristics:
Western clothing, abstinence from coca, and so forth. They
usually speak disparagingly of traits defined as Indian.
They consider themselves *mestizos* and in fact are usually
called *cholos* rather than *indios*. In the Andean region
cholo refers to an Indian who has acquired some "civilization." It is, however, used in an unfavorable sense to

describe the *cholo's* acquisition of *mestizo* characteristics while at the same time calling attention to his supposed ethnic distinctiveness and inferiority.

In Bolivia, the process is one of gradual amalgamation, rather than of sharp and sometimes painful transition. The broad outline of social change is already discernible. Sooner or later the *campesinos* are certain to be absorbed into a new and more heterogeneous *mestizo* culture. The eventual absorption of even the presently isolated *campesino* communities into a generalized national culture, in which Indian and *mestizo* traits persist side by side, is being greatly facilitated by the distinctive nature of the process of change. In Bolivia the process is a communal rather than an individualistic one, and it is based upon a complementary rather than an antagonistic relation between the traits of the two subcultures.

The nature of the emergent culture is more difficult to predict, but a study of the small *mestizo* town of Cliza in the upper Cochabamba valley, together with its immediately surrounding *campesino rancherias* (villages) offers some material for projection. Because the *campesinos* remain strongly attached to their outlying communities, rather than copying the townspeople, it is probable that the social boundary between town and *ranchería* will eventually come to define a class boundary, based on occupations, rather than, as in the recent past, a near-caste division between *indio* and *mestizo* cultures.

The constant use today by town *mestizos* of many Quechua sayings, expressions, and words suggests that a substantial part of that language, naturally supplemented heavily with Spanish words, will be preserved in the amalgamated culture. The low esteem in which most townspeople hold the church and its functionaries, and an incipient anticlericalism which has been noted among the *campesinos*, suggest a continuing trend toward the secularization of customs and attitudes.

There is already a considerable evidence of the decline of fatalism among the *campesinos*, an attitude which has been in harmony with the teachings of the church. In their responses to questions concerning their general evaluation of their economic situation before and after the revolution of 1952, and their attitudes toward their present way of life as compared with that before the revolution, the *campesinos* in many cases showed a measure of optimism which they backed up by specific arguments.

The concept of equality of opportunity is well established among the *campesinos;* it is best indicated by their enthusiasm for building schools and educating their children, despite the added economic burdens. There is an increased interest in taking advantage of opportunities outside their immediate areas, for example, through the program for resettling *campesinos* of the upper Cochabamba valley in the eastern lowlands of Santa Cruz. The opinion is growing that a person can advance by virtue of his capacities, instead of being confined to a predetermined status. The spread of the concept of equality of opportunity is only one aspect, though an important one, of a general reshaping of values. The emerging system of values points away from the older social system, based on inherited or ascribed position, and toward one which will be based on personal achievement.

A further consequence of this new point of view is that more and more *campesinos* are coming to hold a favorable view of the accumulation of wealth. So long as they were dominated by the latifundium system, the *colonos,* or serfs, had little reason to hope for or desire the accumulation of wealth in any form. For one thing, any signs of prosperity usually served only to arouse the cupidity of the *hacienda patrón* or his administrator. In addition, the accumulation of wealth was often regarded by the community as a sign of meanness. It meant that its possessor was not fulfilling his duty to contribute to *fiestas* to the limit of his ability. Now the attitude is changing. According to case studies made of *campesino* households in the Cochabamba valleys, since the 1952 revolution a good many farmers have taken to buying livestock—oxen, sheep, cows—which they regard as a permanent investment. The building up of this substantial investment in livestock is a new and satisfying experience for most farmer *colonos*.

The extent to which accumulated property, or the ability to accumulate it, is becoming a new source of prestige among the *campesinos* is not yet clear. The studies I have made suggest a more direct relation between the new prestige scale and certain personal qualities that have enabled individuals to rise to positions of influence in the new political hierarchy based on the rural syndicates. These qualities are a combination of judgment, reliability, persuasiveness and ability to interpret the new national forces to their fellow villagers and to guide them in the new situation.

Another area in which it is too early to forecast new trends is that of marriage and family patterns. In this generally conservative aspect of social life no clear line of change has manifested itself. Quite possibly, the agrarian reform, which can provide only bare subsistence plots in the most heavily populated areas, will eventually result in the younger family members leaving these holdings in the hands of the older members while they move away to seek more favorable opportunities in other parts of the country. Against this background of turbulent social change, U.S. economic programs have been one of the factors shaping the new environment.

U.S. Technical Assistance and Economic Aid

Over the past several years, U.S. grant aid to Bolivia has been of two kinds: technical assistance, of the type once called "Point Four"; and economic aid, the direct gift of food, fibers, machinery and cash. Technical aid programs are financed by dollar grants from the United States, roughly matched by grants of the Bolivian government in its national currency. The food and fibers provided under the economic aid program are sold in Bolivia, and the proceeds in bolivianos are used for development programs or other forms of assistance within the country. Technical assistance to Bolivia has totaled $22.6 million since 1941, $17.9 million of it since 1952 (see Table 1). Economic aid has cost $112 million, most of it since 1954. The total of this aid exceeds $40 for each citizen of Bolivia. The technical assistance program is one of the largest and most comprehensive in Latin America. The additional economic grant aid given to Bolivia exceeds that provided to

TABLE 1

U. S. Economic Assistance to Bolivia, 1941-1959
(in thousands of dollars)

Fiscal year	Grants			Credits	Total aid
	Technical assistance	*Other economic aid*	*Total*		
1941-45	1,926	5,026	6,952	4,510	11,462
1946	561	25	586	1,200	1,786
1947	493	..	493	7,387	7,880
1948	435	..	435	6,005	6,440
1949	468	..	468	3,200	3,668
1950	361	..	361	980	1,341
1951	409	..	409	7,409	7,818
1952	657	..	657	5,260	5,917
1953	1,264	237	1,501	3,352	4,853
1954	2,924	7,913	10,837	1,701	12,538
1955	1,795	14,062	15,857	1,110	16,967
1956	1,997	16,056	18,053	3,860	21,913
1957	2,855	20,300	23,155	1,041	24,196
1958	3,400	28,694	32,094	26	32,120
1959	3,042	19,690	22,732	764	23,496
1941-59	22,587	112,003	134,590	47,805	182,395

Note: The figures represent expenditure of grants and utilization of credits during each year, not the amounts obligated or authorized.

Sources: U.S. Department of Commerce, *Foreign Aid by the United States Government, 1940-1951* (Washington: GPO, 1952), and *Foreign Grants and Credits by the United States Government,* June quarters, 1951-1959 (Washington: Author, 1951-1959); data for technical assistance, 1953-1959, supplied by the International Cooperation Administration.

any other Latin American country in the postwar period.[16]

Technical aid is administered by four "services" (*servicios*) dealing with agriculture, education, health, and roads. The services are considered agencies of the Bolivian government; they are supposed to cooperate closely with corresponding ministries and are staffed by Bolivian and U.S. personnel. The first service to be established was in health, in 1942, one of the first cooperative programs in Latin America. Education followed in 1944, agriculture in 1948, and roads in 1955. The programs of the U.S. International Cooperation Administration cover several additional fields: civil aviation, a school of public administration, a minerals survey mission, the preparation of a national petroleum exploitation code (now completed), the drafting of a minerals code, a financial survey mission, an audio-visual center, an office of special projects, and programs for training Bolivians abroad.

From 1941 to 1954 almost all U.S. grant aid to Bolivia was in the form of technical assistance. Since 1954 a large program of economic aid has been added through grants of surplus agricultural products, machinery, and cash. The United States has given the Bolivian government, in the period 1955-1959, $70 million worth of economic aid in the form of wheat, flour, lard, cottonseed oil, dried milk, sugar, cotton, aviation gasoline, and other goods.[17] The bolivianos obtained from their sale by the government to Bolivian consumers have been used for irrigation works, livestock improvement, a sugar refinery, potato production, development of manual arts, credit for miners, in-

---

[16] However, if governmental loans (mostly from the Export-Import Bank) are included, the total of U.S. aid to several other Latin American countries is greater than to Bolivia. Before the stabilization loan of 1956, which is discussed below, Bolivia had received only $41.5 million in U.S. loans.

[17] In this five-year period an additional $28 million worth of surplus agricultural products was sold to the Bolivian government under a section of the Mutual Security Act that provides for payment in the local currency and for the use of the proceeds by the receiving government for a variety of economic purposes.

dustrial credit, grain storage, road construction, warehouse construction, airport studies, a National Aeronautics Institute, a school for nurses, construction of the National Industrial School, the vocational school of Muyurina, school repair, and colonization programs.

At the end of 1956 the aid program was re-examined. The urgent need was to bring a halt to an inflationary process that threatened not only the party in power but also its social and economic objectives of increased production and equitable distribution of income. The governments of Bolivia and the United States joined with the International Monetary Fund (IMF), of which Bolivia is a member, to carry out a stabilization program aimed at checking inflation and putting the Bolivian economy in balance, internally and externally. The IMF advanced Bolivia a credit of $7.5 million. The U.S. Treasury provided a stabilization loan of the same amount. ICA, as part of the total of $23.3 million of economic aid allocated to Bolivia for fiscal year 1957, made a special grant of $10 million. For its part, the government of Bolivia replaced a complex system of multiple exchange rates with a single free rate, abolished all controls on foreign trade and on internal prices, restricted government expenditures and private credit, and froze wages at a higher level in anticipation of a rise in prices. To help the government avoid inflationary financing, counterpart funds arising out of U.S. aid were used, along with cash grants, to meet the deficit in the Bolivian budget. In 1957 these funds accounted for 39 per cent of the budget receipts and in 1958 for 34 per cent.

During most of 1957 the stabilization program made modest headway. Inflation was checked, agricultural production increased, and goods that would have been smuggled out of the country or sold on the black market a year earlier were offered for sale in the cities. Demand for foreign exchange was reduced and the drain on the country's foreign reserves eased.

Not all the effects of the new policy were favorable, however. The cost of living shot up as price increases far outstripped the rise in wages. Industrial activity declined when manufacturers could no longer import raw materials at artificially low exchange rates, benefit from illicit sales in the frontier areas of neighboring countries, or obtain credit on favorable terms. At the same time their domestic market contracted with the fall in real incomes. To avert wholesale unemployment, the government prohibited the firing of industrial workers, and the burden of this surplus labor increased business losses.[18] The easing of the government's budgetary imbalance was also brought about at the cost of slowing down investment in its development and diversification program. Many projects already under way came almost to a standstill with the curtailment of government expenditures.

The greatest blow to the stabilization program arose out of Bolivia's dependence on mineral exports. Normally exports of tin and other metals account for 95 per cent of the country's foreign exchange earnings. The collapse of world metal prices in 1957-1958 cut this income nearly in two. When the Soviet Union, for the first time, put large quantities of tin on the world market, Bolivia's own exports were drastically reduced. In the same period its best customer, the United States, imposed quotas on imports of lead and zinc and cut back sharply its purchases of Bolivian tungsten. The result, as Table 2 shows, was a decline of one-third in the dollar value of Bolivia's exports between 1957 and 1958.

In these circumstances the loans from the United States and the IMF could not cover as much of Bolivia's balance-of-payments deficit as had been expected. The sharp de-

---

18 For instance, in December 1958 the British-owned Antofagasta-La Paz-Cochabamba Railroad declared its inability to continue absorbing its large losses. Since the company was not allowed to suspend service, the owners offered to turn it over to the government for a trial period of one year without charge, with a proviso that thereafter the company would receive an annual rental of £500,000. The government refused, and the company eventually withdrew its personnel without reaching an agreement with the government, which now operates the railroads.

TABLE 2

Bolivia's Exports, 1950-1958

Year	Metal exports	Total exports	Metals as per cent of total exports
	(in millions of dollars)		
1950	89.93	93.95	95.7
1951	145.19	150.77	96.3
1952	136.29	142.07	95.9
1953	119.97	124.49	96.4
1954	100.43	103.69	96.9
1955	95.04	99.79	95.2
1956	99.01	106.59	92.9
1957	86.58	96.02	90.2
1958	54.70	63.24	86.5

Note: Exports are f.o.b. Metals are tin, lead, copper, zinc and antimony ores, wolframite, silver; from 1954 to 1958, sulphur and lead and tin bars and ingots are included.

Source: UN Statistical Office, *Yearbook of International Trade Statistics* (New York: Author, various years).

cline in volume and prices of exports inevitably subjected the internal economy to severe strains. The economic planners could not have foreseen that the abandonment of economic controls and their valiant attempts to curb inflation would coincide with a major drop in world demand and prices for minerals. By mid-1958 Bolivia was faced with a depreciating exchange rate and extreme pressure on the balance of payments. One by one the internal anti-inflationary measures were relaxed. Wage increases were granted, restrictions on credit were eased, and some price subsidies were reintroduced.

Even without the decline in the value of metals exports, the effort to end inflation required difficult economic and psychological adjustments. Many interests were affected. In one sector of the society, the tin miners lost the subsidies that had provided them with cheap food. On the other hand, industrialists lost the benefits of subsidization through artificial exchange rates and the reduction of debt that accompanies inflation. The shifts in wages, prices, and profits that accompanied the financial contraction created many strains and difficulties, and the resulting political pressures and agitation threatened one of the objectives of the economic reform: political stability. The export losses sharpened the threat. An advance in metal prices during 1959 and the efforts made to keep the stabilization program from becoming an issue in the 1960 elections have improved the chances of the program's success. Favorable prognoses became more frequent as the first impact of the readjustment wore off. But both the political and economic outcome remained uncertain, not least because of the doubt whether the foreign aid program was effectively reaching down into the roots of Bolivian life.

Some Problems of the Aid Program

One mistake in planning U.S. aid has been encouraged by Bolivia's own revolutionary leaders as they have turned more conservative under the pressures of governmental responsibilities. Both parties to the decisions—U.S. and Bolivian—have fallen into a double error of judgment. They have underestimated the profound nature of the social changes that follow the emergence of the *campesinos* from their previous status as serfs, changes that will make social and economic institutions unstable for a long time. And both parties have overestimated what an aid program, even one of the broadest in the world, can accomplish in imposing stability on an inherently revolutionary process of change.

The majority of Bolivia's population is caught up in this process. The *campesinos* are shedding the lowly status that previously made possible their ruthless exploitation. They, and urban Bolivians as well, are demanding more out of life than they received in the impoverished past. On the other hand, both the Bolivian government and the U.S. aid program have had to be concerned with the internal and external stability of the economy, and with strengthening that sector which is oriented to the world market. In the process they have frustrated some of the immediate expectations of the revolutionary groups. The attempt to meet the new demands without seriously impairing economic stability can succeed only if the formerly underprivileged and exploited majority learns rapidly enough to identify its interests with the world-oriented, exporting-importing sector of the economy. Only then can the government forestall a clash between the economically conservative and the socially revolutionary sectors. While it is true that Bolivia's problems will not be solved until it can put its economy on a healthy footing, it is also true that a healthy economy will not automatically bring about the social development and economic growth that are necessary. Foreign aid contributes to growth by providing more resources than the country can pay for, but it is an instrument of limited scope and flexibility. In Bolivia the root of the dilemma has been that a U.S. aid program of the customary type cannot bring about political and economic stability in a country that is undergoing a social revolution except by slowing down or halting that revolution. And in Bolivia that revolution is still running at flood tide.

After years of radical statements while it was out of power, and after the brief but sweeping changes of 1952-1953, the MNR government has been forced by a combination of many factors to adopt unexpectedly conservative economic policies. In fact, in 1952 the popular pressure for far-reaching changes—expropriation of the mines, land distribution, equal suffrage, and educational reform—was irresistible. Because the MNR rode the wave of revolution successfully, most foreign observers still consider the government "leftist," as, in a somewhat philosophical sense, it is.

In fact, however, recent and present MNR practices are more conservative than we might expect from its pronouncements. In spite of its bankrupt condition, the government has made payments to the Patiño stockholders.

When the government saw that it was not able to run the mines efficiently as a government enterprise, it attempted to contract for their operation by a private foreign corporation, which declined the offer. Likewise, in 1957 the government resumed service on its foreign debt, with U.S. encouragement, thus making good a default that had continued since the financial collapse of 1929.

The preceding administrations steadfastly resisted the disruptive policies of Juan Lechín and the radical efforts of Ñuflo Chávez, removing the former from the cabinet and the latter from the vice-presidency. How far Lechín's election as vice-president, in June 1960, will influence the course of the new Paz administration is a question mark. In any case, during his own period as president, Hernán Siles fought almost singlehandedly and against great odds to bring the currency stabilization plan into operation at the end of 1956 and then to maintain it. With the encouragement of the United States, he concentrated his efforts on checking inflation and achieving some measure of economic stability. Of necessity this policy has meant reduced government spending and a postponement of programs that would contribute to economic development. As the Assistant Secretary of State for Inter-American Affairs told a House Committee: "We had to tell the Bolivian Government that they couldn't put their money into it [the development program] and we weren't going to put ours into it." [19]

Bolivia's precarious situation in the mid-1950's required a solution to the problem of cumulative inflation. In the long run an anti-inflationary policy could help economic growth, but in the short run it posed numerous problems. The curtailment of the MNR program gave rise to a division within the party between advocates of moderate and extreme reform, and this split has in turn heightened rather than lessened political instability. Along with the

---

[19] Testimony of Roy R. Rubottom, Jr., in *Mutual Security Act of 1960*, Hearings before the House Committee on Foreign Affairs, 86th Cong., 2d sess. (Washington: GPO, 1960), p. 847.

loss of metals exports and other misfortunes visited on the Bolivian economy, the curtailment of the program has also involved the United States in a series of bailing-out operations whose benefits have been visible to only a small part of the Bolivian population.

U.S. aid has perhaps been too broadly spread and has attempted to reach into too many parts of Bolivian life, or at least the life of Spanish-speaking Bolivians. Its programs range widely, from training in public administration, to cattle raising in the Beni, to gifts to make up the national deficit. A program that attempts so much is inevitably spread thin; at times it lacks coherence and creates an expectation that U.S. assistance can be counted on to meet every need or overcome every difficulty.

Closely related to this is the tendency of part of the aid program to become linked with institutions that continue to depend upon U.S. support. Some projects have been going on for seventeen years. Begun as limited and temporary undertakings, often advisory in character, they have grown over the years and have acquired handsome physical assets that have then required more and more money to maintain and operate. Sometimes they become too large and too expensive for the Bolivian government to take over and run. By this time the investment in them is so great that it is difficult to contemplate abandoning them in order to assign funds to more pressing needs. Within this category fall the impressive but costly health center in Cochabamba, the experimental station of La Tamborada, and the vocational school of Muyurina.

For reasons of convenience, the aid programs have been directed largely at the Spanish-speaking minority of the Bolivian population. It is difficult to work with the Aymara and Quechua *campesinos*. Their cultures are unfamiliar to most U.S. and many Bolivian technicians, and on their small plots it is impossible to apply the extensive farming methods which account for so many of the activities of the agricultural service. Similarly, locating the health and education services in fixed centers has largely isolated them from the majority of villagers. All three services could facilitate the changes which are taking place among the *campesinos* only if they had more physical mobility.

One unforeseen effect of several programs has been to encourage the already serious exodus of trained personnel from Bolivia. With the best of intentions, the agricultural, education and health services, and the civil aviation mission—among others—have sent Bolivians abroad for training. On their return they have not found jobs in which they could use their new training; or the jobs which are available pay only a small fraction of what they can earn elsewhere, even in neighboring Peru, Argentina, or Chile. As a result many young people who have been trained at great expense seize the first opportunity to leave for greener pastures. Only by planning new training programs in keeping with employment possibilities can this loss of ambitious and skilled people be avoided.

Finally, the U.S. aid program has taken little advantage of the opportunity to promote settlement in the rich and almost unoccupied lowlands of eastern Bolivia. Although the Bolivian government has met with many discouragements in its colonization projects despite the high priority attached to them, this has nearly always been due to its attempt to do too much too quickly. Of course, there are social problems of adjustment, particularly in resettling highland Aymara and Quechua-speaking peasants in subtropical areas, where their new neighbors are ignorant of, and hostile to, the newcomers' cultures and languages. But with patience and understanding these adjustments can be worked out, as has been demonstrated in the successful project of "Aroma." Under this program Quechua-speaking peasants of the Cochabamba valleys have now been permanently settled near Montero in the department of Santa Cruz. One reason why this project has attracted little attention is because it has been carried out with only modest financial aid from outside, apart from the government's help in supplying the most necessary tools. Perhaps the settlers' own investment of time and effort has given them a closer identification with their new colony than in the case of other resettlement projects. At various times the Point Four program began colonization projects in the Caranavi and Inquisivi areas, both near La Paz, only to see them abandoned sooner or later.

The lag in opening up new agricultural lands has been especially serious because in its planning the U.S. aid program relied heavily on the Bolivian government's confidence in its ability to develop the Santa Cruz area rapidly enough to relieve the strains caused by the decline in mining and agriculture. Meanwhile, it is true, a large investment has gone into building the Cochabamba-Santa Cruz highway and extending it to Montero and Portachuelo, and into building the Santa Cruz-Corumba railroad, the Guabira sugar mill, and into constructing the Piray River bridge. All these expensive projects can produce economic benefits for large numbers of people in the near future only if enough people actually move to the new lands. Only then can they produce cane for the new mills, or grow the great variety of subtropical products which can now be shipped out to Cochabamba and beyond. Over the long run these developments will perhaps attract many settlers, but so far there has been a large investment in basic facilities and too little social planning of how to put it to effective use.

In general the U.S. aid experts and the Bolivian government have been equally mistaken in their attempts to interpret the needs of the *campesino* masses. Long-range development programs have too often been stressed, rather than smaller-scale, short-term schemes which would raise living standards for the majority of underprivileged peasants. The *campesino* reaction has sometimes been dramatic. For example, while in theory the agricultural service had four experiment stations, for a time only three were in operation. One station, at El Belén on the *altiplano* had been seized by the *campesinos* who attempted to divide its property for farming land. At La Tamborada, the station in Cochabamba, a number of valuable bulls imported for breeding purposes were slaughtered and consumed by the *campesinos*. The peasants' desire for immediate benefits is a factor that cannot safely be ignored.

To the *campesinos'* desire for seed, land, and water, the agricultural service has too often responded by offering insecticides, sprayers, fertilizers, and a school for training tractor mechanics. These innovations, while potentially valuable, are not adapted to the level of agricultural techniques practiced in most of Bolivia. The agricultural service has suffered from being too close a copy of the U.S. Extension Service.

The operations of the health service are limited by its small staff. Townspeople benefit from the health centers; the great majority of *campesinos* do not. With a more imaginative approach, backed by a small addition to its staff, the health service might cooperate effectively with the provincial medical officers who are required by the government to serve one year in a rural province before becoming licensed physicians. In cooperation, the two staffs together could do much to extend a knowledge of preventive medicine and treatment of disease to the *campesinos*. At the present time the *campesinos* rely mainly on the native curers, the *curanderos*.

Many of the aid programs never reach the *campesinos* simply because their staffs have little contact with or knowledge of the villages. Often the Bolivians employed by the various services are as ignorant of the peasant society around them as are the U.S. experts who arrive with no previous experience of Bolivian rural life.

The hopes of what U.S. assistance could accomplish for Bolivia have often been grossly overstated. It is difficult to believe that any combination of programs, however realistically planned, could slow Bolivia's revolutionary social changes to an even-keeled evolutionary line of development, halt inflation, eliminate exchange and budgetary deficits, provide roads, enlarge credit facilities, improve health, bolster education, develop agriculture—and at the same time avoid creating an overpowering sense of dependence or introducing the new problem of how the programs can be gradually tapered off without giving rise to serious disruption.

The Bolivian aid program has attempted much; its failures have been readily apparent, its successes often lie beneath the surface. A stranger to the country—especially one unfamiliar with the pathetic degradation of a majority of its population before 1952, insensitive to the new aspirations of a generation whose fathers were serfs, or who thinks of Bolivia as simply one more Latin American nation—would see only the failures of the aid program and would feel well advised to wash his hands of a difficult and thankless task. This view would be a narrow appraisal of the meaning of aid, and would overlook the fact that U.S. aid has accomplished well its apparently modest but in fact very difficult original intention: to help a group of men who accept the principles of democracy, who reject totalitarianism, whether exercised by a wealthy elite or in the name of the masses, to build a nation dedicated to true democracy and willing to assume a responsible place in the community of nations. These men were still in power in June 1960, and in all probability they would not have been in power, had it not been for U.S. aid. These men made a revolution which will forever change the course of life of their people. They made a revolution and they are in power eight years later, not a small accomplishment in the eyes of anyone who understands the meaning of revolution.

The inauguration of a new president, in August 1960, marked the third consecutive transfer of power to a democratically elected president, a development unprecedented in Bolivian history. Democratic institutions, which have been tried before and failed, are now succeeding. In a sense the revolution has come full cycle. The man most responsible for the reforms has once more been elected to execute them. The nation, now in its eighth year of experimentation with democracy, is still balanced precariously between a belief that democracy is identified with social justice, and despair that mere men can accomplish the connection.

U.S. aid to Bolivia has, I believe, accomplished its basic purpose and should be continued. Its overriding purpose is to help Bolivia find and follow the path of democracy and responsibility. Other and varying criteria have been applied to the Bolivian programs: Has it increased productivity? Has it raised the standard of living? Has it made friends for the United States? Has it promoted political stability? Has it promoted economic stability?

Some of these questions are answered here, others are not. Some reflect shallow thinking—such as the assumption that aid programs ever make "friends." Others raise complex questions such as that of the whole interrelationship between social change, political revolution, economic development, and the nature of stability. In a larger sense all these questions are irrelevant before the main question: does the program aid a country in its struggle toward democracy and responsibility?

This was broadly the criterion which the United States applied to its Bolivian aid program from 1952 to 1956. From 1941 to 1952 the criteria were strategic and humanitarian. Since 1956 the United States has applied a narrowly economic criterion to measure the effectiveness of aid, as illustrated in the report of the Senate Committee on Government Operations of 1960. Testimony in this report pointed the finger of wrath at an irrigation project which was later called "a worthless project, poorly planned and poorly administered," and the Muyurina vocational school, which was condemned as "an overbuilt, overequipped plant, years ahead of the need . . . and too expensive, too elaborate for Bolivia to operate. . . ." [20] There has no doubt been waste, inefficiency, and sheer ignorance in the

---

[20] *Administration of United States Foreign Aid Programs in Bolivia,* Report no. 1030 of the Senate Permanent Subcommittee on Investigations of the Committee on Government Operations, 86th Cong., 2d sess. (Washington: GPO, 1960), pp. 10, 11.

U.S. attempt to be all things to Bolivia. A generous ob-
server would hope that the United States can learn from
its mistakes, make its programs more pointed and more
effective in line with their immediate economic justifica-
tion. But the people of the United States would be seriously mistaken if it allowed difficulties on this level to put
in question the wisdom of its original and paramount aim,
that of helping a group of courageous men in their be-
deviled and magnificent effort to bring Bolivia from
feudalism to democracy.

Bolivia's Economic Prospects

Bolivia is confronted with problems common to many
underdeveloped countries: dependence on a few basic exports, low productivity, lack of capital, and an absence
of the spirit of enterprise. In addition Bolivia has had a
history of political instability, violent social upheavals, and
demoralizing inflationary cycles that have delayed the
establishment of institutions essential for economic development. At the beginning of the 1960's the prospects
for both political and financial stability seem far more
promising than they were before. The moderate wing of
the MNR has maintained itself in power for eight years,
the country's currency has been stable for a year and a
half, and internal prices have been kept under control.

With these essential conditions for economic health
achieved, Bolivia still faces the hard job of increasing output and productivity in all sectors of the economy if the
country is to live within its income and provide a better
standard of living for its increasing population. Agricultural output must rise so that meager foreign exchange
reserves need not be spent on food and fiber imports. About
two-thirds of the population live by agriculture, but these
people are concentrated in the Andean highlands and
valleys, where land suitable for cultivation is badly eroded
and low in fertility, and where many plots are so small and
distribution channels so undeveloped that little is pro-

duced for market. Some increase in productivity in the areas now under cultivation can be expected with the introduction of more advanced techniques, but the prospects for large-scale increases lie in the plans for opening up the vast and largely uninhabited areas of the fertile eastern lowlands. The Bolivian National Institute of Colonization is engaged in a program of resettlement in the Santa Cruz area, and the UN Special Fund is contributing $283,500 for surveys of the region. (Another contribution of $336,500 will go for training at two agricultural schools.) The Bolivian government has a broad program covering crop diversification, road-building, electrical power installations, and plants to process the products of the region. Exports of tropical products—oranges, bananas, and coffee—are already providing some foreign exchange, and Bolivia's rice and sugar requirements are being increasingly met from domestic supplies.

The future of tin is uncertain; its use has not kept pace with the growth of the world economy. As a high-cost producer Bolivia is at a competitive disadvantage in comparison with other major tin-exporting areas, and the declining grade of its ores and the prospective changes in world demand make reliance on this metal hazardous. In other metals Bolivia is generally a low-cost producer, and the prospects for some of them—particularly gold, antimony, and tungsten—are more favorable. The hopes of extractive industry lie chiefly in petroleum. Drilling concessions were granted to private foreign companies in 1956, and a pipeline across the Andes to Chile has been built. Exports of crude petroleum and gasoline have been rising steadily and an increasing share of the domestic market is being supplied from domestic production.

Manufacturing has made a very small contribution to national income, not only in absolute terms but also in comparison with other Latin American countries. A limited internal market, shortage of capital and skilled labor, dependence on imports for raw material supplies, and high transport costs have all contributed to a low level of industrial activity. The expansion and diversification of Bolivia's manufacturing and service industries are essential since the capacity of the agricultural and mining sectors to absorb additions to the labor force is limited, the first by the difficulties of reclaiming land in the *Oriente* and establishing the settlers there, the second by the surplus labor already underemployed in the mines. Until foreign reserves are larger and foreign funds more readily obtainable, Bolivia will have to develop those branches of industry that require small capital investments—processing of food and fibers, refining of ores, production of materials, such as cement and bricks, that are needed for development work, the manufacture of textiles and household goods. With an advance in agriculture from subsistence farming to the production of cash crops, new domestic consumers will be found for Bolivia's industrial goods.

The expansion of production in manufacturing and agriculture must be accompanied by even larger advances in two basic activities: energy production and transport. Bolivia has abundant hydroelectric and petroleum resources; it lacks the financial resources needed for their exploitation. And few countries have faced the transport problems that altitude and difficult terrain present in Bolivia, or a greater need for improvement in road and rail facilities. Here are two areas essential to economic development, in which foreign funds have traditionally been invested and where, for Bolivia, they are an indispensable supplement to its own efforts.

Another Approach to U.S. Aid

In its relations with Bolivia the United States has a special opportunity to exercise imagination and to answer its critics. Many Latin Americans have fixed ideas about their North American neighbor. One such idea was eloquently expressed in early 1960 by the Students' Federation of Chile in an open letter delivered to President Eisenhower during his visit to four South American Republics. In the name of its 25,000 members, the federation asked President Eisenhower if the United States had become "a satisfied nation which fights for the maintenance of the established order in Latin America." If so, according to the federation, U.S. policy would logically aim to protect the privileges of "a thin layer of the population which controls the power and wealth, surrounded by an ocean of poor people for whom the 'social order' means little or literally nothing. If the injustices of today are all that Christianity or democracy can offer this continent, no one should be surprised if the best children of these nations turn toward communism, seeking those elementary needs which they lack and which are the essentials to morality and civilization: food, shelter, and education." [21]

This is a serious question, asked by a group of men who have considerable political influence in Chile, and in coming years will have more. They are not Communists. They recognize that communism is an alternative they may have to face if the well-established democracies of the world value stability above social justice. They know that the United States is committed to an ideology of nonintervention in the affairs of Latin American countries, but they also know that the United States, by the fact of its existence, deeply affects the internal affairs of the smaller republics in the southern half of the hemisphere. Further, they are aware that the United States maintains programs of aid and possesses powerful economic weapons that have been used in the past and may be used in the future. The economic power of the United States may be used to help a country preserve a system that deprives a majority of the population of the opportunity to achieve higher living standards; or it may be used to assist a country in carrying out changes that put the interest of the majority before those of a minority. The United States cannot escape making a choice. Many Latin Americans, particularly younger ones, believe the United States has

[21] *The New York Times*, March 2, 1960.

chosen to maintain the stability of control by a minority rather than risk the upheavals that often attend the assumption of power by a majority.

President Eisenhower replied to the students' question in a letter of his own: "At once I recognize that you are giving serious thought to hemispheric and world problems; that some of your critical claims are justified; but that other statements indicate a serious lack of comprehension of United States positions and responsibilities." He spoke out more strongly to a group of U.S. citizens in Santiago: "And then I have heard it said that the United States supports dictators. This is ridiculous. Surely no nation loves liberty more, or more sincerely prays that its benefits and deep human satisfactions may come to all peoples than does the United States." [22]

Latin American students, many as familiar with U.S. history as their North American counterparts, do not doubt the President's words. But they and 175 million other Latin Americans would like nothing better than to see the United States actively and effectively assisting a country that has curtailed the power of an oppressive minority and has extended the vote and the chance to attain "those elementary needs . . . which are the essentials to morality and civilization" to millions who never knew them before. Bolivia is such a country.

*　　*　　*

The United States has been successful in the three major purposes that have shaped its aid programs in Bolivia. The modest program from 1941 to 1952 established pilot projects and helped keep a sometimes wavering government on the side of the Allies during World War II. From 1952 to 1956, U.S. aid almost certainly was instrumental in keeping the moderate wing of the MNR in power. From January 1, 1957, into 1960, the government's austerity program, undertaken on the recommenda-

---

22 Same.

tions of the United States and the International Monetary Fund, and supported by their aid, has contributed an important element of stability to the Bolivian economy, albeit at great cost. The time is certainly ripe for a more dramatic, a more active, plan.

A more dramatic program need not necessarily cost more money. Allan R. Holmberg's study (see above) vividly demonstrates the extent to which self-help and true cooperation can stretch dollars. At the same time scores of projects, from that at Vicos to the resettlement program near Montero in Bolivia, suggest that the sense of participation that comes from the aid recipients becoming involved in all stages of planning, operation, and support may be the key to the success of the program and to mutual respect between the cooperating parties.

In the last few years the U.S. program in Bolivia has suffered from faulty administration and inadequate supervision of aid-supported activities. In many instances inexperienced personnel, both Bolivian and American, have failed to evaluate with sufficient care the requirements of an area for which an aid project was planned and have exercised poor judgment in the supervision of the operations once they were under way. Charges of irregularities, wasteful and inefficient procedures, and misuse of funds have come from the U.S. Congress and from many Bolivians, who were dismayed by the shortcomings of some of the projects. The most serious complaints have centered on the failure to estimate the feasibility of projects in terms of existing conditions and on the injudicious procurement of equipment, sometimes greatly in excess of needs, sometimes ill adapted to the purposes for which it was to be used.

The aid program has shown a number of major weaknesses. It has been spread thin, mainly over the Spanish-speaking population. It is too rigid and too elaborate in its institutional structure, and patterned too closely after U.S. models. Its impact is not sufficiently felt by the mass of *campesinos*. Even those programs intended to benefit large numbers of people lack direct and immediate impact on those groups that they are designed to benefit. The United States, forgetful of its own history, has shown too little sympathy for the Bolivian government's compulsion to push its frontier down from the densely populated, inhospitable highlands into the plains of the eastern lowlands. Finally, many programs have created dependence. Instead of becoming self-sustaining, they are still too expensive for the Bolivians to carry forward by their own efforts.

The technical assistance program, in which the possibilities for direct contact with large numbers of Bolivians are greatest, has displayed a fundamental weakness. It has become crystallized around the structure of the *servicios* instead of achieving the flexibility and widespread local participation that it needs. The health, agriculture, education, and roads services have been for the most part inflexible in their planning, administratively top-heavy, preoccupied with policy, and too often dependent for their contact with the Bolivian people on a handful of nationals who have made a profession of dealing with North Americans. They have disregarded the psychological value of stressing local participation.

These defects are not inevitable. They could be largely overcome by putting more stress on the needs of specific communities or areas and by making each project a focus of local activity. Teams composed of both Bolivians and North Americans could be made mobile, instead of being tied, like most of the aid projects, to a few favored localities. Their main function would be to provide materials and direction that are not available in the local community, and to utilize fully the local resources of leadership, materials, and labor, not only for obvious economic reasons, but even more importantly for the intangible reasons of strengthening local identification with the project and encouraging local responsibility. Persons respected in the town or village should be brought into the planning of each project at the earliest possible time, and they should feel that their views are known and respected.

This is, admittedly, not the most efficient way to build a school, a road, or a sugar mill, but there are many advantages not apparent at first. One is a kind of "social multiplier" effect. The spectacle of work going forward in one community may stimulate another community to try its hand at a similar project. For example, the construction of an impressive school building by the Indians of Vicos in Peru prompted a nearby *mestizo* town to install a water system. Even more impressive is the widespread knowledge of the Vicos project in the remotest parts of Peru. The Peruvian Indigenous Institute has scores of painfully composed letters from Indian communities asking how they too can become like the Vicosinos. Another advantage of the focused project is the weakening of attitudes of paternalism—the lethargy of waiting for "the government" to "give" the town a road. Only thus can the tradition of dependence be weakened and eventually destroyed. The sharp definition of goals has propaganda value, and the North American personnel in the field are much more real symbols of U.S. good will than any number of cases of dried milk labeled "From the People of the United States of America."

The ultimate and perhaps crucial advantage of the project approach is that it can be expanded and contracted in accordance with the vacillation of the degree of U.S. interest in Bolivia's development in a way that will do the least harm to that country and to relations between it and the United States. Five school-building projects would be good. Fifty would be better. The eradication of malaria in Guayara Merim is a lasting and well-remembered fact. The eradication of malaria in a hundred settlements of Santa Cruz and the Beni is possible, and it would leave behind a permanent respect for the United States. The ideal answer, of course, is that the United States should understand the great impact its existence and its aid programs have on a country such as Bolivia. With this under-

standing there would grow a sense of obligation in the
United States to vote aid, once decided upon, for a number
of years at a time. In the meantime, the more flexible
project approach can do more than the present program to
enlist the efforts of Bolivians in recognizing and meeting
their felt needs for local development.

*   *   *

A new emphasis on community projects is not the
whole answer to Bolivia's problems, nor will it meet all
the goals of the U.S. aid program. It can help significantly
in Bolivia's economic development and it is an important
way of dramatizing U.S. sympathy and cooperation. In
money terms, however, the other elements in the aid program have been greater than technical assistance. They
have also been deeply involved in the dilemmas the United
States faces in its aid to Bolivia.

U.S. aid has been of crucial importance in keeping the
moderate leaders of the MNR in power. Since 1956, however, aid has been intimately linked with the stabilization
program, which has provoked serious political reactions.
In effect, U.S. aid, as well as the loan from the IMF, has
been conditioned on Bolivia's persisting in its program
of austerity and economic readjustment. This has been
judged necessary to prevent the economy from being en-
gulfed by inflation, to lay the foundations for future
stability and growth, and to ensure the most productive
use of aid as well as of Bolivia's own strained resources. It
has created, however, a set of political dilemmas for all
concerned.

The help of the IMF was sought, at least in part, to
reduce the political strains on the Bolivian government
and on U.S.-Bolivian relations by giving the stabilization
program an international status and backing. Though it is
"nonpolitical," the Fund cannot be indifferent to the
political fate of the member government with which it is
cooperating. The Bolivian government in turn has felt it
could not abide by all of the conditions stipulated in its

agreement with the IMF and still remain in power. It has moderated some of the austerity measures, but the freezing of prices in the miners' commissaries has dangerously strained relations between the miners and the *campesinos* when the *campesino* militia was used to break a strike of the miners against enforcement of the stabilization plan. The MNR moderates have become increasingly identified with the United States, whereas the left has found it increasingly effective to be anti-American. One can understand the poignancy of President Siles' complaint to the head of the IMF mission in Bolivia: "The United States has given me just enough rope to hang myself."

The United States faces the dilemma of its dual interest in fostering a stable and moderate government and in strengthening a sound economy in Bolivia. Concern for the long run and the short, for politics and for economics, has created for U.S. policy the paradox of publicly supporting the moderates while making its aid conditional on economic measures that may prove to be their political undoing. Like the Bolivian government, the United States has adjusted some of its stern economic requirements to meet the sterner political requirements.

In spite of vigorous disapproval of the handling of aid and some suggestions that it be discontinued, the U.S. Congress concluded in the spring of 1960 that the aid program had enabled Bolivia to weather a crisis without a major upheaval in its economy or political structure. There was hope that the re-examination of the aid program, brought about by unfavorable criticisms of its past operations, would lead to more effective use of both the U.S. and Bolivian contributions. This will mean the reorganizing of administrative procedures and the elimination of uneconomic practices.

But major problems will persist. The United States will have to provide aid to help Bolivia find new sources of livelihood to replace tin exports that will never again support the country's foreign trade. To escape the basic dilemma, U.S. aid policies must become flexible enough to reconcile the requirements of economic stability and moderate government in a revolutionary situation. This will require finding the means of easing the austerity program without plunging the country into a new spiral of inflation, of keeping the most important economic gains thus far achieved while enabling the moderates to gain political strength, of maintaining the present level of aid to Bolivia without imposing conditions that are beyond the ability of the government to fulfill. Otherwise the United States must face the virtual certainty that eventually Bolivia will be governed by the MNR left, with Juan Lechín as most probable president—a man who has built his career on hostility to the United States. Finally, and urgently, the United States must dramatize its friendly purposes to the *campesinos* who, having emerged from four hundred years of serfdom, now hold Bolivia's future in their hands.

This multiple task takes more than money. It requires, on the part of both the United States and the representatives of the Bolivian people, a more profound understanding of the Bolivians' culture, their newly emerging society, and their aspirations for a future very different from the past.

Four

THE BRAZILIAN REVOLUTION: SOCIAL CHANGES SINCE 1930

by CHARLES WAGLEY

BRAZIL OF THE mid-twentieth century seems to live in a state of feverish crisis. While one economic crisis leads to the next, Brazilian industry expands rapidly but monetary inflation continues its painful course. A building boom is under way in all the big cities, but shantytowns continue to sprawl. The tortuous course of Brazilian politics is hard to follow. A dictator, Getulio Vargas, overthrown in 1945, in 1950 was elected president of the republic in an orderly and honest election. Despite the scandals that brought this same ex-dictator to suicide in August 1954, his political party and political heir were victorious in the elections of 1955. An ex-governor of the rich state of São Paulo, who received over two million votes in the presidential election of 1955, fled the country when a São Paulo court found him guilty of malfeasance in office. Cleared of these charges by the Supreme Court, Adhemar de Barros returned to be elected mayor of the city of São Paulo in 1957. Meanwhile, crises afflict amost every facet of Brazilian life—transportation, food supply, water, electricity, schools.

An earlier version of this study, *A revolução brasileira: Uma análise dos mudanças sociais desde 1930,* was published by the Fundação para o Desenvolvimento da Ciências na Bahia (Bahia, 1959).

177

Specialists in different fields of study explain this continued state of crisis in different ways. An economist wor-
ries about the adequacy of capital formation, the pressure
of inflation, and the recent upsurge of industrialization.
A political scientist with an historical bent may attribute
the confusion in political life to the disintegration of
Brazilian political institutions and parties during the fifteen years of Vargas' dictatorship. A demographer could
point to the explosive rise in the population, the amazing
growth of the cities, and the disorderly migration of people
from one region to another. As a social anthropologist, I
am inclined to emphasize the shifting alignment of social
classes, and the appearance of new social and economic
groups, as crucial factors. Each specialist would in a sense
be right. Each describes but one aspect of a basic transformation in Brazilian society, a transformation which began
during the early years of this century, has been felt with
increasing intensity since 1930, and has not yet run its
course.

This process of transformation, which I shall call the
"Brazilian revolution," is at once an economic, a political,
and a social revolution. It has not taken the form of armed
rebellion or civil war, nor is it expressed in a set of consciously planned policies and ideals such as those that
developed out of the Mexican revolution of 1910.[1] Rather,
it has happened, and is still happening largely without plan
or ideology, except as each political administration attempts to solve the more urgent problems which arise out
of the process of change. From an essentially agrarian,
rural, semifeudal, and patriarchal society, Brazil is now
in the process of becoming a modern, industrial, urban-
centered, capitalistic society. Brazil is midway in a process
of changing from its "traditional" structure of the nineteenth century to a "new" Brazilian society of the future.
The process is painful and often costly. It makes the policy
of the United States, or any other nation, toward Brazil

---

[1] Cf. Nathan L. Whetten, *Rural Mexico* (University of Chicago Press,
1948), p. viii.

difficult to chart. At the same time, it is all the more important that we chart it wisely if we wish to insure that this "new" Brazil will emerge as a strong and prosperous democracy.

Traditional Brazil

In the first decade of this century, Brazil was a relatively poor and isolated nation. It had less than eighteen million people; only about 25 per cent of them were literate. The purchasing power of the great mass of people was so low that few industries were able to develop. Almost everything but the barest necessities had to be imported. Brazilians of higher incomes had learned to depend upon Europe for practically every manufactured article—for the material for their clothing and even for many food items, such as tinned butter. Brazil's economic life was based on a few commercial crops and the gathering of native products from the land. In the Amazon valley, a rubber boom, based on the collection of wild rubber in the jungle, was in full swing, only to collapse in 1912, when Asian plantations came into production. In the northeast, the sugar plantations were frankly in decline, and cotton, which had brought a temporary prosperity, had already lost out to the competition of cheaper production in the southern United States. Cocoa production in southern coastal Bahia constituted a growing but limited enterprise. The only significant factor of expansion was the planting of coffee in São Paulo and Minas Gerais.

Communications between different regions were sadly lacking. Transportation between coastal cities was by boat, and it was often just as expensive and time-consuming to ship cargoes from a southern to a northern port within Brazil as it was to Europe.[2] Communications with the interior hardly existed at all. Although Brazilians had, throughout the colonial centuries, penetrated into the heart of the country in their search for gold and gems,

---

[2] Limeira Tejo, *Retrato sincero do Brasil* (Pôrto Alegre: Globo, 1950), p. 195.

establishing towns and even cities there, large pockets of unknown territory were left behind near the coast. In 1910, hostile Indians were actually making war on Brazilians within two or three hundred kilometers of the main coastal cities. A tribe, known as the Kiangang, were attacking the construction workers engaged in building the Northeastern Railroad less than two hundred kilometers inland from the city of São Paulo, in what are today rich coffee-producing lands. Another tribe made war on Brazilians not far from the city of Vitória in the Rio Doce valley, the route to the rich iron deposits of Itabira. Because of the lack of communications, and because of very different environments contained in the vast area which is Brazil, a strong sense of regionalism had developed, each region preserving its own variety of the national culture. The strength of regional interests was reflected in Brazil's economic and political life. It was almost as if there were several Brazils, but loosely held together as a nation. And, yet a basic set of Luso-Brazilian traditions and the Portuguese language provided a minimum unity for the nation.[3]

At the turn of the century, Brazil had just recently abolished two important institutions. In 1888, slavery was abolished and in 1889, the monarchy was replaced by the republic. "The ironical thing about the simultaneous disappearance of the two institutions of slavery and monarchy," Gilberto Freyre has written, "was that the former slaves found themselves men and women who had neither an Emperor nor an autocrat of a 'big house' [mansion] to protect them, and who in consequence became the victims of a deep feeling of insecurity. . . . It took years for political leaders to understand the real psychological and sociological situation of these former slaves, disguised as free laborers and deprived of patriarchal social assistance that had been given them in their old age or when they were sick by the 'big house' or, when that failed to do them justice, by the Emperor or the Empress, or the im-

---

[3] Charles Wagley, "Regionalism and Cultural Unity in Brazil," *Social Forces*, no. 4, 1948, pp. 457-464.

perial Princes." [4] Thus, the republic, as Freyre points
out, at first fraternalistic, "soon . . . imitated the monarchy which it had replaced and became paternalistic." [5]
Throughout Brazil a group of "traditional families" sup-
planted royalty and the landed gentry of the empire and
came to dominate the country's economic, political, and
social life. To a large extent, they carried on the paternalistic role of the upper class of the empire toward the lower
classes.

Some of these influential families, who formed what I
call the "traditional upper class," were descendants of the
titled nobility of the empire and of the landed gentry.
Other families had gained high position after the establishment of the republic, through newly acquired wealth or
political position. By the early twentieth century, both
these groups of families had fused through intermarriage
into a clearly defined upper class into which admission was
difficult, but, of course, not impossible. Members of the
"traditional upper class" were able to cite the surnames of
those who belonged to it, not only in their own region but
in other parts of the country as well. The genealogies and
family connections of friends were known and recounted.
Membership in one of these large "good families" was often
an indispensable prerequisite to economic, professional,
political, or social success. Although often highly patriotic
and public-spirited, many members of the traditional
upper class suffered from what the talented novelist, Viana
Moog, has described as *mozambismo*—a tendency to look
down on or even disdain anything Brazilian and to look
with almost worshipful eyes toward Europe, especially
France. "Politically, in Brazil, with exceptions, he [the
mozambo] tended more toward authoritarian regimes than
democracies. Liberalism in his opinion was all right . . .
for France and for peoples with a high cultural level. But
in Brazil with the crass ignorance of the majority of the

---

4 "Slavery, Monarchy, and Brazil," *Foreign Affairs,* July 1955, p. 631.
5 Same, p. 630.

population . . . this was not possible." [6] This class valued a stable and closed society in which their privileges and special rights were guaranteed. Indeed, the educational system reflected the aristocratic and European values of the traditional upper class. Brazil's secondary schools and universities, patterned after the classical tradition of France, aimed to train a small elite.

Except perhaps in the extreme south of Brazil with its numerous European immigrants, a middle class hardly existed in Brazil during the first decade of this century. There were professional people, army officers, public officials, small businessmen in the cities, as well as businessmen, minor white-collar employees, and landowners in the rural areas, whose level of education and standard of living seemed to place them in a middle class and who by family connections were not members of the "traditional families." Yet, as they so often tend to do today, they identified themselves with the values of the traditional upper class. In the cities, they formed, in a sense, a group marginal to the traditional upper class. In the rural areas they were a provincial and local upper class. Just as the traditional upper class was oriented toward Paris, the provincial upper class in the small towns looked toward Rio de Janeiro, Bahia, Belém, Recife, or other coastal cities. Sons of the provincial upper class often came to these cities to study, mostly to study law, the channel to political and administrative careers. Sometimes, through success in business or politics, or through marriage, they managed to become members of the traditional upper class.

The great majority of Brazilians belonged, of course, to the lower-class groups. They were largely illiterate and in one way or another dependent on the traditional upper class. In the cities, they were the artisans, domestics, and manual laborers. In the rural zones, they were the workers in the cane fields and on coffee plantations, the cowboys on the ranches of the northeast and the open *pampa* of the

---

6 Clodomir Viana Moog, *Bandeirantes e pioneiros: Paralelo entre duas culturas* (Rio de Janeiro: Editôra Globo, 1955), p. 152.

south, the rubber collectors in the Amazon valley, share-croppers on large estates, and frequently squatters on other people's lands, living by subsistence agriculture. Usually these people had a *patrão,* or "boss." The householder was the *patrão* (the feminine *patroa*) of the domestics, the land-owner the *patrão* of the sharecropper, and the ranch owner the *patrão* of the cowboys. Even in factories and commercial establishments, the workers had a protector, usually the owner, who was their *patrão.* Essentially, the *patrão*-worker relationship was an economic one, between employer and employee. It was also highly exploitative, for payment for the labor of these lower-class groups was notoriously small. Yet, the *patrão*-worker relationship was something more than economic. It involved a sense of *noblesse oblige* and paternalism on the part of the employer toward the worker which had survived out of the paternalism of slavery and the monarchy. On the part of the worker, it involved a sense of loyalty to the *patrão.*

Furthermore, by extension, a *patrão* was not necessarily an actual employer. Landholding peasants were often tied to a *patrão* storekeeper by debt or past favors, or a wild-rubber collector to the trader who gave him credit in merchandise and purchased his rubber. Frequently, the local political leader, the *Coronel,* or "colonel," served as a sort of *patrão* for his followers who had received favors or who expected future favors. A lower-class worker without a *patrão* was a man without a protector in time of need. The *patrão* provided some measure of social security—generally the only form available to the worker. Often, the *patrão*-worker relationship between lower-class families and a particular traditional upper-class family endured for generations. A domestic in the home of such an upper-class family, for example, might be the daughter or grand-daughter of a former slave who had been the property of that family's ancestors. It was an intimate and highly personal relationship in which each individual, the upper-class *patrão* and the lower-class dependent worker, had close, warm ties with the other and each treated the other as an individual, not as an impersonal member of a mass. Sometimes, the lower-class individuals, long after they had left the employment of an upper-class family, still considered them to be their *patrões* and returned to seek help in securing new employment or other favors.

These traditional *patrão* relationships have persisted in many relatively isolated parts of Brazil. It is still the basic form of relationship between people of different social classes in the rural communities of northern Brazil.[7] In the Amazon valley, the rubber gatherers and small farmers have as their *patrão* a trader who provides them with credit advances and purchases their produce. The *freguêzes,* or customers, of a particular trader, live on and exploit lands owned or controlled by the trader. The center of their social ties is his trading post, or *barracão,* situated at a strategic point such as the mouth of a tributary stream. The people attached to a particular trading post often form a neighborhood within which there is mutual help and constant visiting. While such people are regularly in debt to the trader, they are also tied to him in other ways. Often the trader and his wife are the *compadre* and *comadre* of the collector and his wife, by becoming godparents to their child. As elsewhere in Latin America, this form of ritual kinship involves a series of mutual obligations and rights between the two couples. Generally, the rubber collector owes a series of past favors to his *patrão* and *compadre.* Perhaps the trader may have continued credit advances in a year when the collector was ill. Perhaps the trader arranged to send a member of the collector's family to the nearest source of medical aid on

---

7 An anthropological study, jointly sponsored by the Department of Anthropology of Columbia University and the Fundação para o Desenvolimento da Ciências of Bahia state, carried out studies of four communities: one in the arid northeastern region; one in a sugar cane producing community near the coast; one in the mountainous region where mining was formerly important; and one in the cocoa area of southern Bahia. A fifth community study previously undertaken in the Amazon valley added a great deal to our data. References to these studies will follow.

the river boat that comes to load rubber and restock the trading post.

Each fortnight the collectors or small farmers who form the *freguesia* or clientele of a trader come to the trading post to secure new supplies and to pay off some of their debts with their produce. This day of trading, known as the *quinzena* (fifteen days), is equally a day of social intercourse during which the men drink and the women gossip. Likewise, on the trader's birthday, on a saint's day, or on election days, there are social gatherings at the trading post and the trader may offer a dance. The trader-collector relationship in the Amazon valley is not an impersonal economic bond, and, if a customer succeeds in paying off his debt and takes his produce elsewhere, the trader feels this as an act of personal disloyalty.[8]

Likewise, a study of a family-owned sugar plantation in the Recôncavo area of Bahia has shown that the relations between owners and workers are social as well as economic. On this plantation, the owners were clearly members of the old traditional upper class, and most of the permanent workers had been born on that or neighboring plantations. The workers were paid in cash and the relationship between the owner and his workers was basically that of employer and employees. At the same time, their relationship was paternalistic, highly personal, intimate, and often based upon a lifetime of close acquaintance. When the plantation owner returned from a stay in the city, he came loaded down with many small purchases requested by his workers. The workers' wives called on the wife of the *fazendeiro,* or plantation owner, upon her return. They were not asked to sit down, for a rigid barrier of social class is maintained, but the lady of the house asked after their children, each of whom she generally knew by name. They inquired about her relatives who lived in the city or about her children who had remained at school in the city. Here, too, the workers were often *compadres* to their

---

8 Charles Wagley, *Amazon Town: A Study of Man in the Tropics* (New York: Macmillan, 1953), p. 96ff.

patrão and obligated to the *patrão* for many past favors. On his birthday or on Christmas Eve, the *patrão* often provided a festival for the workers on the plantation. Under these patriarchal conditions, it was rare for a worker to leave a plantation to seek work elsewhere.[9]

Similarly, the *vaqueiro,* or cowboy, on a northeastern cattle ranch stood in a traditional *patrão* relationship to the ranch owner, but it was a less intimate one, for the owner often lived far away in the city, visiting the ranch only on the occasion of the division of the herd. As our recent anthropological studies show, the relationship still survives, as described at the turn of the century by Euclydes da Cunha in his classic study of the northeastern *sertão:*

Like the landed proprietor of colonial days, he [the ranch owner] parasitically enjoys the revenues from vast domains without fixed boundaries, and the cowboys are his submissive servants. As a result of a contract in accordance with which they receive a certain percentage of what is produced, they remain attached to the same plot of ground. . . . They spend their entire lives in faithfully caring for herds that do not belong to them. Their real employer, an absentee one, well knows how loyal they are and does not oversee them; at best, he barely knows their names.[10]

Marvin Harris observed: "One of the most recurrent themes for businessmen, miners, farmers and artisans alike is the plaintive search for the 'boss' *(patrão)*—the fatherlike figure who gives people work, provides them with raw materials, lends them money, and buys their products before they are produced." [11]

Throughout Brazil, analogous *patrão* relationships existed in the past, and still survive in many localities. Un-

---

9 Harry W. Hutchinson, *Village and Plantation Life in Northeastern Brazil* (Seattle: University of Washington Press, for the American Ethnological Society, 1957), pp. 57-62.

10 *Rebellion in the Backlands,* tr. by Samuel Putnam (University of Chicago Press, 1944), pp. 95-96. Also, Ben Zimmerman, *Montesserat: A Sertão Community,* in ms.

11 *Town and Country in Brazil* (New York: Columbia University Press, 1956), p. 57.

like Indians of the highland countries of Central and South America, whose corporate and landholding communities offered them some measure of security, the Brazilian rural lower class had no close-knit community to turn to for support. Small neighborhoods within Brazilian communities were often strongly united by kinship among the residents, the custom of mutual aid, and even dependence upon the same *patrão*. But most observers agree that the rural community itself is amorphous, weakly organized, and split by class alliances. As T. Lynn Smith has put it:

In Brazil, as in the plantation South of the United States, there is a great difference in the locality-group attachments of the upper landowning class and the families who live and work on the estates. The former have contacts with and attachments outside the neighborhood and local community. . . . The latter are likely to live in a world whose horizons end with the neighboring *fazendas* or the nearby village or town.[12]

Since the upper landowning class supplies the local leadership, the lower class often is almost without leadership of its own. Even more in the past than at present, upper-class people have felt a closer affiliation with their upper-class associates in the cities than with the lower-class members of their local community. Lacking the support that might otherwise have been supplied by a strong local structure, the Brazilian lower classes have depended even more upon a *patrão*—a planter, a trader, a commercial man, or a politician—for some measure of security in their difficult world.[13]

---

[12] *Brazil: People and Institutions* (Baton Rouge: Louisiana State University Press, 1954), p. 522.

[13] I have purposely omitted the subject of the racial composition of the Brazilian classes and I have also omitted the subject of the effect of the Brazilian revolution on race relations and the changing racial composition of the socio-economic classes. This aspect of Brazil has been rather intensively treated in recent years in such studies as *O negro no Rio de Janeiro*, Biblioteca Pedagógica Brasileira, Série 5, Brasiliana, 276 (São Paulo: Editôra Nacional, 1953), by L. A. Costa Pinto; *Les élites de couleur dans une ville brésilienne* (Paris: UNESCO, 1953), by Thales de Azevedo; *Relações raciais entre negros e brancos em São Paulo* (São Paulo: Editôra

The Brazilian Revolution

During the first decades of this century, these isolated, semifeudal, and stable societies of the early republic began to be transformed slowly and almost imperceptibly into something quite different. Then, during the regime of Getulio Vargas, between 1930 and 1945, and especially since the end of World War II, many changes that had only cast their shadows before have come to be felt with greater intensity. At present, Brazil is in a frenzy of continuous crisis as the traditional gives way to a new type of society. This revolution has been felt with varying degrees of intensity in different regions. In many rural zones, in northern Brazil especially, the traditional patterns still largely dominate the way of life. Even near some of the large cities of the north, there are isolated areas as yet little influenced by the new trends. In the central and southern states—Rio de Janeiro, Minas Gerais, São Paulo, Paraná, Santa Catarina, and Rio Grande do Sul—these new trends have been felt more sharply. There one can see emerging the outlines of a new Brazilian society.

What are the forces and changes that are bringing about this profound reshaping of Brazilian society? To discuss them in any detail would require an intricate analysis of the history of Brazil, especially since about 1930. However, even a brief review of some of the interrelated developments that have set off this Brazilian revolution will help to make clear the drastic changes which have swept the Brazilian people from their traditional moorings.

Anhembi, for UNESCO, 1955), edited by Roger Bastide and Florestan Fernandes; and *Race and Class in Rural Brazil* (Paris: UNESCO, 1952), edited by Charles Wagley. It is enough to say here that broadly the traditional upper class was white and the lower-class groups were Negroes, mulattoes, or mixed (American Indian with Negro or white). In accordance with Brazil's traditional tolerance in regard to race, the new social classes are far from racially homogeneous.

POPULATION GROWTH AND THE NEW CITIES

Brazil's total population has more than tripled since 1900. As compared with only some 17,318,000 Brazilians in 1900, there were 30,635,605 in 1920; 41,565,000 in 1940; 52,645,000 in 1950; and an estimated 67,200,000 in 1960.[14] Brazil has one of the most rapidly growing populations in the modern world. Immigration is only a secondary cause of the estimated net increase of over 1,320,000 people each year. In terms of population, there is no doubt that Brazil will become one of the major nations of the world.

While Brazil is still predominantly a nation of villages and hamlets, its cities have been growing much faster than the rural areas. According to the criteria used by the Brazilian census of 1950, only 36.5 per cent of the population, or a total of 19,197,686 people, were urban.[15] But totals tell only a part of the story. In 1900 the city of São Paulo had about 240,000 inhabitants; by 1950, 2,198,000 inhabitants; and in 1957 over 3,230,000. Rio de Janeiro, which had approximately 500,000 in 1900, had reached 2,377,500 in 1950, and was close to three million in 1957. Other cities have been growing at great speed, and by 1950 there were twelve other centers with more than 100,000 people, including Belo Horizonte (352,700 in 1950; an estimated 514,200 in 1957), Pôrto Alegre (394,150 in 1950 and 522,700 in 1957), and Recife (524,700 in 1950 and over 718,600 in 1957).[16]

The rapid growth of the cities has created a serious crisis. Urban systems of water supply, electric power,

[14] Unless otherwise noted, statistics have been taken from official Brazilian and U.S. sources; 1960 estimate, Brazilian Embassy (Washington), *Survey of the Brazilian Economy 1958* (Washington: Author, November 1958), p. 4.

[15] T. Lynn Smith reduces this figure by some 2,784,762 people through subtracting from the "urban" category the "urban" population of some 3,198 places of less than 2,000 inhabitants. (See *Brazil: People and Institutions*, cited, p. 166.)

[16] Brazil, Ministry of External Relations, *Brasil* (Rio de Janeiro: Author, June 1958), p. 5.

sewerage, and transportation, hardly adequate in 1920 and 1930, have been suddenly outpaced by populations that have expanded to several times their previous size. No matter how fast such facilities are expanded, and they have not expanded fast enough, they never seem to catch up with the growing urban population. A further result of this turbulent exodus from the rural areas to the cities has been to accentuate the already strong contrast between rural and urban conditions of life. In the cities a large proportion of the people participate in the modern world by means of the radio and television, cinema, magazines, and newspapers. In the isolation of rural life such things are a part of a distant and strange world. The contrast between the two worlds in turn reinforces the attraction of the cities as people realize that only there can modern conveniences and amusements be acquired.

INTERNAL MIGRATION AND IMMIGRATION FROM ABROAD

In addition to the rural influx into the cities, there have been important migrations between different parts of the country. In the first decade of this century, many villagers migrated from the arid northeast to the Amazon valley. Then, with the collapse of rubber-collecting along the Amazon, the current shifted to São Paulo, where coffee-planting offered new employment. Later, southern Mato Grosso and Goiás attracted many settlers, not only from the northeast but from Minas Gerais and even São Paulo. From 1900 to 1939, at least one million Brazilians, mostly from the northeastern states, which are often drought-stricken, came to work on plantations and farms in São Paulo state. This migration, both to the rural areas and to the capital of São Paulo, continues even today at the rate of over 100,000 people per year. And the migration from São Paulo to the south and into the west pushes ahead even more strongly. More recently, northern Paraná has become the mecca whither thousands flock each year to seek work or buy rich lands. Between 1940 and 1950, the number of people born in other states but living in Paraná increased from 214,256 to 661,456, and in Goiás from 155,480 to 281,364—indicating a strong westward movement.

Migrants from the north come crowded into trucks carrying thirty, forty, and even fifty people over dusty and bumpy roads for more than a thousand miles. Many come by train through Minas Gerais and into São Paulo state. Although most of them are males hoping to send home funds and perhaps to accumulate enough money to go home, a surprisingly large proportion consists of entire families. From 1935 to 1939, for example, over 75 per cent of the migrants who lodged at the Hospedaria de Imigrantes, or immigrant station, maintained in the city of São Paulo, journeyed as members of families—and these families average five persons.[17] As Smith describes it, "the current migrations to São Paulo are more reminiscent of the flight from the 'dust bowl' toward the West, or the expulsion of the Mormons from the Middle West than to any other chapters in the history of migration in the United States." [18] This migratory movement, as well as providing laborers for the cities has changed the social scene in the rural areas of São Paulo and other central states.

Although the great bulk of the population expansion results from the excess of births over deaths, Brazil has received over 4,000,000 immigrants from abroad since 1900. The presence of this relatively large mass of people who did not share in the values of traditional Brazil has been an important influence upon the development of the country and a factor in the Brazilian revolution.

During the nineteenth century, colonies of Italians and Germans were established in the hope of forming the nucleus of a group of small farmers engaged in diversified agriculture and thus overcoming the predominant plantation monoculture of the country. But only after the abolition of slavery, when the state of São Paulo set up a

17 Smith, cited, p. 278.
18 Same.

method of systematic recruitment and subsidization for immigrants, did the mass of European immigrants come to Brazil. Even then, compared to the same period in the United States and Canada, the number who immigrated to Brazil was small. The six countries that contributed most in numbers have been, in order: Italy, Portugal, Spain, Japan, Germany, and Poland. Relatively few in number, but important in their economic and social impact upon Brazil, have been the "Turcos," as they are called in Brazil; actually, they are Arabs from Syria and Lebanon.

The majority of these immigrants from abroad first settled in the rural areas, mainly in São Paulo and the southern states. But lately, their descendants, too, have flocked to the cities. In recent years—except for the Portuguese who may enter almost at will—immigration has tapered off as the Brazilian government imposed a quota system. From 1944 to 1957, only 570,674 immigrants entered Brazil; of these, 228,933 were Portuguese.[19]

COMMUNICATIONS

Brazil still suffers from the lack of communications among its various regions. In early 1957 there were only 37,000 kilometers of railroads and 467,500 kilometers of motor roads. The various railroad systems run on five different gauges and they lack easy interconnections. Many of the motor roads are so poor that they are impassable for a part of the year, and by far the largest part of the road system consists of local or county roads. Even so, in the last decades there has been a "revolution" in the Brazilian communications system. Most cities and towns today are connected by telegraph or radio. Road-building proceeds apace, and today there is an excellent highway between the two metropolitan centers of Rio de Janeiro and São Paulo.

---

19 Brazil, Conselho Nacional de Estatística, Instituto Brasileiro de Geografía e Estatística, *Annuário Estatístico do Brasil* (Rio de Janeiro: Author, 1957), pp. 53-54; data for 1957, Banco do Brasil, *Relatorio 1957* (N. p.: Author, March 1958), pt. 3, p. 45.

The Via Anchieta between São Paulo and its port city, Santos, is considered a masterpiece of modern engineering. It is possible to travel by road from Rio de Janeiro to all of the southern states, to the rich central states of Minas Gerais and Goiás, and through Bahia into the northeastern states. These roads have allowed the penetration of trucks —one of the main carriers of modern Brazil—to the hinterland. Today, trucks not only carry merchandise from the hinterland to the city and return, but also provide local transportation for freight and passengers between towns in the back country.

More remarkable, Brazil seems to have jumped from the age of the ox cart to the age of the air. In this vast country, air travel has become not just a convenience but a necessity. In 1938, Brazilians were already flying 41,504,000 passenger kilometers per year, and by 1957 this number had risen to 2,289,492,000. In 1957, over 89,000,000 tons of cargo were transported by air, and the total was probably larger since there were many unchartered (and uncounted) flights. Brazil is perhaps one of the most air-minded countries in the world—many little towns have their own "Air Club," and young Brazilians who have never driven an automobile have "soloed" in the air. On a map, Brazilian-owned and operated airlines look like a spiderweb as they connect not only the cities of the coast and capitals, but also the smaller cities and towns of the interior. It is no longer a trip of two weeks or more from Rio de Janeiro to Belém by coastal steamer, but a flight of only several hours.

INDUSTRIALIZATION AND AGRICULTURE

Although Brazil is still predominantly an agricultural nation, there has been a marked upsurge of industry, particularly during the last fifteen years. The last ten years have seen the country break away from a heavy dependence upon the outside world for manufactured articles and begin to manufacture most of its own needs. Now producing a large percentage of its own consumer goods,

Brazil adequately supplies its own needs of clothes, shoes, glassware, pharmaceutical supplies, canned foods, and other necessities. Other industries are rapidly expanding. For example, the first cement plant was built in 1926; by 1957 domestic production had reached 3,376,000 metric tons, and Brazil had become self-sufficient in cement.

Automobiles have been assembled in Brazil largely from imported parts since the 1920's. In the early 1950's, the government took a series of steps to increase the use of domestically produced parts, with the aim of giving Brazil its own automotive industry. A 1952 ban on imports of parts obtainable in Brazil and a 1953 regulation virtually prohibiting imports of finished vehicles were major steps in this process. An industry-government group was formed to encourage domestic vehicle output. Pressure plus incentives have encouraged firms to expand the manufacture of vehicles in Brazil. Subsidiary industries supplying component parts have been stimulated. Under an elaborate plan, imports of parts are to decline in relation to the production of vehicles until by mid-1960 90 per cent (by weight) of all parts used in Brazilian vehicles are to be domestically produced. By 1958 there were some 1,200 automobile parts factories, of which 150 were of substantial size. Subsidiaries of sixteen motor companies—American, English, French, Italian, German, and Japanese—were in operation or had their projects approved by the government. Output of vehicles of all types increased from 6,000 in 1956 to 30,700 in 1957 and an estimated 61,000 in 1958. The official goal for 1960 is 170,000 vehicles; the industry hopes to do still better and aims at a total output of 210,000.

The most impressive part of Brazilian industrialization has been the progress in two fundamental sectors: steel and hydroelectric power. The great Volta Redonda plant alone, which first went into production in 1946, was producing over 800,000 tons of steel ingots in 1957, about half the national output. By 1960 it was expected to produce over 1,000,000 tons, and the goal of the entire steel industry was 2,300,000 tons in 1960, and 3,500,000 tons in 1965.[20] Brazil's hydroelectric potential is one of the highest in the world, but until recently its power development lagged behind its industrial growth. In 1939 hydroelectric capacity was 888,600 kilowatts; ten years later it was 1.4 million and, by the end of 1957, 2.7 million. Because power shortages have been a severe handicap to industrial expansion, electrical development has held a major place in the government's Economic Development Plan, which calls for a total expenditure—federal, state, and private—of Cr$83 billion between 1957 and 1966; the goal is a generating capacity of 8 million kw. by the end of 1965. By early 1957 the Paulo Alfonso station in northeast Brazil and the Peixoto project in Minas Gerais were in full operation, supplying 200,000 kw.; the state of São Paulo had made plans for a program which would add 434,000 kw. to its power capacity; the upper reaches of the São Francisco River had been selected as the site for the Três Marias Dam, with a capacity of 480,000 kw. The most ambitious project has been the Furnas Dam on the Rio Grande in south central Brazil; it will be the largest of nineteen dams to be built on the river. With an ultimate capacity of 7.5 million kw., this complex of dams and reservoirs will supply power to the most industrialized part of the country. The first stages of construction are being financed by a World Bank loan of $73 million, extended in 1958.

Compared to that of the most industrialized countries of Western Europe and the United States, Brazilian industry is still in an infant stage, but there are clear signs that a tremendous transformation of the basic economy is just beginning. Perhaps as a harbinger of this transformation, foreign investments are flowing into the country at a volume that is increasing rapidly. According to the Brazilian Ministry of External Affairs, the inflow of direct foreign investment rose from $51.3 million in 1955 to $55.7 million in 1956 and over $108 million in 1957. Roughly

---

20 *Survey of the Brazilian Economy 1958,* cited, pp. 22, 24.

two-thirds of this went into basic industry, according to the ministry's classification. Although the total value of foreign direct investments is not known, it is estimated at over $3 billion. Of this, U.S. investments were $1.3 billion at the end of 1957, half in manufacturing enterprises and the remainder in petroleum marketing, public utilities, trade, and mining. Brazil has been able to draw private and public capital from a number of other sources, including Canada, Germany, France, the United Kingdom, Italy, and the World Bank.

There has been a considerable increase in the production of basic food products in Brazil during the last two decades. The annual production of rice, for example, increased from 1,484,514 tons in 1939 to 4,076,273 tons in 1957; beans increased during the same period from 789,722 tons to 1,685,091; and cane sugar from 19,987,772 tons to 46,576,491 tons. It would seem at first glance, then, that agriculture has developed as rapidly as industry, but this is far from the actual picture. Instead, there is a crisis in foodstuffs. Production has not kept up with the mushrooming population and with the expanding purchasing power of large segments of the population.

The production of wheat illustrates well the changing pattern of food consumption. For many years Brazil has imported wheat, but, in recent years, as the consumption of flour increased, foreign wheat has been a heavy drain on the supply of foreign exchange. To counteract this drain, the government has made serious attempts to restore the country's once relatively large wheat production, particularly in the southernmost state of Rio Grande do Sul, by extension and research work and by a price-support program. Between 1939 and 1957 national wheat production increased from 101,000 tons to 1,199,000 tons. By 1957 the acreage in wheat was six times larger than in 1939, and the average yield per acre had doubled. In spite of the growth in output, however, wheat and flour imports have increased; in 1939 they amounted to 1,012,000 tons and in 1957 to 1,474,000 tons. The only agricultural products imported to any significant extent, wheat and flour, are a continuing drain on Brazil's foreign exchange. An agreement with the United States in 1956 provided for the purchase of 1,800,000 tons of surplus wheat over a three-year period, payments to be made in cruzeiros over forty years. The U.S. government is using some of these cruzeiros to meet its expenses in Brazil, but, if it follows its practice in other countries, it may lend a large part of them to Brazil for use in economic development projects, among them the expansion of Brazilian wheat production.

The increasing demand for wheat reflects not only a growing population but also a change in food habits. In the past manioc flour has been more important to most Brazilians than bread. Bread is a food of the towns and cities, manioc the food of the countryside. As the cities grow, as people increase their incomes, and as they acquire new city ways, they change their food habits. Even so, production of manioc has been increased rather steadily, from 6.7 million tons in 1939 to 15.8 million tons in 1957. There is now a shortage of other foods, however. The production of dairy products, vegetables, and even fruit has not grown fast enough to keep up with increasing population, rapid urbanization, and higher purchasing power.

The agricultural problem is further complicated by the failure of commercial agriculture, which produces mainly for export, to expand its total output in the last twenty years. From prewar years to 1957 the production of coffee, Brazil's prime export, has hardly increased, while the production of cotton, another important commercial crop, declined. Troubled by fluctuations in world prices, Brazilian commercial agriculture is also technologically backward. Gradually, though, giant *usinas,* or sugar mills, surrounded by corporation-owned sugar plantations with thousands of workers, have begun to appear, as well as extensive coffee plantations with numerous workers. These "factories-in-the-field," though they are few in number, must be counted as part of the Brazilian revolution, for they represent a markedly different kind of agricultural enterprise from the family-owned plantations and ranches of traditional Brazil.

RISING INCOME AND INFLATION

It would take a skilled economist and better data than now exist to trace the tenuous balance between the spiraling inflation in Brazil and the rising incomes of the various segments of the population. As Brazilians increase their incomes, they are repeatedly robbed by inflation and by the constant rise in the cost of living. Still, most observers agree that in some degree the purchasing power of the Brazilian public has been increasing. Each year a larger number of people enter the national market, and the large mass of people who make up the "economic zeros" of purchasing power seems to diminish.

There are no cost-of-living data on a nation-wide basis, but some indication of the inflationary trend can be seen in the index of consumer prices in São Paulo. There the cost of living in early 1958 was nearly fifteen times greater than in 1939. Inflation, however, is no stranger to the Brazilian economy. An average yearly rise of 18 per cent in the cost of living from 1950 to 1957 came on top of a spiraling of prices in the late 1930's and the war years. Since the war the requirements of a developing economy have meant that the price level has outdistanced the supply of goods and services, and in an effort to protect living standards the government has had to yield on such anti-inflationary measures as wage stabilization. In 1956 and again at the end of 1958 it set higher minimum wage standards; for the unskilled worker the monthly base wage was set first at 3,800 cruzeiros and then at 6,000. (In terms of U.S. dollars, the increase became a decrease, from $60 to $43.) Yet the important fact remains that a minimum wage even exists and that salaries in government and industry are considerably above this figure. Furthermore, the government has made a faltering but valiant effort to control prices. Most observers would agree that wages have

pulled themselves somewhat above the cost of living. The
latter has risen from an index of 100 in 1953 to 206 in
1957 while average monthly industrial wages in the Federal
District have in the same period gone from 100 to 275.

Nevertheless, relentless inflation continues to haunt
prosperity and economic development, with its varying
impact on different segments of the population. Industrial
labor and the mass of government employees have been
granted increases in wages only to see them wiped out,
entirely or in part, by higher prices. The "middle-class"
white-collar workers and professionals suffer as the de-
valuation of the currency and the rising cost of living out-
distance their more slowly rising incomes. The owners of
capital tend to invest in urban real estate. As a result of
the enormous building boom, created both by the housing
shortage in the burgeoning cities and by the desire to invest
in real estate, great fortunes have been made on paper in
real estate.

The Brazilian government's development program has
meant expanded credits to industry for projects which will
not always provide income in the near future. Its agricultural policy has involved it in a program of bolstering
domestic production and living standards of producers
through buying up unexportable farm surpluses. The
ambitious power and transport goals of its economic plan
have turned the government into a large-scale producer
and investor. The result has been that the government's
expenditures regularly exceed its revenue, and the difference is made up by printing more money. Labor unrest
and the demands of business firms have made it difficult
to enforce wage and price stabilization measures. Attempts
to institute an austere tax program have been handicapped
by the maneuvering of political groups. While Brazil, with
large mineral deposits, rich agricultural lands, and enormous power potential, has many investment opportunities,
foreign capital is faced with uncertainties arising from the
government's import and exchange controls, recurrent
threats to the repatriation of profits and capital, and re-

strictive legislation with respect to the exploitation of mineral resources.

The efforts to industrialize have increased the pressure for imports but have not yet brought about an expansion of exports. Whereas a trade surplus was the rule in Brazil until the postwar period, in eight of the eleven years after 1947 there were ever-growing deficits which had to be covered by foreign credits. Imports, especially machinery and petroleum, are essential if the development program is to succeed, but to pay for these vital imports Brazil is largely dependent on the export of a few major products —coffee, lumber, sugar and cocoa head the list—whose prices in the world market fluctuate more widely than prices of the products which must be imported. In petroleum, for example, Brazil has increased its own production and refining operations, so that in the space of ten years domestic needs, instead of being met almost entirely by imports, were in 1957 supplied in part (nearly 15 per cent) by domestic production. However, consumption has increased so rapidly in postwar years that the cost of petroleum imports in the mid-1950's amounted to between 15 and 20 per cent of the total import bill.

Historically, coffee has been the mainstay of Brazilian trade. Earnings from its sale abroad have equaled or exceeded all other export earnings, but the prospects for the future of coffee—and of the other traditional exports, cotton and cocoa—are not good. Producers are faced with severe international competition and plagued by recurrent price declines. Coffee and cocoa exports have not increased in volume since 1946, and cotton shipments have declined. Sugar, an unimportant trade item before the war, has come to have a significant place in exports of foodstuffs, but the main hopes for a long-run improvement in the trade balance lie in the expansion of production of minerals, fats and oils, timber, meat, and industrial products. In the latter field Brazil is already building up export markets, chiefly in Latin America, for its processed foods, textiles, chemical and pharmaceutical products, and vehicle parts.

Mineral exports, especially manganese and iron ore, may
some day replace agricultural products as major earners
of foreign exchange.

EDUCATION

Despite the fact that in 1950 more than half of the
total population was still classed as illiterate, it would
seem on the surface that Brazil has undergone nothing
short of a major revolution in its educational system during
the last two decades or so. The progress in providing
educational facilities and in spreading education has been
magnificent. In 1933, only 27,770 primary schools claimed
matriculation of 2,107,619. In contrast, in 1957 the record
shows 80,178 primary schools with an enrollment of more
than 5,400,000 pupils. The record scored by secondary
education is even more remarkable. In 1933, only 417
schools offering regular academic secondary education
could be found in all of Brazil, and only 66,420 students
regularly studied in them.[21] By 1954, in contrast, 535,775
pupils were attending almost 2,000 secondary schools.
Thus, almost five times as many secondary schools could
be counted, with over eight times as many students attending them. The program in higher education has been
equally striking. In 1930, opportunities for higher education were found in a small number of isolated faculties,
mainly of law, medicine, pharmacy, engineering, and the
like. As late as 1940, there were only slightly more than
20,000 students registered in courses of higher education
in all of Brazil. By 1957, there were nineteen organized
universities in Brazil and numerous faculties, schools, institutes, and programs offering advanced education in law,
engineering, medicine, pharmacy, nursing, dentistry, music,
social work, industrial chemistry, architecture, library
science and numerous other specialized fields. Almost the
full range of technical, scientific, humanistic, academic,

---

21 Included are both levels of secondary schools: *Ginásio,* or "middle
school," equivalent roughly to junior high school in the United States,
and *Colégio,* roughly equivalent to the senior high school.

and professional schools found in the United States are present nowadays in Brazil. In 1957 the number of students registered in Brazilian universities and other institutions of higher education exceeded 75,000.

Yet, such progress in education must be set against the rapid population growth in the last three decades and against the exceedingly low "baseline" situation of Brazilian education in the 1930's. Brazil has not yet overcome these disadvantages and the educational system still acts as a drag on the formation of the new Brazilian society. The educational system does not meet the needs and the demands of the Brazilian population. The educational philosophy and pedagogical methods inherited from the past are still aimed at educating an elite. Even in 1958, less than half of the population of elementary school age was attending school, according to a survey of a Brazilian government educational office.[22] The economically backward northern states suffer most from lack of educational facilities. Despite strong efforts to extend education to rural zones everywhere, as late as 1950 there were 2,026,235 children enrolled in elementary schools in urban districts, compared to only 1,872,388 in rural districts, although only 36 per cent of the total population was classified as "urban." Many rural schools provide only one or two grades rather than the regular four-year primary sequence, and distances are so great and transportation so difficult that attendance in rural schools is very low. Yet, even city schools are terribly overcrowded; in Rio de Janeiro and São Paulo, for example, multiple sessions—sometimes three and four—are necessary in primary schools.

Some of this crowding results from the rigid pedagogical system. Theoretically standards are exceedingly high, but teaching is often unskilled. Many pupils come from illiterate backgrounds and cannot count on their families to help them with their studies. Rules of promotion to the next grade are strictly applied beginning with the first

---

22 *Bulletin de CAPES* (Companha para Aperfeiçoamento Pessoal de Nivel Superior), no. 73 (December 1958), pp. 7-8.

grade, and a very large percentage of children in each grade fail. In 1958, 52.3 per cent of all elementary school children were in the first grade, 22.1 per cent in the second grade, 15.5 per cent in the third grade, and only 1.3 per cent in the fourth grade. Only a small percentage of children entering elementary school finish the fourth grade which, after an entrance examination, prepares them to enter a secondary school. Furthermore, "repeaters" in the lower grades block the entry of the seven-year olds into the already crowded schools and are a heavy drain on educational budgets. It has been estimated, for example, that, in 1957, of some 1,200,000 students in the elementary schools of São Paulo state about 300,000 failed to pass their grade and were made to repeat it. This is said to have cost the state about Cr$750 million and to have blocked the entry of 100,000 new students into the first grade.[23]

Despite the small number of children who finish the four-year elementary schools, there is a tremendous demand for secondary education in Brazil today. It has been estimated that in 1954 only 6 per cent of the population between twelve and eighteen years of age were in secondary schools.[24] Yet, the secondary schools again work as a "filter" eliminating the majority of students from further education. The secondary curriculum is based fundamentally on the French *lycée* system and is aimed primarily at training an elite. Many students fall by the wayside. Thus, in 1954, while there were 168,009 students enrolled in the first year of the *Ginásio* (middle school), there were only 18,115 enrolled in the last year of the *Colégio* (senior high school).[25] Only about one-third of the secondary schools offer the *Colégio* course and furthermore the vast majority of all secondary schools are private. Although the government offers scholarships and subsidies to support secondary education, cost is a barrier for the great majority of Bra-

23 Same, p. 10.
24 Jaime Abreu, *A educação secundária no Brasil* (Rio de Janeiro: CAPES, 1955).
25 Same, p. 10.

zilians. In addition, the problem of location deprives many potential students of the opportunity to attend a secondary school. In 1955, well over 50 per cent of all secondary schools were located in Minas Gerais, Rio de Janeiro state, São Paulo state, and the former Federal District (now renamed the state of Guanabara)—that is, in the most urbanized regions of the country. Even there, most secondary schools were located in big cities and towns. The rural population generally does not have access to secondary education.

The situation in higher education presents another Brazilian paradox. There seems to be an overwhelming demand for admission to schools of higher education and the facilities have expanded enormously. Yet, this demand seems to be selective; while there are many more candidates than places, there seem to be fewer candidates able to pass the entrance examinations than most schools of higher education could admit. The largest number of candidates for admission are still in law, medicine, engineering, and other traditional professions. Fewer candidates seek admission to nursing, agronomy, veterinary sciences, public administration, and other newer fields. A survey carried out in 1957 of 358 schools and faculties of higher education showed that there were 7,883 candidates for admission to eighteen medical schools which had but 1,175 places for first-year students. Yet, only 1,015 of these candidates passed the entrance requirements. The situation is similar in engineering. Even in the faculties of philosophy which prepare secondary-school teachers, there were twice as many candidates as places to be filled; yet only about one-third of the candidates passed the entrance requirements. Schools of nursing and agronomy were not filled to their capacity.[26] Obviously, the entrance examinations to universities and technical schools are so administered as to cut down the huge number of candidates to fit the number of students they can receive; it is also clear that, despite

---

26 *Bulletin de CAPES*, no. 60 (November 1957), pp. 11.

the high level of their curriculum, the secondary schools do not prepare students to carry on university work.

There is a veritable rash of expansion of institutions of higher education in Brazil. Between 1955 and 1959 at least one hundred faculties of philosophy (liberal arts colleges) have been established throughout Brazil. Each month brings announcements of the formation of new faculties of law, dentistry, pharmacy, and the like, as well as of expanded facilities in already established schools. Brazil sorely needs professionals, technicians, and teachers. The greater opportunity for higher education in modern Brazil is a far cry from that in the isolated Brazil of the beginning of this century. Nevertheless, the educational system is still oriented toward the training of a relatively small elite and is thus out of step with the needs of a changing Brazilian society.

MASS MEDIA

Another important feature of contemporary Brazil, at once a result and a cause of the Brazilian revolution, is the rapid development of mass media during the last two or three decades. The dates of the founding of periodicals (including newspapers and magazines) show the rapid expansion of the use of the printing press over the past thirty years. Between 1900 and 1910, only 92 new periodicals appeared. Between 1910 and 1919, 146 new periodicals were founded. Between 1920 and 1929, 263 appeared; from 1930 to 1939, there were 546 new periodicals, and 853 from 1940 to 1949; and finally, in the four-year period 1950-1954, another 953 were established. The 261 daily newspapers issued in 1954 had a total circulation of only 3,351,762, which is small compared to that of West European countries. Yet, today Brazil supports newspaper chains such as the Diários Associados, which has dailies in several large cities. The voice of the press is now important in forming public opinion.

Other forms of mass media have spread rapidly. In 1930, there were only sixteen radio stations; by 1948 over two hundred were functioning. Rio de Janeiro and São Paulo are now served by television stations. In 1954, there were 3,142 *Casas de Espetáculos* (mostly cinemas), and these had 1,747,767 seats. In the same year, 3,721 films were examined by the censorship.[27] Of them, 1,751 were produced in the United States, although among "feature films" shown an even larger proportion were of North American origin.

Publishing is still weakly developed, when compared to many other countries, and Brazilians complain that sales of ten to fifteen thousand copies of a popular book are insignificant compared with those of "best sellers" in the United States. Just the same, new publishing houses appear each year and the traditional companies thrive. Many outstanding Brazilian writers of fiction have appeared in the last thirty years—Jose Líns do Rego, Erico Verrissimo, Jorge Amado, Viana Moog and others—and their work has come to be widely read at home and abroad. North American and European fiction is widely published in Portuguese translation. Unlike the past, when a well-known writer could say that "Portuguese is the tomb of thought," and when the reading public of Brazil depended upon European books, today Brazilian writers have a wide and interested audience and are important in forming the new Brazilian values.

POLITICS

The current political situation of Brazil is more a reflection than a cause of the Brazilian revolution. A few changes in the electorate and system of politics will bear out this observation. For one thing, there has been a tremendous expansion in the electorate, despite the automatic disqualification of the more than one-half of Brazilians who fail the literacy requirement. It has expanded despite the fact that those who came of age during the Vargas dictatorship, between 1933 and 1945, when voting was sus-

---

27 All films are censored for the purpose of grading them according to their propriety for the ages of the viewers.

pended, had never voted until the elections of 1945. For the National Constitutional Assembly in 1933, 1,466,700 people voted; for legislation in 1934, 2,659,171; for president and state legislatures in 1945, 7,459,848; for president and legislative offices in 1950, 7,459,432; and for state and legislative offices in 1954, 15,104,604. The proportion of Brazilians participating in elections, and thus their political awareness, have obviously grown much more rapidly than the population itself.

In the second place, there has been a remarkable development of political parties and of modern techniques of political campaigning. Although even today political parties tend to be regional in their scope and interests, there are several important national parties—the União Democrática Nacional (Democratic National Union), the Partido Trabalhista Brasileiro (Brazilian Labor party), Partido Social Democrático (Social Democratic party), as well as the National Socialist party and the Communist party (presently illegal but obviously still active). Only with the 1945 elections did anything resembling truly national political parties appear.

With the lack of transportation and communications and because of the highly charged regional interests, it was almost impossible to organize political campaigns on a national basis before 1930. The political scene was marked by a multitude of local parties in almost each state, and the balance of power seemed to be determined by local parties in São Paulo and Minas Gerais states. But by the time of the 1945 and 1950 elections, Brazil had changed, and a new type of political campaign was possible. Where in the past, politicians in the national capital and in São Paulo and Minas Gerais had to depend entirely upon local political bosses—the so-called "colonels"—to carry the vote, they could now appeal directly to the electorate. Particularly in 1950, and again in 1955, the candidates for the presidency of the republic traveled extensively by airplane from north to south Brazil. They spoke to the voters over the radio and appealed to them through cinema shorts. In 1955, television was used in a political campaign for the first time, and "television personality" became an important factor. Political leaders and campaign managers could now move easily from one distant city to another, and political propaganda could be put out on a national scale. In cities and small towns loud-speaker systems blared forth recorded appeals almost day and night. Local political bosses and local machines continued to be important in these campaigns, and in some isolated areas the old traditional *Coronel* carried the electorate as he did in the past. Still, a new kind of political campaign had come to the fore.

These economic, educational and political developments are but a few of the trends that are now changing the entire structure of Brazilian society. Nothing has been said of the development of public administration, which has been eagerly promoted during the last twenty years. Nor has anything been said about legal forms. Since 1946, the country has lived under a new federal constitution. And, of some importance are the changes that have resulted from economic and political relations with other countries; Brazil's increasing international trade and its growing role in international organizations are closely related to its internal affairs. Yet, the major trends which I have sketched will, I hope, make it clear that only now is Brazil going through the same kind of social and economic revolution that most Western European countries experienced in the nineteenth century. But with this important difference: Brazil is undergoing its revolution in the midst of the accelerated changes and profound tensions of the mid-twentieth century. If the industrial revolution exerted both disruptive and creative influences on the society of nineteenth-century Europe, how much more disruptive and creative is its Brazilian counterpart in the middle of the twentieth century?

Modern Brazil

Out of the apparent chaos engendered by the Brazilian revolution a new society is emerging. Certain main lines of its development are even now apparent. It is clear that Brazil will some day be one of the world's most important economic powers and that its economic system will be a modified form of industrial capitalism. Politically, Brazil is allied with the West, and much of its past and present political thinking points to a democratic form of government. Culturally, it has by tradition looked to Europe, first to Portugal, and later to France. Isolated by language and traditions from Hispanic- and Anglo-America, it has only in the last decades really come to know and be known to its American neighbors. More recently the United States has grown to be its most important foreign market and its most important source of imports. As trade has turned to the United States, Brazil has also sought technological inspiration there, and nowadays thousands of Brazilians, who in the past would have gone to Europe, travel to and study in the United States. Probably the United States, more than Europe, will influence the emergent Brazilian society.

What is the new society that is beginning to emerge in Brazil? Fundamental to any understanding of this future society is the recognition of the growing importance of four social and economic groups: the urban lower class, the rural proletariat,[28] the middle class, and the new upper class. These are not entirely "new" segments of the social structure. For a long time there have been many lower-class workers in the cities; a small middle class has existed since colonial times; wage workers on large plantations became usual about with the end of slavery; even in the colonial period the upper class was always fed by *arrivistas,* or new arrivals. What is significant now is the added numerical

---

[28] I have borrowed this term from Sidney Mintz ("The Culture History of a Puerto Rican Cane Plantation 1876-1949," *Hispanic American Historical Review,* May 1953, pp. 224-251).

force of these four groups and the new values and ways of
life they seem to be acquiring.

THE URBAN LOWER CLASS

During the past twenty years migrants from the rural
zones to the cities have been of all social classes. The great
ambition of youths of the small-town middle and local
upper classes has been to move to the city where life is
more convenient and more stimulating. Obviously, however, the majority of rural migrants are from the lower
class, and in the city they continue to perform manual
labor. Many of them have come from the distant "interior"
—most often from the arid northeastern states—directly to
the large cities of São Paulo and Rio de Janeiro. Single
males may go directly to work in the building trades, living
in the skeletons of the very structures they are helping
to build. At night they sleep in hammocks on the job.
Sometimes they even cook their meals on open fires in the
reinforced-concrete structures. Then, too, one also finds
in Rio de Janeiro and São Paulo, entire families who have
recently migrated there from distant rural zones. Families
of newcomers have trouble in finding any form of housing;
often they end up living in *favelas* (shanty towns) or in
remote suburbs. The largest number of rural migrants to
the cities seem to come from nearby rural areas. In the city
of São Paulo, for example, the great majority of recent
migrants have come to the city from São Paulo state.[29]
Then, as nearby rural inhabitants move to the large cities,
their places are often filled by migrants from more distant
regions. Thus, migration to the cities usually takes place
by a series of steps, rather than all at once. Most of the
recent arrivals in the city know something of urban life
and what is expected of them.

Nevertheless, studies that have been made of small
communities not far distant from the large metropolitan

---

[29] Vicente Unzer de Almeida, and Octavio Teixeira Mendes Sobrinho,
Migração rural-urbana (São Paulo: Secretaria da Agricultura, Estado de
São Paulo, 1952).

centers of São Paulo and Rio de Janeiro indicate that even there the rural population is thoroughly rural in its outlook.[30] It is obvious that the members of this enormously swollen urban lower class, who work in industry and in the booming building trade, do not make up an "urban proletariat" in the European sense, holding urban values and "born and bred" to the city. The vast majority of them are, in a sense, peasants living in the city. Many of them live in the city with a false dream of some day returning to their small towns and farms after they have saved enough money. They are paid poorly by U.S. or even by European standards, but still they earn three or four times more than in the rural areas.[31] Furthermore, they have steady work rather than the intermittent employment which is all they often can find at home. Their real wages increase, yet slowly they acquire new necessities and are beset with a whole new set of problems. In the rural areas, housing and transportation are seldom serious problems. In the city, to find any kind of dwelling within their means is very difficult indeed. A worker may have to spend two to three hours, or even as much as five or six hours, traveling between his home and work. But gradually these rural migrants come to acquire a taste for city things— the occasional movie, the parade on Independence Day, and other forms of recreation—and they always have before them examples of people who live better than anyone in their home towns or rural areas. Few even return to the hinterland; when they do, it is rarely for long.

This recently formed urban lower class has lost the social institutions that gave its members a sense of security and stability in their rural communities; but they have not yet developed a new set of institutions to replace the old system. In the city, there is seldom a storekeeper to extend

---

[30] Emilio Willems, *Cunha: Tradição e transição em uma cultura rural do Brasil* (São Paulo: Secretaria da Agricultura, Estado de São Paulo, 1947); and Donald Pierson, *Cruz das Almas: A Brazilian Village* (Washington: Institute of Social Anthropology, Smithsonian Institute, 1952).

[31] Jacques Lambert, *Le Brésil: Structure sociale et institutions politiques* (Paris: Colin, 1953), p. 44.

them credit. There are political leaders, to be sure, but
the *Coronel,* the traditional political boss of the country
people, is not present to tell them how to vote. They work
for a company or corporation; thus they no longer have
a *patrão* in the traditional sense. They live the impersonal
life of the city without the kinsmen and lifelong friends
of the same neighborhood. Their chief form of security
must be derived from the well-conceived, but imperfectly
functioning, labor code. When they need help they turn
to the *sindicato* or labor union, and the *Fiscal,* or inspector
of the Ministry of Labor, who ultimately controls the
union. These quasi-legal associations and government
organizations hardly take the place of the highly personal
patrão. Many of these recent migrants are illiterate or
semiliterate and they are bewildered with the com-
plexities of the bureaucracy. Often they are unaware of
the laws that protect them and at a loss about how to claim
their rights. It is not surprising that there are frequent
demonstrations and protests which have even resulted in
the burning of street cars as a protest against an increase
in fares and the miserable transportation service.

It was to this urban lower class that Getulio Vargas and
his Partido Trabalhista Brasileiro appealed and from
which he drew most of his support. Not only did his government promulgate the labor code, establish minimum wages,
and establish (and control) the labor unions during the
so-called "New State" (1937-1945), but also Vargas himself
had a deep emotional appeal to these people. They saw in
him an image of the father-like *patrão* and protector. He
was called affectionately "The Father of the Poor," "The
Old One," or just "Getulio." When Vargas spoke to them
over his "Hour of Brazil" on the radio, he addressed himself to the *trabalhadores do Brasil* (workers of Brazil). To
them he represented security in the new impersonal world
of the city. Never did these workers become fanatic, semi-
fascistic followers of their leader as did Perón's *descamisa-
dos* (the "shirtless ones") in Argentina, and as did many
followers of similar charismatic leaders in Europe. Rather,

they were passive but loyal to their protector in whom they
recognized many faults, just as they had in their *patrão*
in the rural areas and on the plantations.

Vargas was admired for his astuteness and his daring.
His electoral following was not shocked when he used
doubtful political methods to gain power or when he deprived the country of political freedom. After all they were
accustomed to the rigged elections in the rural areas. They
were not upset when Vargas surrounded himself with
capangas (toughs), when his relatives were accused of en-
riching themselves through his favors, or when during
World War II he opportunely shifted his support from the
Axis powers to the Allies. To them, this was a familiar
pattern of behavior. After all, in traditional Brazil and
in the rural areas, the upper-class *patrão* had lived ostenta-
tiously while the lower classes lived miserably. The *patrão*
had obviously exploited them, even while he provided
them with some measure of security. The important thing
to the new urban lower class was that Vargas proclaimed
that he fought for their interests against the new impersonal upper-class groups of the cities and that he could
point to some evidence that he had acted in their favor.
Deprived of the slight security that the old social structure
of traditional Brazil had afforded them, they looked for
a new *patrão*, and Vargas seemed to fulfill that role. Even
after his death in 1955, they continued to rally to the
support of his political party, electing his political heir,
João Goulart, vice-president of the republic.

It is natural for this new urban lower class to be vulnerable to extreme right- or left-wing movements as its members seek for leadership and guidance in an unfamiliar and
impersonal world. Through similar causes the Brazilian
Communist party garnered almost 600,000 votes in 1945,
electing one senator and fourteen deputies. Even today,
although it is illegal and "underground," the Communist
party undoubtedly has considerable influence. Yet, despite
the glamor exercised by the Communist leader, Luis Carlos
Prestes, and despite the leadership provided by some intel-

lectuals, it is doubtful that the Communist party has any wide support among the urban lower class.

This new class is still rural in its orientation and to a large extent traditional in its point of view. Its members do not see their situation as a product of a "class struggle." They are Catholics and are influenced by the church, and they are looking for a *patrão* for their protection, not for an internationally oriented political movement. Even when they turn from Vargas or his party they vote for such candidates as Adhemar de Barros, and for Janio Quadros, both past governors of São Paulo state. Both these men, like Vargas, appeal to the half-felt need of the urban lower class for a protector, and they proclaim their support to this group against the upper-class "exploiters." Even so, the urban lower class might easily be swung to new charismatic leaders; as long as their plight is serious, they will be vulnerable to extremist influences. For the time being, they are mild and relatively passive—a heritage of their recent past—but they might easily learn to be violent.

THE RURAL PROLETARIAT

Similar to the urban lower class, but numerically less strong, is a new rural segment of the Brazilian population, the workers on the large mechanized plantations. Like the urban lower class, these wage laborers have been separated from their traditional way of life. They no longer have a *patrão* in the traditional sense. On the large sugar cane plantations and in the sugar mills of São Paulo, Bahia, and Pernambuco, on the large coffee plantations of São Paulo and Paraná, and on the few large cocoa plantations of southern Bahia the workers are employees of corporations. Their immediate supervisors are also corporation employees and administrators. It is often true that the shareholders in many of these corporations are relatives, and that such corporations are "family affairs." Still, the corporation must be run as a "strictly business enterprise." In a study of community life in a sugar cane producing area of Bahia, Harry W. Hutchinson describes the new pattern of work:

These two new managers (employed by the corporation) have put the relations between management and labor on a strictly business basis and have removed all elements of paternalism. Upon taking over, they dismissed most of the older, higher-level factory, field, and office workers. Administrators, mechanics and bookkeepers, most of whom had seen twenty years or more of service, were dispatched. New people came to take their places and some of the vacancies were filled by promotions. Time clocks were installed, and the system of authority was reinforced all the way down the line. Social legislation—a new factor in rural, agricultural Brazil—was invoked to take the place of paternalism.[32]

On these large agricultural establishments, the workers are more numerous and more heterogeneous than on the older and smaller family-owned plantations. The field hands, skilled labor, office workers, and executives no longer form a close-knit neighborhood, united by kinship and many years of close acquaintance. They come from many places and they frequently move on after a time, seeking work elsewhere.

Usually these large agricultural establishments are closely integrated into the national marketing system. By necessity, they are connected to the larger metropolitan centers and ports by adequate systems of transportation and communications. On them, the houses of the workers, generally provided by the corporation, form small towns; there are stores, a school, a chapel or church, generally a soccer field and club, and a system to supply water and electricity. The corporation furnishes medical assistance, and there is a clinic—sometimes a small hospital. As Hutchinson found, the workers are not protected by social legislation, and labor unions are active among them. Many of these workers are recent migrants from more distant rural zones and many are illiterate. Like their fellows in the cities, they hardly know how to cope with this new impersonal world and its many regulations. In another and older setting, they were accustomed to look for protection

---

[32] Cited, p. 107.

to a *patrão:* a landowner, a storekeeper, or even a political boss. Now, they must depend upon "the government," that is, laws, and on political leaders for help in securing their rights. In the political arena, they, like the urban lower class, are vulnerable to the appeal of a charismatic leader or even of a demagogue who promises protection and support in an impersonal world.

It is difficult to judge the numerical force of this rural proletariat. Certainly, it forms a much smaller group throughout the country than the urban lower class and the more numerous but isolated peasant farmers. Brazil has not developed large-scale mechanized "factories-in-the-field" comparable to the sugar plantations of Cuba or Puerto Rico or the banana plantations of Central America. In fact, in the southern states and particularly in São Paulo, there has been an increase during the last twenty years in the number of farms owned or worked by single families. Nevertheless, following the 1940 census, T. Lynn Smith estimated that almost 10 per cent (or 178,326) of the agricultural establishments in Brazil were operated by administrators, and these establishments were relatively large, including almost 23 per cent of the total acreage under cultivation.[33] Hendrik Meijer estimated also on the basis of the 1940 figures that 17.5 per cent of the agricultural and cattle-raising establishments were owned in *condominio,* or by multiple owners, and 10.3 per cent by *pessoas jurídicas,* mainly corporations.[34] The same census figures showed that almost 1,500,000 people lived on plantations operated by administrators. Without doubt many of these "administrator-operated" plantations are relatively small and of the traditional family-owned type, but particularly in the sugar-producing regions of the country there has been a marked trend during the past fifty years toward large corporation-owned enterprises, which combine the growing of cane with milling and refining of sugar.[35]

33 Cited, p. 382.
34 *Rural Brazil at the Cross Roads* (Wageningen: Veenman, 1951), p. 52.
35 Gileno dé Carli, *O processo histórico da usina em Pernambuco* (Rio de Janeiro, 1942), in Smith, cited, p. 440.

It is difficult to predict whether or not the future trend of Brazil's agricultural development will emphasize the "factory-in-the-field." Several well-trained observers feel that the small-farm pattern similar to that common in the United States and in the south of Brazil, will spread throughout the country.[36] The growing system of tenancy in São Paulo and other states and the subdivision of enormous states on the Paraná frontier is resulting in the formation of a large class of farmers who work the land themselves. As communications improve, this large class of rural farmers will also, along with the rural proletariat, be drawn into the mainstream of modern Brazil. For the time being, however, it seems that the effects of the Brazilian revolution are filtering from the cities into the rural zones mainly through the channel of the workers on large plantations. This segment of the rural population has already broken with the old traditions and institutions, but the shape of its new life is not yet fixed.

THE NEW MIDDLE CLASS

Ever since the early nineteenth century, Brazil has had a small group of people who might be classified as "middle class." These were the families of men who were clerks in government offices or had other white-collar occupations. In small towns, there has long been the provincial "upper class," distinct from the landed gentry; it was composed of people who made their living as municipal and state employees, from commerce, and sometimes from small-scale landholdings. From the mid-nineteenth century, the immigration of Europeans added to this small middle group, especially in southern Brazil. Traditionally, the army, rather than being truly "aristocratic" and controlled by the landed gentry, has been a means of upward mobility and has been dominated by the middle class.[37] Until very re-

---

[36] Smith, cited, p. 443.

[37] This is often misunderstood by those who know Spanish America but who are less well acquainted with Brazil. They see the Brazilian army as an instrument of the old traditional society of the nineteenth century as it often seems to be in other Latin American countries. But in Brazil,

cently this middle segment has been insignificant in numbers, and until recently it tended to identify its outlook with the aristocratic values of the landed gentry.

The size of the present-day middle class is difficult to determine. Yet to anyone who has known Brazil during the past fifteen years, it is apparent that this group has increased many times over and that it is growing with every year. Its new role is reflected in the enormous increase in demand for consumer goods, the expansion of housing in the middle-income brackets, and the rapid development of services of all kinds for middle-income groups in the large cities. Perhaps, the best index of growth is the increase of "white-collar" jobs, for the middle groups still consider manual labor in any form as "lower class." The rapid growth of federal, state, and municipal civil service has opened up many "white-collar" positions, and government employment has been perhaps the most important single road to membership in the middle class. With the rapid growth of industry and commerce, numerous jobs have also opened up in offices and in stores. Furthermore, with the growth of the population as a whole, there are greater opportunities in the professions and there is an urgent demand for specialists in chemistry, nursing, engineering, surveying, and the like. Social mobility in Brazil today is rapid and the demands of its expanding economy call for white-collar workers and specialists as well as for labor.

This growing new class finds itself in a difficult situation. Its members have learned to expect a higher standard of living than they can actually afford. Their economic problem is very acute. They live in a modern world of the radio, television, cinema, and the theater. They have learned to want, even to need, telephones, electric iceboxes, washing machines, typewriters, automobiles, and a multitude of industrial products and gadgets. They want better and more modern homes, and they are extremely conscious of

the army, which is no less politically potent, represents a new growing middle class.

and eager for good clothes. They are prey to modern advertising and fads; fashions come and go among this group
as they do in the United States or in Europe.

The difficulty is that few of them earn enough to acquire
what they have been taught to regard as modern necessities.
A few professionals and some very successful businessmen
can afford to purchase cooperative apartments in the city
or houses in the suburbs, electrical appliances, and other
things of the kind; but the lower echelons of the new
middle class earn very poor salaries in relation to their
aspirations. A 1948 study of *comerciários,* or commercial
employees—mainly clerks and the like—in Rio de Janeiro
showed that 60 per cent of them earned less than 3,000
cruzeiros per month (about $60 U.S.), 33 per cent earned
between that amount and 6,000 cruzeiros, and only 7 per
cent earned over 6,000 cruzeiros.[38] At the same time, a
librarian at the National Library, after many years of service, might be earning about 5,000 cruzeiros ($100 per
month), and a secretary in a government office or a schoolteacher about the same. By comparison, at that time, a
small electric icebox cost 15 to 20,000 cruzeiros ($300-
$400), or the equivalent of five or six months' salary for
the majority of these people. Other prices were equally
high in relation to income.[39] The same study of the commercial employees showed that they spent on the average
as much as 40-45 per cent of their income for food and
less than 3 per cent for recreation.[40] It is not surprising
that many middle-class families buy "on time" and that
many are in debt. They are truly "economically frustrated."

The aspirations of this class and their frustrations are

---

[38] L.A. Costa Pinto Instituto de Economia, *Pesquisa sobre a padrão de
vida do comerciário no distrito federal* (Rio de Janeiro: Author, 1949),
p. 107.

[39] Since then, salaries in all categories have been increased but prices
have also increased almost as much. Although Brazil now produces more
of the items that the middle class wishes to buy (electric iceboxes, for example), national products are high in price, almost as high as imported
items.

[40] *Pesquisa sobre a padrão de vida . . . ,* cited, p. 169.

reflected in the educational crisis. This new middle class places a high value on education. Through giving their children secondary and higher education, they hope to consolidate or improve for their children the positions they have won. For example, in a study of the 1,353 students in seventeen "middle schools" (Ginásios) it was found that the parents of 40.5 per cent of the students were high-ranking employees in commerce and government and the parents of 24.2 per cent of the group were bookkeepers, clerks, salesmen, primary-school teachers, and other lower echelon "white-collar" commercial and government employees. Taken together, the two groups, clearly of the new middle class, accounted for 64.7 per cent of the secondary students in the sample. The parents of 18.6 per cent of these students belonged to the upper class (landed gentry, high-prestige professionals, etc.) and the parents of only 8.4 per cent were manual laborers and artisans. The remaining students were children of professionals of less prestige such as dentists, teachers, pharmacists, army officers, and the like—a group that has been middle class for several generations.[41] Another study carried out in the state of Rio de Janeiro indicated that by far the preponderant number of secondary students came from this new middle class.[42] In this desire to educate their children they are often frustrated, for secondary schools, mainly private, are costly in relation to the income level of the group that is most anxious to profit by them.

The new middle class shares many values with the small group which, in earlier days, formed the Brazilian middle class. Essentially, they have not yet developed their own middle-class ideology or values in the same way as the European and North American middle classes. Fundamentally, they still identify their aspirations with older and aristocratic values, except in the extreme south of

---

41 Juarez Ruben Brandão Lopez, "Escolha ocupacional e origem social de ginásios em São Paulo," *Educação e Ciências Sociais* (Rio de Janeiro), August 1956, pp. 43-62.

42 Unpublished notes of the author.

Brazil, where European influences are strong. They are "white-collar" groups, and they have a deep disdain for manual labor. In the study of the secondary-school students in São Paulo already referred to, more than 60 per cent of them still hoped to become either medical doctors, engineers, lawyers, or plantation owners—the four most traditional and prestigeful occupations of traditional Brazil. This indicates, according to the Brazilian author of the study, "the permanence of traditional Brazilian values relating to work (or occupation) in an environment in which economic development demands new specialties." [43] Likewise, it is customary for most families of this class, even though they may be having a difficult time making ends meet, to have at least one domestic servant. And, although it cannot be expressed statistically, the hospitality of this middle class often reaches an ostentatious level that is far beyond their economic means. In brief, they are not ideologically a "middle class." They aspire to the old aristocratic values of the landed gentry of the eighteenth and nineteenth centuries. This is not only impossible economically for them but also out of keeping with the needs of modern Brazil.

The Brazilian middle class is, in a sense, the most conservative social segment of their society. Because they are insecure in their position, they make a point of preserving most of the old Latin American values and traditional patterns of behavior. Yet, they cannot maintain many of these values and behavior patterns, either because the world around them is changing or because they lack the economic basis to support them. They believe that a woman's place is in the home, and yet their daughters, even their wives, often work in business or in the government. They value the large Latin American family with its close ties among kinsmen and its large family gatherings, but many of this middle class have lost touch with their kinsmen through migrating to the cities or through their

43 Brandão Lopez, cited, p. 61.

new social and economic mobility. They value the traditional Brazilian emphasis upon a humanistic education, but at the same time they are highly materialistic. They want a higher material standard of living, and they are aware of the importance of technology and of a scientific education. Nationalistic and patriotic, this group believes strongly in the past and future of their great country. They are quick to take offense at any slight or disparagement of Brazil. Like the middle class in the United States, they might be called "isolationist" or "ethnocentric." And then, these are the same people who flock to English language classes in most of the big cities, follow the lives of American movie stars in their fan magazines, and readily adopt the latest American fashion or fad. To them, the United States symbolizes a higher standard of living and the type of society, at least materially, to which they aspire.

Even now, this middle class is changing rapidly. As it grows in numbers and as it consolidates its economic position, it will probably develop its own social and political ideology and values. It will no longer identify its ambitions with the traditional upper class or copy its aristocratic values. Already it is divided politically. Many owe their economic positions to the Vargas regime, under which the bureaucracy was greatly expanded, and many support his party. But most middle-class people looked with critical eyes on the excesses of the Vargas regime and on its suppression of political and civil liberty for almost ten years. Like the traditional upper class, they are not above seeking special privileges for themselves or their relatives; it is part of the normal course of life to make use of a *pistolão*, or "pull," if one has important friends or relatives. But this middle class also values "honesty." Thus, in 1950 it voted in great numbers for Carlos Lacerda, the journalist critic who exposed the excesses of the recent Vargas regime, when he ran for deputy. Its members voted for Eduardo Gomes in 1945 and 1950 and for Juarez Távora in 1955— these were the "honest" candidates for president who represented to them the traditional values of Brazil. Although he often performed like a demagogue, they voted for Janio Quadros when he ran for governor of São Paulo state, because he promised to "clean house" and wipe out graft. Still, although it is perhaps the most articulate segment of Brazilian society, this middle class is hardly large enough to dominate the electorate. It is far outnumbered by the urban lower class and by that part of the rural population which is still under the influence of a *patrão* or of a political machine. This was especially evident in the 1955 election when, according to most observers, it was the combination of the urban lower class and the *patrão*-dominated rural vote that defeated the candidates of the middle class. But as the economy and the educational system expand, the middle groups will grow in size and influence. Their role will be crucial for the future of the country.

THE NEW UPPER CLASS

Finally, the Brazilian revolution has changed the face of the country's upper class. The "traditional families" of the beginning of the century are still important in Brazilian life and their names continue to appear in high business circles, in political and public life, in the diplomatic corps, and in the intellectual life of the country. But during the last twenty years an increasing number of people from the middle class have moved into the upper class through acquiring wealth, political influence, education or professional competence. The Vargas regime brought many new names into national prominence. The expanding economy of the last twenty years has opened up numerous opportunities for amassing new wealth, and success stories of "rags to riches" are often heard in Rio de Janeiro and São Paulo. Many of the European immigrants who arrived in Brazil during the late nineteenth or during the first decade of the twentieth century have prospered and have even made great fortunes. Such names as Matarazzo in industry, Jaffet in industry and banking, Lunardelli in coffee, Santos Vahlis in real estate, and Klabine in paper manufacturing are but a few people of non-Luso-Brazilian origin who are now of great importance in their respective fields. Second-generation immigrants have entered widely into the scientific, artistic, and even the political life of the country.

Many of these new upper-class members are *arrivistas,* or recent arrivals, and, like the "new rich" everywhere, they often shock the traditional upper class, and even the middle class, by their ostentation, their manners, and their unscrupulous methods. It might almost be said that some in this group have no traditional values. They have achieved their exalted positions by astuteness and hard work, not by inheritance or family position. These are, as Gilberto Freyre has pointed out, "transitional figures" arising out of the rapid changes in the economic system. As he also points out,

The transitional figure is just as common among Brazilians of Portuguese origin as among those of non-Portuguese origin. Their transition has been from the agrarian North to the industrial South, from country to city, and sometimes from positions of weakness and poverty to positions of power and wealth. In such circumstances, moral controls break down, and the influence of one's ancestral environment, whether it be a farm in Brazil or a farm in Italy, no longer affects one's behavior.[44]

Such people have only partially understood the values of the Brazilian gentry and, in fact, they may be said to aspire only partially to acquiring traditional Brazilian upper-class values. They are far more interested in acquiring the high material comforts of the rich of New York and Paris than in the old family-oriented Brazilian upper-class traditions, yet they continue a long Brazilian tradition of the love of ostentation and luxury.

It must not be thought that this "new upper class" stands

44 Gilberto Freyre, "The Brazilian Melting Pot," *Atlantic Monthly,* February 1946, p. 107.

apart and is rebuffed by the traditional families of Brazil. Nor must it be thought that all of its members behave as *arrivistas* and "new rich." Among them many are as malleable and as mobile socially as they have been economically and politically. One has only to look at the increasing number of non-Portuguese names in the society columns of the large cities and at the frequent announcements of marriages between individuals of traditional upper-class families and the new upper class to understand that their success is not confined to the market place or the political arena. The new upper class is, in fact, rapidly fusing with the old traditional upper class to form a new dominant segment of Brazilian society. This is taking place even in the traditional sugar plantation area of Bahia. Harry W. Hutchinson describes vividly how a new upper-class family, the "Helvetians," took over control of an important sugar mill from the old traditional family, whom he calls the "Condes":

Usina São Pedro was described earlier as a family corporation, owned and operated by the members of one extended family (i.e., the Condes). At one time in the last five years, this family was obliged to take into the corporation a large amount of capital representing a second family enterprise, considerably larger in scope than the first. Within a short time, the second family achieved complete control of the factory through a series of financial manipulations. As a result, Usina São Pedro passed from the Conde family's ownership and direction and is now just one element of a large commercial firm. . . . The second family, the Helvetians, is a second-generation immigrant family. . . . The Helvetians have taken a place in the upper ranks of Bahian society, representing new money and economic power. Their history is important. The original immigrant married into a Bahian family of "good name" and all of his sons have done the same. One of them married a daughter of the *Coronel,* founder of the Usina São Pedro. It was through this marriage that the transfer of the factory was channeled.[45]

---

[45] Cited, p. 180.

This process is not a new one in Brazilian society, for the traditional upper class has never been a truly closed social class; it has always been fed by the assimilation of newcomers from the lower and middle classes and from abroad. During the empire and the early republic, the aristocracy was enlarged by newcomers who through inter-marriage soon became part of the traditional upper class. Foreign names of German, Polish, English, French, and Italian origin are not infrequently as familiar as Portu-guese surnames. In the past, it has been the traditional upper class that has absorbed the newcomers, thereby pre-serving and transmitting its aristocratic values. With the shock of the new Brazilian revolution, the newcomers into the upper economic and social echelons of society are to-day more numerous than ever before. As a consequence, the dominant segment of Brazilian society may take a new form, one more like that which prevails in the United States, where the values of the power group derive from commerce, industry, and capital rather than from politics and landowning.

The changes in the upper class have made themselves felt intensely in political life. The party that has been in strongest opposition to Vargas and his heirs from 1945 to the present has been the União Democrática Nacional (UDN). Its leaders have come mainly from traditional upper-class families, such as the Melo Franco family, long prominent in Minas Gerais. Its candidates for the presi-dency have been from middle-class and traditional upper-class families. Its electoral following has also probably been made up largely of the middle and traditional upper class, and of voters living in small towns and rural areas, where the values of these "traditionalist" classes persist. On the other hand, the new upper class has often been allied with the Partido Social Progressista led by Adhemar de Barros, and with the Partido Trabalhista Brasileiro founded by Getulio Vargas, both of which also appeal strongly to the urban lower class. Many members of the new upper class owe their advancement to the Vargas regime, and others

hope for special favors after new elections. Some others no
doubt give their support out of a fear of the rising power
of the urban lower class or a suspicion of the continued
power of the traditional upper class. Thus, one finds an
unusual political alliance in modern Brazil—an alliance,
in many cases, between the wealthiest segment of the
population, the new business and industrial groups, and
the urban lower class who often live in outright misery.
For different reasons, both seem to be united against what
they consider the special privileges of the old oligarchy.

Brazil and the United States

The makers of U.S. policy toward Brazil as well as those
who work face to face with Brazilian problems must understand the process, the trends, and the full import of the
Brazilian revolution. Policy toward any country must be
based on an awareness of dynamic trends and new forces,
and this is especially true of Brazil. From the turn of the
century, and especially since 1930, Brazilian society has
changed profoundly, and this revolution has not yet come
to an end. In fact, it is only now in full swing and the
changes in the next two decades will surely be more drastic
than those of the recent past.

Brazil is in a stage of transition from a society essentially
agrarian and rural, with a rigid class system, to one that is
industrial and urban-oriented, in which older class lines
are fading and a new social, economic, and political order
is beginning to emerge. New socio-economic segments have
already appeared in some key regions, but throughout most
of the country, particularly in the north and in remote
rural areas, the traditional social and economic class system
persists. There most of the population still depend upon
a *patrão* for economic security and for direction in political
affairs. In these less-developed parts of the country, and
to a certain extent through the country, the traditional
values of the past continue to function and to determine
individual behavior and the relations between individuals

and groups. To understand this "traditional Brazil" one must understand the great value placed on the family and kinship relations, on old social class associations, on personal relations and personalism in all forms, and upon transcendentalism and humanism.[46] These old Luso-Brazilian values are still very much alive in Brazil, and they help to explain both the present and also the clash between the old and new forces in Brazilian society.

It is in the south of Brazil, however, and especially in the large cities, as well as in the smaller cities of between 50,000 and 100,000 people that are appearing with increasing frequency on the map, that the trends of the future are most apparent. Here masses of people have broken with the traditional values, and the old class structure is giving way to new social and economic alignment. Social organization is fluid, and people are striving eagerly to improve their status. A new set of values and a new set of social institutions have not yet fully appeared to replace those of traditional Brazil. Members of the urban lower class and their rural counterparts, the so-called rural proletariat, so far have received only nominal protection through the labor and social welfare laws and through the new labor unions. And they no longer have the minimal protection of a rural *patrão*. Nor have they developed a class ideology or associations in keeping with the urban scene. Still, this segment of the Brazilian population is politically powerful. If the present trends of the Brazilian revolution continue, they will increase in numbers and in political awareness and power. In their striving to improve their lot they are vulnerable to the appeals of demagogues of the extreme left or extreme right; they also respond to the extension of true democratic processes when that offers them the opportunities they seek.

Likewise, in these cities, large and small, and in small towns, the Brazilian middle class is growing rapidly, but it is slow to acquire a middle-class ideology and a system

---

[46] Compare John Gillin, above, pp. 28 ff.

of middle-class values. At least the lower strata of this new middle class, and to a lesser extent most of this class, are frustrated by the conflict between their new material wants or "necessities" and the inadequacy of their small incomes, which are further diluted by inflation. To date, it cannot be said that the middle class forms "the backbone of the nation," but, in my opinion, this is the social segment that will be most important in determining the Brazil of the future. The traditional upper class is ill at ease with the upheavals which have riven their traditional society and with the appearance of the "new upper class" based upon industry and commerce. They often tend to become *saudosistas* (nostalgic) about the Brazil of the past. The new upper class is still too busy consolidating its financial, political, and social position to be concerned with public responsibility. It is the middle class who are seeking secondary and higher education in large numbers. Out of this class are emerging the leaders in science, public health, education, public administration, and even in politics. As the members of the middle class grow in numbers and in economic power, they will develop a new set of Brazilian values differing from the traditional values of the aristocracy as well as from those of the middle classes in North America, but adapted to an impersonal, modern, and urban world. They will be the Brazilians of the future.

Both the growing urban lower class and this middle class are the new social segments to be considered above all in the conduct of our future relations with Brazil. In the past it was easy to deal with a small upper-class group who had firm control over the economic, social, and political destinies of their country, but this class no longer exists. Likewise, it is easy to set forth a program for Brazilian development that focuses upon the vast rural population. In terms of numbers, Brazil is still predominantly rural. Certainly no country as basically rural as Brazil can truly develop its resources unless the way of life of the rural population is improved and brought into the orbit of national life. However, a program of "grass roots" diplomacy focused on Brazil's rural population can easily be misspent. Out of our own North American past, it is easy for us to look upon the stability and security of the rural community as a sound basis for political and economic life. But the Brazilian rural community in reality provides little basis for the development of a new dynamic society. It is in the large towns, in the numerous small cities, and in the great metropolitan centers that the future of Brazil will be determined.

There is every reason to believe that at the end of this century, Brazil will have become one of the great powers, not only large in area and population, but also in providing a high standard of living for its people. The new capital, Brasilia, dedicated in 1960, is a symbol of Brazil's determination to bring the undeveloped interior into the national society. It is also a symbol of Brazilians' national pride. By tradition, Brazil is allied with the United States. The direction of its internal development as well as its international policies are important to us. Brazil will need the help and understanding of the United States to live through this most important epoch in its history. "The little solutions" or *jeitinhos*, so common in Brazil, will not be enough. The Brazilian revolution demands far-reaching changes. But, with its long tradition of peaceful solutions, there is every promise that Brazil will overcome its "growing pains" and emerge as one of the world's strongest democracies.

Five

SOCIAL CHANGE IN GUATEMALA AND U.S. POLICY

by RICHARD N. ADAMS

DURING THE DECADE following the Second World War, U.S. newspapers brought, with increasing frequency, reports of the emergence of a strong Communist leadership, supported by sympathetic presidents, in the small Central American country of Guatemala. Most readers probably never took this whole train of events very seriously. Everything was wrong about it: small countries were unimportant; communism could not take hold in our own backyard; and where was Guatemala, anyway? Subsequent events made clear, however, that small countries could be very important; that communism could gain a foothold if it was suitably encouraged; and that Guatemala's location turned these developments into a threat to inter-American solidarity and security, as well as a blow to U.S. prestige throughout the hemisphere and the world.

Today the newspapers focus their attention not on Guatemala but on Cuba. While history seldom repeats itself in all particulars, the conditions in these two cases are sufficiently similar that an examination of what happened in Guatemala may provide us with a better grasp of what is happening today in Cuba and may happen tomorrow in the Dominican Republic or elsewhere.

To Americans in the first half of the twentieth century, Guatemala was one of several "banana republics." In the popular mind, these countries consisted of little more than steaming jungles, peopled by Indians, revolutionaries, snakes and O. Henrian consuls, all equally picturesque and equally unimportant. In the eyes of the government, however, the little Caribbean countries had a disconcerting habit of ruining their treasuries in periodic revolutions, defaulting on foreign debts, and thus offering European powers an occasion for threatening to send in their troops. More than once the United States sent marines into Caribbean countries to protect American investments, thereby forestalling any similar action by European powers. Action to "protect life and property" was central to U.S. policy until 1933, when the Roosevelt administration, under the newly proclaimed Good Neighbor policy, agreed that armed intervention in the affairs of other American states was no longer permissible.

At the beginning of the Good Neighbor era, Guatemala was coming under the control of Jorge Ubico, who was to maintain his dictatorial control for a decade. The country he ruled was one of the larger republics in Central America, as well as the most populous among them. Although most Guatemalans were independent subsistence farmers, many worked on the numerous coffee farms that produced Guatemala's main export, and some were employed on the banana plantations.

Guatemala's territory falls into three major zones. In the south, the Pacific coastal plain has been sparsely populated since pre-conquest times except for a small area held by the banana interests. In the north, the inland mass of the *Petén* has similarly been underpopulated since the days when the classic Mayan civilization held sway from its fabulous ceremonial centers of pyramids and temples. In the middle, running from Mexico to Honduras, lies a broad series of mountain ranges, flanked on its southern rim by a line of volcanoes. It is in the interior valleys, intramountain plateaus, and southern piedmont of this highland region that most of the Guatemalans live.[1]

Despite the effects of the world-wide depression and a low level of economic activity, Ubico succeeded during his decade of rule in paying off the government's foreign debt and promoting the country's foreign trade. Although he embarked upon some limited social reforms, Ubico's policies strongly favored the coffee and banana producers and neglected other needs for internal development, except that of keeping the roads in good order. Labor regulations operated in favor of the big producers. There was no effort to guide the people as a whole into an era of economic and social advancement. Individuals who protested against Ubico's policies were escorted out of the country or otherwise denied all influence. In Guatemala Ubico was *la política,* and this was made plain to anyone who ventured to question it.

The Impact of World War II

Ubico's rule might well have continued for some years longer, had it not been for the impact of World War II. As a friend of the United States, he immediately sided with his northern neighbor, sequestered Axis-owned properties, and made available facilities for the enlarged defense of the Panama Canal. The United States sent in several thousand troops to build and man air bases and devoted a good deal of effort to advertising the cause of the Allies, together with the Atlantic Charter, the Four Freedoms, and similar lofty goals. In the Guatemala of Ubico, one did not generally advertise any freedoms, much less four of them, without evoking some invidious comparisons, and younger

[1] For a general background, C. L. Jones, *Guatemala, Past and Present* (University of Minneapolis Press, 1940); K. H. Silvert, *A Study in Government: Guatemala,* Publication 21 of the Middle American Research Institute (Tulane University, New Orleans, 1954); *Integración social en Guatemala,* Publicación Numero 3 (Guatemala City: Seminario de Integración Social Guatemalteca, 1956), a collection of papers and discussions presented at a conference held at Guatemala City in June 1956.

Guatemalans were quick to respond. As more and more Guatemalans began to feel that it was their own future freedom that was at stake, Ubico decided that the course of greater wisdom lay in stepping down. In 1944 the aging dictator retired to New Orleans, where he died shortly thereafter. On his departure, the struggle for power flared up in a revolution. By 1945 there had emerged a new government, a new constitution, and a mass of literate and illiterate Guatemalans filled with enthusiasm for a future of social justice and progress.

The revolution of 1944 and its sequel have been recognized by most observers to be a genuine social revolution, a type of upheaval which has been rare in Latin America. A progressive and constitutional government, under the newly elected president, Juan José Arévalo, embarked on a vigorous program of social, economic, and political reforms. During his tenure, the U.S.-sponsored aid programs, begun during the war and continued after its end, were increasingly ignored or deprecated. The United States was accused with growing frequency of economic and other forms of imperialism and prominent Guatemalans voiced loud approval of the ideology and programs of the Soviet Union and Communist China. Jacobo Arbenz Guzmán, who followed Arévalo in 1951, initiated a program of agrarian reform and came increasingly under the influence of Communists. The excesses of the Arbenz regime brought on a new revolution, in 1954, led by an army officer, Colonel Carlos Castillo Armas.[2]

---

2 For various accounts and interpretations of these events, Daniel James, *Red Design for the Americas: Guatemalan Prelude* (New York: Day, 1954), a journalistic account; John Gillin and K. H. Silvert, "Ambiguities in Guatemala," *Foreign Affairs*, April 1956, pp. 469-482; Philip B. Taylor, Jr., "The Guatemalan Affair: A Critique of United States Foreign Policy," *American Political Science Review*, September 1956, pp. 787-806; *Penetration of the Political Institutions of Guatemala by the International Communist Movement* ... (Washington: Department of State, June 1954); Stokes Newbold, "Receptivity to Communist-Fomented Agitation in Rural Guatemala," *Economic Development and Cultural Change*, July 1957, pp. 338-361; also Silvert, cited. There has also been a rash of anti-United States polemics in Spanish from members of

The advent of Castillo Armas marked a sharp swing to the right. The Communist party was outlawed, and most of the major political figures in the two previous regimes fled the country. The new government appealed to the United States to revive its aid program. Agrarian reforms were continued on a more limited basis, but labor unions were suppressed, as well as all political parties. In the summer of 1957 Castillo Armas was assassinated by one of his bodyguards. After eight uneasy months of interim governments, a new election resulted in the choice of Miguel Ydigoras Fuentes, who had been the leading candidate against Arbenz in the less-than-free election of 1950. The new president took office in March 1958.

The Impact of U.S. Aid Programs

During World War II the United States initiated economic and technical aid programs in Guatemala, as in many other countries of Latin America, through the Institute of Inter-American Affairs and other governmental agencies. The decisions as to the kinds of technical assistance to be given stemmed from a laudable but politically shortsighted philosophy that only long-range and "basic" problems should be tackled—hence the great emphasis on primary education, agricultural extension, and public health. In themselves, these programs were of considerable value, and of them Guatemala received more than its proportionate share. Between 1946 and 1950, for example, it received from the Office of Foreign Agricultural Relations alone more dollar assistance than any other Latin American country.[3]

Under these programs, little or no attention was paid to whether or not the segments of the population at which these efforts were aimed were politically influential. It

the Arévalo and Arbenz regimes. These have received wide circulation in Latin America; so far as I know, none has become available in English.

[3] Arthur T. Mosher, *Technical Co-operation in Latin-American Agriculture* (University of Chicago Press, 1957), Table 2, p. 20.

sufficed that the groups to be helped were in a precarious
economic position. The new political leaders who were
coming to power in Guatemala were more realistic. They
knew that within their country there were different kinds
of people, with different sets of problems, needs, and hopes.
Since the new leaders had also risen out of segments of the
population whose existence was scarcely known to U.S.
policy-makers, either in Washington or in Guatemala
City, no effort was made, apparently, to enlist their understanding or cultivate their good will.

Between 1946 and 1950, the Guatemalan government
showed an ever declining interest in working with the
U.S. technical aid missions. In 1950 it ordered the public
education mission to leave the country and effectively
restricted the activities of the agricultural and public
health specialists. Meanwhile, political activities were growing, and many changes were under way within Guatemala.
Not all were congenial to U.S. ideals and interests. Labor
unions, for example, were increasingly dominated by leftist leaders, who made Guatemala's big northern neighbor
their favorite whipping boy for all ills. To anyone who
observed the organizing activities, the agitation and propaganda directed at the urban workers, the laborers on large
farms, and the residents of small towns and villages, it was
obvious that the new leading group was intent upon drastic
changes and that in these changes U.S. aid and influence
were, to put it mildly, unwelcome.

The failure of U.S. policy was not due primarily to
inadequate personnel and financing, or to insurmountable
problems of economic and technical development. The
difficulty stemmed, rather, from the involvement of the
United States in a struggle between competing ideologies.
Opposing U.S. policy was a local group of increasingly
influential Communist and Marxist ideologists and leaders
who were intent upon converting their people to their
own allegiance—to the discomfiture of the prestige of the
United States.

With the establishment of the Castillo Armas government, which it had helped into power, the United States
gained a new chance to play an effective role in Guatemala's development. During the first two years of the new
regime, Washington poured almost $20 million into aid
programs for Guatemala. But from this outpouring of
funds there came very little in the way of effective development. A variety of projects was initiated, but, aside from
the effort to improve the highway system, the programs
had trouble in getting off the ground. Once again, the U.S.
government failed to give a strong lead in directing the
program at the politically significant sectors of the population. Perhaps policy-making in Washington was more at
fault than the officials stationed in Guatemala; in a bureaucracy it is difficult to know where to place final responsibility. In any case, it was Guatemalan pressures and
Guatemalan decisions that, after 1954, gave a new impetus
to agrarian reform and launched a new and promising rural
development program, and it was the World Health Organization that pushed forward the program of public
sanitation. In 1957, just as technical assistance activities
seemed to be getting under way, the assassination of
Castillo Armas and the subsequent confusion threw the
picture out of focus once more. As the sixth decade of the
twentieth century drew to a close, the United States was in
serious danger of bungling its second chance to help the
process of social change in Guatemala move forward along
constructive paths.

Among the major changes that have been going on in
Guatemala over recent decades, there are some that U.S.
foreign policy-makers have either failed to perceive or, for
reasons unknown, have chosen to ignore. Not all these
changes affect all Guatemalans, but there are two factors
that go far toward explaining why some segments of the
Guatemalan people have been more receptive to Communist patterns than to those of the free world. One of
these new factors is the nature of the change that has been

taking place. In Guatemala, as in many other parts of the world, we are witnessing an ever accelerating rate of change, which constantly demands new decisions, one after another, without breathing spells. The other factor is the source and sequence of these changes within Guatemalan society. Most theories of social development assume that changes take place first in the area of technological innovations, followed by secondary effects in economic, social, and political life. In Guatemala today, change is appearing first in the field of political action, with consequences which then spread to the social, economic and technological fields. And it is in the area of political organization and action that the Communists are most experienced and most zealous. The experiences of Guatemala point to the urgent need for the United States to re-examine its attitude toward social change. If it hopes to provide an alternative to communism it must formulate policies with the dynamic qualities necessary to compete successfully against the appeals of that hostile philosophy.

Who Are the Guatemalans?

In Guatemala, as elsewhere, the population is made up of many segments and the differences between them are often of critical importance in predicting how they are going to act. We must therefore find out who "the Guatemalans" are. Only after examining the various segments, each with its own pattern of behavior, can we say anything intelligent about the changes that are taking place today within Guatemalan society.

A MAJOR DIVIDING LINE: INDIANS AND "LADINOS"

A fact of prime importance is that one-half of the three million Guatemalans are Mayan Indians. The other half, called *Ladinos,* are a Spanish-American population, predominantly of mixed racial descent and clearly stratified in a number of social classes. The Indians, differing in customs and language from the *Ladinos,* constitute a classless society organized in distinctive communities.[4] Within the total population, Indians are considered by *Ladinos* to constitute the lowest class, but Indians generally regard themselves as being different from, not inferior to, *Ladinos*.

The Indian population occupies the western and northwestern highland region, extending as far as the southwestern coast. Indian communities are also scattered throughout the eastern highlands and along the southeastern coast, and in the vast northern third of the country, the *Petén*. The more traditional Indians live in villages and scattered rural communities. Their settlements are marked by extreme localism, frequently by separate local dialects, by distinctive costumes for women (and in some areas for men), by a largely subsistence agricultural economy with some regional specialization in handicrafts and vegetable produce. Typically, Indians have a very low per capita income and depend closely on local natural resources for most of their daily living. However, the Indians also depend to some extent upon a wider market, national and even international, to earn some cash income and to procure certain items of importance: metal hoes, machetes, adzes, and other tools; certain medicines; dyestuffs, needles and thread; and, oddly enough, seeds for planting their vegetable and flower crops.[5]

Many elements of Indian life and thought have been taken over from the Spanish conquerors and their Spanish-American descendants and woven into an integrated system

---

4 See Sol Tax, "The Municipios of the Midwestern Highlands of Guatemala," *American Anthropologist*, July 1937, pp.. 423-444; Sol Tax, ed., *The Heritage of Conquest: The Ethnology of Middle America* (Glencoe, Ill.: Free Press, 1952); Richard N. Adams, "Guatemala," *Cultural Surveys of Panama, Nicaragua, Guatemala, El Salvador, Honduras*, Scientific Publication no. 33 (Washington: Pan American Sanitary Bureau, 1957), pp. 261-412; Guatemala, Dirección General de Estadística, *Sexto censo general de población* (Guatemala City: Author [1953]).

5 Sol Tax, *Penny Capitalism: A Guatemala Indian Economy*, Publication no. 16 of the Institute of Social Anthropology (Washington, 1953); Sanford A. Mosk, "Indigenous Economy in Latin America," *Inter-American Economic Affairs*, no. 3, 1954, pp. 3-25.

of social, religious and political beliefs. Except for some Protestant converts, the Indians are staunch Catholics, but their Catholic outlook stems from the colonial era rather than from the present-day Catholicism of Western Europe and the United States. Today, as the Indian culture is changing, fewer and fewer generalizations can be applied to "all Indians."

Whereas the Indian population is segmented regionally in individual and generally isolated communities, the *Ladino* population is segmented both by regions and by social classes. In the colonial period, the term *Ladino* was used to describe Indians who had given up their native idioms and adopted Spanish customs. Now it is applied in Guatemala to almost the entire non-Indian population. Some people, it is true, still use it to identify the lower class of the non-Indian population; here it will be used in its more widespread meaning of "non-Indians." While having varying degrees of Indian racial descent, the *Ladinos* are different in culture from the Indians. While one can often tell by his dress from what town or region an Indian comes, it is impossible by that test to determine even whether a *Ladino* is a Guatemalan or not. Dress and other characteristics serve basically to distinguish the major social and economic strata among *Ladinos*. The *campesino* or countryman often goes barefoot and wears ill-fitting or homemade clothes for farm work, as well as the inevitable straw hat. As people rise in the social scale, shoes become obligatory, together with white shirts and collars, suits and pegged trousers. In the upper brackets, tailored suits are the rule, and today sport shirts are worn by almost all classes.

Regional characteristics vary among the *Ladinos*, depending upon whether or not there are Indians living nearby. In the predominantly Indian regions of western Guatemala, there are few *Ladinos* who can be classified as *campesinos*. There, most *Ladinos* belong to a local upper class of landowners and tradesmen, economically dependent upon the lower-class Indian. In non-Indian regions, however, this agricultural lower class is made up of *Ladino* countrymen, and in some areas this is a fairly stable group, cultivating independently owned farm plots. Elsewhere it is a mobile population, having arrived only within a generation or two as a result of the demand for labor or because of overpopulation in its localities of origin. In predominantly *Ladino* regions it is not uncommon to hear middle- and upper-class *Ladinos* refer to their countrymen neighbors as "Indians," thereby indicating that, culturally speaking, the latter have only recently made the transition from the Indian group or that, socially, they are identified as a lower class, along with the true Indians.

The confusing variation in the use of the term "Indian" stems from the important fact that in Guatemala any Indian can become a *Ladino*. Originally, the word *Ladino*, as I have noted earlier, referred to an Indian who had taken on the Spaniards' way of life; today the term refers to a group into which an Indian can move. If two Indian parents move to the city, their children may grow up as *Ladinos*. This involves no racial change; the terms used today refer to habits, customs, and patterns of life rather than to biological heritage.

Other lines of cleavage within the Guatemalan population arise out of differing patterns of settlement. In addition to the capital city, an urban center of over 300,-000 people, there are also provincial centers (usually departmental capitals), local towns serving their rural areas, scattered rural settlements, corporate farms with settled labor, family-owned farms with settled labor, and temporary rural settlements for seasonal and migrant agricultural labor. Within these types of settlement we find different social relationships and different class and ethnic elements. In general, these differences have less meaning within the Indian population than among the *Ladinos*, but even the Indians' way of life and their status are influenced by the type of settlement to which they belong. Migrant Indian labor, for example, while less widespread than *Ladino*, is still migrant labor, and it is affected by the same general breakdown of social controls as among the *Ladinos*. Dwellers in the capital city, whether *Ladinos* or the far fewer Indians, are subject to demands and influences which do not reach out to people who live in scattered rural homesteads and who are more likely to return to old customs, whether they are Indians or *Ladinos*.

Among other factors, differences in ethnic composition and settlement patterns tend to set apart a number of segments of the population, each with its own consistent pattern of behavior. These segments may conveniently be called "components" of the Guatemalan population.[6] An essential thing to keep in mind is that these components not only behave differently today in response both to felt needs and to outside stimuli, but also are undergoing different kinds of change.

THE "LADINOS"

Most Guatemalans, as we have noted, fall into two broad groupings, Indians and *Ladinos*. However, when we look at the distinctive groupings within the *Ladino* half of the people, the picture turns out to be far more complex. Among *Ladinos,* at least seven main components can be identified: the cosmopolites; the local upper class; the emergent middle class; the independent farmers; the mobile rural laborers; the stable rural laborers; and the urban laborers.

Within the Indian half of the population, more specifically among the Maya Quiche Indians, I have identified three major components, defined mainly by the degree to which their way of life has changed to resemble that of the *Ladinos*. These three components are: the traditional Indians; the modified, independent Indians; and the modified Indian laborers.

---

6 Richard N. Adams, "Cultural Components of Central America," *American Anthropologist,* October 1956, pp. 881-907. In this reference and elsewhere I have used a more detailed and complex classification of the Guatemalan populations and especially of the Indians. For present purposes a simplified treatment is sufficient.

One further grouping, small in number, comprises a number of ethnic minorities, such as Chinese-Americans, Black Carib Indians, East Indians, and Euro-Americans. Only the last-named group has some importance in a study of the implications of social changes for foreign policy.

What are some of the changes that these different parts of the population have been undergoing in recent years? What are the implications of these changes for the future of Guatemala and for the formulation of U.S. policy?

The Cosmopolites. This small and exclusive group includes the "old families," and also families of recent wealth that maintain a strong orientation toward European values. Individual families show some cultural differences, depending upon the European country of origin or preference. This social component has traditionally looked to coffee-growing for its wealth, although some individuals have turned to other crops or to import and export trade. Formerly, many cosmopolites were resident on their plantations or in provincial capitals. In recent decades, as more of them have congregated in the national capital, absentee ownership and indirect management of rural *haciendas* have become common. Within the capital, some cosmopolites still cling to colonial-type residences near the center, while others have moved to the edge of town, now made easy of access by the automobile. Place of residence, income (both source and amount), education, and manners—the usual attributes of an upper class—set off the cosmopolites from their compatriots. This background has led many U.S. businessmen and officials to associate by preference with the cosmopolitan segment. Then, when newly influential elements of Guatemalan society pile an active political hostility toward the cosmopolites upon their traditional feeling of social estrangement from them, this antagonism is readily transferred to the representatives of U.S. business and government.

As the name indicates, the cosmopolites have more in common with similar groups in other Latin American countries than with the Guatemalan lower class. Their numbers are few and their wealth probably does not compare with the fortunes found in some other countries of the region. Since the mid-nineteenth century, the political power of this group, with its understandably conservative outlook, has been weakened by the growing strength of the middle class and, more recently, of the workers. It lost its direct control over the government long ago; today its influence rises or falls, depending upon the politics of the regime in power. Since 1954 this group has supplied some cabinet members and has exercised some further degree of influence through important lawyers and counselors on policy. The cosmopolites also influence national policy through their important role in economic life.[7]

On the economic side, the foreign investment in banana and coffee production, mining, transportation, and power has led to the building up of alternative sources of wealth and to the creation of new power centers which influence governmental policies. For a long time the native families of wealth stuck to coffee-planting, leaving the banana industry, railroads, and shipping to outside interests.[8] The new and old centers of economic power were not in direct competition; in fact they tended to complement each other. Nevertheless, the cosmopolites' political power declined as new economic interests made their weight felt.

While coffee still remains the principal source of cosmopolite strength, various members of this group have ventured into speculative farming, which, unlike coffee, depends neither on a permanent labor supply nor on a single long-term crop.[9] Decisions to grow the next crops, such as corn, cotton, lemon grass, or sesame, can be adjusted flexibly to meet shifts in supply and demand. Shifting from one of these crops to another can be accomplished more rapidly since, unlike coffee, they do not require

---

7 Bert F. Hoselitz, "Economic Development in Central America," *Weltwirtschaftliches Archiv* (Hamburg), no. 2, 1956, pp. 281-282.

8 Same.

9 Francis LeBeau, "Agricultura de Guatemala," in *Integración social en Guatemala,* cited, pp. 296-301.

many years to mature. The speculative farmer, while equally dependent on distant markets for his profit, can gauge the market more readily than can the coffee grower. One consequence of diversification in agriculture has been the growth of new relationships with labor and new attitudes toward property. The ownership of vast areas of land may no longer be desirable; it may be more profitable to rent land for a single year to raise a quick crop, and then forget about it. In this new situation, labor has no permanent attachment to the *hacienda* and its owner, and, very likely, cannot count on a predictable amount of seasonal work. The new flexibility and mobility of labor, which destroy the workers' local attachments, also change their social and political role.

The Local Upper Class. This stratum is prominent today in most small towns and all provincial capitals. Its members are the well-to-do, literate portions of the local community; they are engaged in farming with the use of hired labor, sometimes also in nonfarming occupations, such as running local stores, inns, or transport services. Formerly rooted firmly in landholding, this social component is now made up both of descendants of an older provincial upper class and of recently established upper-class families in new communities. When its members leave their local communities, they may move into the newly forming middle class. If successful in economic or political activity, or a mixture of both, they may enter the fringes of cosmopolite society. In some cases, they may be reduced to poverty and be absorbed into one of the lower classes. For this reason, the local upper component is a peculiarly local class; unlike the cosmopolites, it survives only in its own community setting. This group has generally had little direct contact with U.S. businessmen and officials.

The local upper class formerly played an important role in the Guatemalan system of social controls and sanctions. Until the development of political parties in the late 1940's, it was through this channel that political control was exercised over most of the small-town and rural population. In the absence of any elaborate network of informal political control, the concurrence of this component with the cosmopolites in their basic philosophy was the principal means by which the local laboring and peasant population was "kept in place." Since both rural laborers and smaller independent farmers had various reasons to be strongly dissatisfied with their conditions of life, the local upper class provided until recently an essential cement in the social and political structure.

One of the most important changes since 1944 has been the breaking down of the social control formerly exercised by the local upper class. During the time of Arévalo and Arbenz, the establishment of new and powerful groups—political parties, a national peasants' association, agrarian committees for the allotment of land under the agrarian reform program, and labor unions—created for the first time informal networks of influence and control linking the national capital directly with the individual rural dweller. Some members of the local upper class, it is true, joined these new networks, but in so doing they ceased to function as a local upper class, and became merely a link or strand in the new and more centralized structure. The individual countryman now came under the control of the local party boss or the regional or local labor union head, or of the municipal government, and, in the later years of the Arbenz government, under that of the increasingly powerful land-reform committees.

The Guatemalan local communities have been launched, for better or for worse, on the first steps toward their assimilation into a national structure. They are now aware of the vulnerability of the local upper class, and of the potential strength of new nation-wide forces. For most Guatemalans, their class, ethnic or cultural groups, and their local communities no longer set the limits of social awareness. New types of national organizations have been tried, reflecting a growing centralization of political and economic power. The introduction of banana-growing and railroads was the first step in the loss of power by the cosmopolite component; more recently, the introduction of new networks of centralized control has marked the first step toward loss of its power by the local upper class.

The Emergent Middle Class. This is, in one sense, the most important component of all.[10] The use of the term "emergent" does not mean that a middle class did not exist until recently in Guatemala. In the nineteenth century there were, in Guatemala City, in the larger provincial towns, and on the larger *haciendas* persons who belonged neither to an upper class nor to the laboring group. Including the more specialized artisans, foremen, and minor governmental employees, this embryonic middle stratum was of slight political importance, dependent as it was on the good will of the more educated, more traveled, and independently wealthy upper class.

Over the past half-century there has been developing a new middle class which draws its membership not only from the earlier middle class, but also from the local upper class, some of the laboring groups, the independent farmers, and even the cosmopolites. This new stratum has appeared in many parts of the country but is strongest in the national capital and other administrative centers. It includes local businessmen, clerical and other semiprofessional personnel, government employees, foremen and supervisory personnel, skilled workers with a steady income, and, of particular importance, many army officers and the schoolteachers. Although the strength of the middle group is not based on landed wealth, its members often purchase large farms as a form of security. The desire to acquire wealth is strong among members of this component, and government service, the military profession, teaching (a form of government service), and business are the chief channels for entering this new stratum.

In some respects the emergent middle component may

---

[10] See particularly the study by John P. Gillin, Essay One of this volume; also Gillin's "Cultura emergente," in *Integración social en Guatemala,* cited, pp. 435-459.

be regarded as a successor to the local upper class. It has taken over from it the principal functions of social control. It supplied most of the personnel for the extragovernmental channels of political control which were established under the Arévalo-Arbenz regimes. In this new function its members have acted, not as part of a local social structure, but as cogs in a national political system. Individual members of the "emergent middle" stratum often come from small provincial centers but they do not necessarily maintain close ties with their home communities as they move up the political and social ladder.

Although it is still undergoing significant changes in structure and outlook, the emergent middle class is a well-established entity today, and it is active in promoting changes in other segments of Guatemalan society. Along with some cosmopolites, members of the emergent middle are increasingly participating in speculative agriculture, often using government credits and favors to help finance their enterprises. Of greater importance, however, is the influence which this component has had on the reshaping of the Guatemalan body politic. It is most vocal in its nationalism and in pressing its views on forms of government, on issues of social justice, and on communism and democracy. The emergent middle supplies the intellectual leadership for the labor movement, and for the government's programs of economic development. It staffs the political parties, the extension services, the schools, and, indeed, all the agencies which are actively engaged in remaking the country.

The Independent Farmers. This group comprises those who work for themselves on their own land, both subsistence and small cash-crop farmers, as well as those who, lacking sufficient acreage, either rent land or hire out as laborers from time to time. This group attaches strong values to economic independence. It clings to this independence, or perhaps to the illusion thereof, despite the realities of a marginal agriculture and a technology which is not much more advanced than its native and medieval

European models. While these farmers receive some assistance from the government's extension service, their independence still rests upon subsistence agriculture, not on cash crops in which they can scarcely compete with the large plantations and speculative entrepreneurs.

Politically, the independent farmers have never been a very significant group. Their partial dependence upon part-time or seasonal employment and a low level of capital investment and returns leave little time for them to take an interest in political activities at the national level. Some independent farmers may hold municipal posts, but, if some individuals among them become particularly active, it is usually because increased wealth has enabled them to enter the local upper class or become a part of the emergent middle component. During the Arévalo-Arbenz period, the early attempts to control the independent farmers through political party channels had but slight success since they were not easily swayed by mere political propaganda. Later efforts through other mass organizations, such as the land-reform committees, were more successful.

Today the independent farmer finds himself in an increasingly difficult position. The development of the national economy makes the future of subsistence farming a precarious one, even though the government and various technical services are trying to increase the output of such crops as corn and beans for local consumption, as well as to diversify agricultural production so that small farms can earn a larger cash income. Another factor of change is the undermining of social solidarity among the small farmers. Traditionally the subsistence farmer has coped with peak work loads through the reciprocal exchange of labor or the hiring of his socially equal neighbors.[11] Now, with more intensive methods of production and greater emphasis on production for the market, this traditional way of organizing work is losing ground, with a consequent decline in solidarity within the communities of small farmers.

---

11 See Adams, "Guatemala," cited, pp. 299-302.

One of the aims of the Castillo Armas government and its successor has been to strengthen the independent farmers. Programs for colonizing the Pacific piedmont, as a means of supplementing agrarian reform, are designed to provide the new settlers with adequate allotments of agricultural land, together with credit and technical aid, so that they will form a stable part of the rural population. What this may mean for the future development of local social controls is not entirely clear. In any case, these newly settled independent farmers, like those less fortunate in landed wealth and government aid, must learn to apply many new techniques and to take many new decisions. Inevitably, increased pressure for production will force the less efficient independent farmers off the land and into the rural or urban labor market.

The Mobile Rural Laborers. Within the rural labor force two components have been distinguished, the mobile and the stable. The distinction between the two, important in the past, is likely to become more marked as speculative farming expands. The difference between the two lies in the nature of the social and residential relationships that prevail between laborers and employers.

Stable rural labor is permanently resident on a plantation. In the past this has brought with it a mutually recognized interest of laborers and owners in the prosperity of the farm and in the well-being of the workers. A stable labor force has been especially typical of the coffee plantations.

The situation of the mobile laborer is a very different one, in that he seldom remains long on any one farm. The causes of this increased mobility vary. The introduction of banana plantations led to some increase in the stable labor force, but it also touched off a great expansion in the numbers of mobile laborers through the wide fluctuations in the total demand for workers. Their ranks have been enlarged by the rapid growth of population, typical of all of Latin America.[12] In addition, many newly acculturated Indians have left their traditional communities and have joined the uprooted labor force.

The mobile rural labor component has been particularly susceptible to labor and radical agitation.[13] Under the Arbenz-sponsored agrarian reform, the demand for land was pressed with special vigor by mobile laborers, even though many of them later abandoned their new allotments to move elsewhere. It was this social group that provided the agrarian committees with forceful support in the revolution of 1954; in the region of the southern coast, it was the element most receptive to Communist agitation.

The Stable Rural Laborers. This component has evolved in a somewhat different manner. It supplied the recruits for the numerous rural labor unions which were set up under the Arévalo-Arbenz administrations. In many areas, however, the rural laborers clung to the older pattern of employer-employee relations (the *patrón-mozo* relationship) with its somewhat paternalistic tradition and resisted the interference of union organizers. Backed by the power of the government, however, the rural labor unions finally became established on most family-owned and corporate farms. Through them the government set about "re-educating" the stable labor groups to demand wage increases and improve labor conditions, and to press the employers to submit to union demands, while stepping up its own political propaganda with a strong emphasis on Communist and antiforeign themes. The success of this effort to mold the rural populations into an effective political force varied considerably, but, in general, stable laborers—except those on government-owned farms—seemed less receptive than mobile workers.

In the long run, however, the effects of the labor unions

---

[12] UN Department of Social Affairs, *The Population of Central America (including Mexico), 1950-1980,* Population Studies no. 16, 1954.XIII.3 (New York: Author, 1954).

[13] Newbold, cited.

on the stable labor group will probably be of far-reaching significance. Between employer and mobile labor, social ties and paternalism have never been so strong as between employer and stable labor. The creation of labor unions among mobile labor was not as drastic a step as it was among the stable laborers. By the time the Arbenz government was forced out and the labor unions were thrown out with it, the former paternalistic ties of mutual interest and custom between employer and stable labor had been so effectively broken that it is doubtful that they will be restored. Stable rural labor, while perhaps less susceptible to radical doctrines, has nevertheless become aware of its potential power, and this experience is one it is not likely to forget. At the same time, the employers, who formerly relied on paternalistic methods to solve most labor problems, have come to realize that the older methods will no longer work now that their labor force is controlled from outside the individual plantation.

The changes within both the stable and the mobile labor segments are but a part of the general transition of Guatemalan society. The rise in speculative cash-crop farming among the cosmopolitan and middle groups represents in part an answer to the new labor problems, as well as an adjustment to the demands of the world market. In turn, this development demands large numbers of mobile workers and makes less probable the growth in absolute numbers of stable labor. Most plantations are refusing to hire any more stable labor, thus forcing surplus workers into the mobile rural and urban labor forces. The resulting unrest among the uprooted labor groups has not been assuaged by several nation-wide wage increases enacted over the past fifteen years, for the higher wages have largely been swallowed up by rising prices.

The Urban Laborers. The urban labor group has scarcely been studied by sociologists. However, its way of life and its general outlook are strongly influenced by its largely rural background. This group forms a large part of the population of Guatemala City, whose population

increased between 1893 and 1950 twice as fast as that of
the country as a whole.[14] A large proportion of the new
city people were originally natives of small towns and rural
areas.

Politically, the urban labor force has been of greater importance than its numbers would suggest. Its accessibility
to propaganda and the special importance of labor organizations among urban workers have made it easier to
establish urban than rural unions. As voting blocs and
participants in mass meetings, urban labor is easier to
control. Although organized labor went into a temporary
eclipse during the Castillo government, it seems inevitable
that, as urban labor expands in numbers and influences,
more individuals drawn from its ranks will play a role in
the development of a national labor movement and in the
state bureaucracy.

THE INDIANS

Among the Mayan Indians—53.5 per cent of Guatemala's
population in 1950—we can distinguish two major stages
of conversion to the Spanish-American way of life. One
large stratum—the "traditional Indians"—has held most
strongly to a culture and a society apart from the *Ladinos*.
Usually these groups speak only an Indian language. Another large number of Indian communities have accepted
Ladino customs, the most obvious being the supplementary
or exclusive use of the Spanish language, and these groups
we can call "modified Indians."

The degree to which Indians retain their own languages
is a crude index to the maintenance of an entire way of
life which distinguishes the Indian from his *Ladino* countryman. Within the category of "modified Indians," a
further distinction must be drawn between independent
farmers and farm laborers. No such distinction applies
among the traditional Indians, for they move rapidly into

---

[14] The census of 1893 and the census of 1950 report city figures as
71,527 and 284,922, and total republic figures as 1,364,678 and 2,788,122.

the "modified" category as they come to depend on finding employment at wage labor.

In Guatemala an Indian community is easily identified. Everyone knows who are its members and who are outsiders. Each community is organized along family and neighborhood *(barrio)* lines, supplemented by the bonds of religious fraternities or sodalities. Indian communities fall into several physical types: compact villages of close settlement; small village centers with a rural hinterland; and scattered rural homesteads centered around what Sol Tax has called an "empty town"—a town in which no Indians live but which serves as a ceremonial and trading center.

The social integrity of traditional Indian communities rests upon the continuous functioning of a political and religious hierarchy and is reinforced by a general reliance upon the decisions of elders in matters of community importance. So long as this social structure remains intact, the adoption of *Ladino* ways proceeds slowly. From time to time, however, there may occur a series of events, usually arising outside the community, which weakens or even destroys the communal bonds. When this happens, there is a general shift toward a *Ladino* way of life. The Indian language may be given up, and there may be marked changes toward adopting *Ladino* ways of dress and adjusting to the *Ladino* political system. A community classified as "traditional" in one generation may become a "modified" one in the next. When the Indian structure is on its last legs, little more is left than a few minor religious sodalities to distinguish Indians from *Ladinos*.[15]

The Indian communities play rather different political roles, according to whether they are traditional or modified and whether they are primarily made up of laborers or independent farmers. Politically the traditional commu-

---

15 See Richard N. Adams, comp., *Political Changes in Guatemalan Indian Communities: A Symposium*, Publication 24 of the Middle American Research Institute (Tulane University, New Orleans, 1957), pp. 1-54; and "La ladinoización en Guatemala," in *Integración social en Guatemala*, cited, pp. 213-244.

nities are of little significance precisely because they have insulated themselves so successfully against incursions of *Ladino* culture. When it comes to voting for a particular candidate, they can usually be controlled, but they look on politics with a certain amount of indifference.

Traditional communities begin to become politically important as they cease to be traditional. Modified Indian communities composed mainly of independent farmers develop many of the political characteristics of similar *Ladino* villages. Among Indians a stable rural labor force is found principally on family-owned plantations. Mobile Indian labor, on the other hand, can hardly be regarded as a significant factor. An Indian who cuts his ties to his community is rapidly *Ladino*-ized and absorbed into the stratum of *Ladino* mobile rural labor.

The Indian rural laborers are more important in politics than the independent Indian farmers for the same reasons that *Ladino* labor makes its weight felt more than do the independent *Ladino* farmers. Both laboring groups can be reached more easily by political propaganda and can be mustered more readily to the polls. Under the Arévalo-Arbenz administrations, labor, acting through unions and agrarian committees, was considerably more vocal than were the independent farmers.

In terms of where the Indians stand today, the two significant facts are: the distinctive pattern of their culture and their gradual assimilation into the *Ladino* way of life. In entering the general population, Indians do not form a separate ethnic segment but are absorbed into a broader social stratum. This process, however, is a slow one; the total Indian population is still growing faster in absolute numbers than it is losing individuals and communities to the Spanish-American way of life. However, the *Ladino* segment is growing even more rapidly, and at some time in the not distant future the Indians will begin to shrink in absolute numbers. At that stage the resistance of their traditional way of life to *Ladino*-ization may decline rapidly, and Guatemala may cease to be a nation of two cultures.

One rather common notion holds that an Indian who "loses his Indian heritage" becomes "deculturated," a lost soul, receptive to any kind of propaganda. True, some individuals who move from the status of Indian to that of *Ladino* within a single lifetime may go through periods of extreme stress, and may fall into socially aberrant forms of behavior. However, this does not apply to the large numbers of Indians who shift to a *Ladino* status while remaining members of their own community. For one thing, this type of cultural change proceeds slowly. In addition, when the change affects an entire community, the individual who changes with his own group does not feel detached from his village or deprived of a "magnificent" Indian heritage. In these cases the Indian heritage is, in fact, so thoroughly lost that the entire village is unaware of what it was once like.

The Indian population of Guatemala is not a monolithic social bloc, resisting change and holding back the development of the country. Rather, the Indians are increasingly responsive to the same political issues as the *Ladinos*. At the same time they tend to lose their separate Indian identity as they enter more and more into the *Ladino* way of life.

THE EURO-AMERICANS

The development of banana-growing and railroads and, in recent years, of many small industries and large commercial activities has been sponsored by foreigners and others of recent foreign, usually European, descent. While weak in political terms, this component exerts a considerable measure of indirect influence, greater than many of the national components. The role of foreigners has changed perceptibly over the past three decades. Early in the century some foreign firms (for example, the Swedish match monopoly) were given special privileges, or special tax exemptions. The 1944 revolution was followed by an upsurge of antiforeign and particularly anti-U.S. attitudes and policies. As far as official policy is concerned, this trend was sharply reversed with the revolution of 1954, although there has been no return to the fairly wide-open system of privilege that prevailed up to 1944.

The Euro-American component is playing a variety of roles in the process of social change within Guatemala. Aside from an obvious interest in promoting the increased importation of foreign products, from films to tractors, it also exercises an important influence through the technical assistance programs as well as through its official and un-official influence on the administration. On the other hand, the tendency of Euro-American groups to maintain their identity as foreign colonies largely prevents their being assimiliated into the national population, even though some individual foreigners are absorbed in each genera-tion. In this respect, the Euro-Americans resemble the cos-mopolites, who likewise maintain closer ties with the nationals of other countries than with other strata of Guatemalan society.

A New Factor: The Continuous Character of Change

In Guatemala almost every major group of the popula-tion has, as we have seen, been undergoing far-reaching changes. Now we must look at these separate changes in a broader framework; we must see how they are related to each other. When we examine the process of change in Guatemalan society as a whole, two striking features leap to the eye. In the first place, the nation is in the throes of changing over from a discontinuous set of regional cul-tures to a continuously evolving and nationally centered culture. In the second place, this change-over is being initiated by political and social innovations, rather than arising spontaneously out of changes in production and technology.

The concept of continuous or open-end change is a new one to Guatemalans, and they are far from coming to terms with it. Most of them think of their past experience as "normal" and of change as something exceptional and limited in scope. When the Spaniards began to colonize Guatemala, they did so under a general set of policies formulated by the Spanish Crown. The form villages were to take, the relationship to be established between the Spanish *conquistador* and the native population, the economic exploitation of the new land, the specific form of local government—these and many other general and specific matters were prescribed in Spain. That the rules were often ignored did not alter the fact that, from Spain's point of view, the prime purpose of the conquest was to establish colonies that would be economically useful to the mother country. Under colonial rule the surviving Indians gradually adopted Spanish ways in varying degrees and formed more or less stable communities.

During this long period each series of changes was in most respects discontinuous. Each new change was followed by a new adjustment in economic and social organization; once this had happened, a new stability set in. Over most of history, this is the kind of change to which people have been accustomed. If a priest succeeded in converting a community of Indians to Catholicism, the change was considered to have been accomplished, and further effort was limited to maintaining worship as prescribed by doctrine. If Spain needed wheat, then the job was to introduce wheat and produce the amount that was needed by the mother country, without attempting to spread its use among the population of the colony. When coffee was introduced, the trend was to set up the plantations as permanent organizations, inflexible in practices and social structure. Each of these changes was discontinuous. In each instance, the effort was directed, not toward achieving an infinite series of changes, but toward introducing a specific set of practices in order to attain a predefined and limited goal. Thus coffee plantations oriented to the world market existed side by side with self-sufficient Indian and *Ladino* villages.

The discontinuous nature of change was due, in part, to

a number of circumstances that no longer prevail today. There was plenty of land and rainfall, and population was sparse. The commercial sector of the economy could rely on a fairly steady demand from abroad. Of course, when demand shifted, the readjustment was sometimes fairly violent. Cacao, a major piedmont product in the early nineteenth century, was displaced late in the century by coffee. However, the general social structure, resting on a large Indian population of independent farmers, provided all the cheap labor required, without imposing any responsibility for its maintenance if it was no longer needed; this made it easier for the plantation owners to shift from one crop to another. Some areas of life reflected a tradition of strongly paternalistic rule; in others, the Indians were free to pursue their own economic activities. Both Guatemala's culture and its economy were strongly regional in character. Each major region developed, survived, or declined economically, depending on its direct relationship with the outside market. For example, Cobán, in the northern highlands, grew into an important coffee center; its coffee growers dealt directly with the merchants of nearby ports, having little or nothing to do with Guatemala City.

In the twentieth century these conditions have gradually disappeared. Immigration and, more important, the rapid natural increase in the population led to overcrowding on the land in some regions. The southwest piedmont, an important coffee region, filled up and the *Ladino* population in particular grew at a phenomenal rate. The remaining areas of unoccupied land were scarce and isolated from major transportation routes. After World War I, foreign markets became less dependable, and coffee farmers were especially hard hit by the depression of the 1930's. As coffee prices rose before and after World War II, Tanganyika, Brazil, Mexico, and other areas encroached on Guatemala's traditional markets. More important, the lack of suitable new areas for coffee, combined with increasing labor problems, led some operators to venture

their capital only in speculative agriculture, thus undermining the traditional economic and social balance still
further.

The introduction, following the 1944 revolution, of a
labor code and labor unions, as well as welfare measures
for the general population—all this combined with political
radicalism—began to erode the social structure, based on
paternalism and cheap labor, in which coffee-farming had
developed. The substitute—speculation in quick crops such
as corn, cotton, sesame, and lemon grass—freed the entrepreneur of the burden of supporting a resident labor
force in good times and bad; and it offered a way around
the long-term commitments involved in coffee-growing.

By the end of World War II, Guatemala, like many
other Latin American countries, was experiencing a new
surge of nationalist ambition. Guatemala City, the political
capital, had displaced Cobán and Quezaltenango as the
country's coffee capital. The expanding road system reflected national rather than regional needs. One sign of the
growing ease of communication within the country can be
traced in the pattern of the revolution of 1954, which was
hatched not in some outlying province but in a neighboring country behind the protective shield of a national
boundary. Improved transportation has strengthened the
role of the capital city and weakened the forces of political
regionalism.

By the mid-twentieth century change of a new, continuous type was in the air, stimulated by the conjuncture of
internal events with external forces. Population was increasing rapidly, in great part because of the beginnings of
a public health system. Instability in the world market,
with the now chronic precariousness of coffee-growing,
placed new strains upon the country's economy. Above all,
new concepts of social order, from Arévalo's fuzzy "spiritual socialism" to communism, were propagated vigorously
after World War II by intellectuals who, returning from
long years of exile under Ubico's rule, brought with them
new ideas and new slogans, both idealistic and self-seeking.

Within this general context of open-ended change, what are the paths along which contemporary Guatemala is evolving? How are the changes affecting its people? What is their meaning for U.S. policy?

The Impact of "Ladino"-ization

Ladino-ization, that process by which an Indian becomes a Spanish-American, has been going on ever since the arrival of the *Conquistadores*. In the past, however, as Spanish or other European elements of culture were introduced, they were incorporated gradually into the life of the people and thus fused with the Indian culture. Among these transplantations were the *cofradías*, religious associations which were introduced in the colonial period as a means of bringing the Indians within the orbit of the church. *Cofradías* place on members of the community certain responsibilites for sponsoring the *fiesta* of a saint. Under a stable social organization, the *cofradías* worked well, for each generation trained the next to accept and carry on these duties. Similarly, new crops and domestic animals were taken over and incorporated into the Indian way of life. Chickens, fruit trees, flowers of European origin, vegetables, wheat, broad beans, the machete, the hoe, and numerous other postconquest innovations have become embedded in the Indian way of life. The spirit world has likewise been peopled impartially from European and Indian sources. When a man takes sick of a sudden fright because his soul has been seized by the spirit of the local mountain, prayers are offered both to the Christian God and saints, and to the Mayan mountain spirits, to regain his soul and ward off death.

The incorporation into the Indian culture of Spanish and other foreign elements was possible so long as the changes were gradual and did not threaten the Indians' basic family and community organization. The past half-century has seen a new type of change, one which requires the Indian community not to incorporate new elements,

but to give up being Indian, to accept an ever increasing
dominance by the national political structure. The changes
demanded are no longer fixed, each with its definable and
visible goal; they are open-ended and infinitely complex.
The shift from the *cofradía* to a political party as a means
of organizing community life is not a simple substitution.
It involves putting an end to a fixed local and unchanging
structure in which control rests in the hands of the Indian
village elders. It creates a new structure in which fresh
demands for further change are constantly being made
from without and control is located far beyond the bounds
of the village.

The new medical practices, for example, no longer involve the simple application of a well-known remedy to a
familiar ailment. They introduce all sorts of progressively
more complex changes. Milk must be drunk, blood—with
its magic connotations—must be given to medical people,
new measures obeyed, all for no clearly understood reasons.
Even the doctors, who are supposed to know so much, cannot handle such everyday maladies as "fright" without
employing excessively long treatments, even removing the
individual from his village—a thing that of itself causes
"fright." Medicines highly recommended one year are rejected as dangerous the next. Thus, in the world of disease
and cure, certainty gives way to the expectation of uncertainty, of continuing and unpredictable change. A similar
uncertainty enters the spirit world, as Protestant mis-
sionaries have brought new concepts and purposes, while
Catholic reformers enter the fray to combat both Protestant innovations and inherited Catholic practices which
are no longer congenial to the church of today. Thus, in
one sphere after another, fixed, meaningful habits crumble
and open the way to seemingly infinite, open-ended process
of change.

The Indian culture cannot forever go on incorporating
changes of this variety and magnitude. Sooner rather than
later it is sure to break down. Political and religious demands on the social organization, technical and economic

demands in agriculture and handicrafts, public health and resettlement demands on the individual, each of these, and all of them together, are undermining the older structure to such an extent that the Indian way of life cannot continue indefinitely as a separate sector in the Guatemalan society. Inevitably, the Indian half of the people will eventually be assimiliated into a uniform *Ladino* society and nation.

The Impact of Technological Change

The pattern of continuous changes through which the Indians are being *Ladino*-ized has its parallel in the experience of the *Ladino* countrymen. The latter have also been draw into the millrace of sequential change; the effect on them is less startling because, unlike the Indians, they have not previously maintained themselves as a society apart. Nevertheless, the introduction of new crops and fertilizers, a new religious ferment, new definitions of illness and cure, and new political organizations are also setting in motion an endless series of adjustments for the traditional *Ladinos*, whether villagers or townspeople.

In agricultural technology the new demands are especially visible, but here their impact has been slowed by the lack of material wealth required for rapid innovation. Extension agents have come to both cosmopolites and independent farmers in order to help them improve their farming techniques. For the cosmopolite planter, the shift to new ways requires a degree of personal attention that he is often unwilling to give, and an increasing investment in his agricultural properties that he often does not want to make. For the independent farmer, change means acquiring plows; plows require oxen; to feed oxen requires higher production; higher productivity needs better seed; new seed often brings new forms of plant pests and sicknesses; and these require still better seed and fertilizers, and new insecticides. All this in turn requires more money and therefore more produce to sell. And so it goes, each change taking the countryman farther and farther from his traditional subsistence farming.

Continuous change permits of no resting spells. Once started, change begets change and demands a further series of adjustments. Arthur Mosher has aptly described the essence of this change in agriculture:

> The opposite of traditional is "choice-making." The process of decision-making is at a minimum in any traditional culture or method of production. Thus, encouraging farmers to move from traditional agriculture to progressive agriculture requires the development of a wholly new habit of thinking, a new way of living. . . . Farmers must . . . be induced . . . to shift from an attitude of tradition to one of continuous choice-making in economic and political fields as well as in the narrow realm of farming practices. . . .[16]

Among the tradition-minded components of the population, whether Indian or *Ladino*, laborer or independent farmer, few find it easy to adjust to a progressive, continuous process of change. In this adjustment, there must be some dynamic element that is converted, as it were, into the promoter of change. Of all the components, it is the emergent middle group that has assumed this role. It has taken the lead in the introduction of new technologies, new political structures, and new religious ideas. It also provides the personnel to staff agricultural extension and public health programs and, above all, for teaching and government service.

The emergent middle component has responded actively to the growing pressures for change which have been exerted from within and without the society. The cosmopolites had too many vested interests to assume this role of leadership. The local upper group was limited by its regional horizon. The subsistence farming and laboring groups were limited in their outlook, and their widespread illiteracy left them helpless in the realm of ideas. Within each of these groups some individuals have found the

---

[16] Cited, pp. 248, 249.

processes of change congenial, and have moved into occupations that were formerly open only to the older middle class. These "new men," differing widely among themselves, cannot be defined as a social class; following John Gillin's terminology, I shall speak of them as the new "middle mass."

In the introduction of change, another factor of critical importance has been the continuing flow of foreigners who bring with them many new ideas. Those who come as individuals are usually engaged in import and export trade. Beginning many years ago with the efforts of the Rockefeller Foundation, and especially under U.S. and United Nations programs, Guatemala has received increasing numbers of foreigners, especially North Americans, engaged in providing technical aid.

In their role as promoters of change, technical specialists from abroad have come face to face with the great problems which Guatemala and its neighbors encounter in attempting to promote a continuous and interacting series of changes in a hitherto unchanging or slowly changing society. Resistance to innovations, they have frequently discovered, is not confined to the traditional Indians; it is also strong among the cosmopolite and local upper components, as well as in the bureaucratic structure in which the emergent middle groups play a prominent part. While change meets with resistance everywhere, the factor that distinguishes the new efforts at directed technical aid from earlier innovations is the attempt, at times unrecognized by the specialists themselves, to institute an infinite and open-ended sequence of changes rather than merely to achieve a limited change that can then be digested by the society and incorporated into its basic structure. This new type of change, which by its structural effects brings with it many further changes, is causing the vast "shaking up" of all segments in Guatemalan society. What is taking place is not merely a realignment of power, a change in the roles of social classes, or the emergence of a new class. Instead, the entire social structure is being reshaped in response to the new dynamic of continuous change.

The Primacy of Political and Social Change

Were the changes being experienced in Guatemala only those that usually result from introducing a progressive technology, they would be readily comprehensible to North Americans. However, the reshaping of the Guatemalan way of life has another and less readily understood aspect. Many Guatemalans are more concerned with establishing a new social order than with bringing about basic economic and technological changes. It is not that they are not interested in economic change. But in comparison with the history of Western Europe or North America during their industrial revolutions, Guatemala and much of Latin America are pressing for a different order of priorities.

Within North American society the process of change has usually been generated first by technological and economic innovations. The coming of the factory altered earlier patterns of settlement, and the automobile changed them again out of all recognition. The family is not the same as it was a century ago. The fundamental structure of our present-day social order, its occupational groups, its political organization, and its religious activities have, in one degree or another, been remolded by the accelerated technological changes typical of the past two centuries. In this process new social forms have developed and matured —business and managerial structures, labor unions, and numerous professional groups.

Living in the midst of the process of technological change, North Americans of the present generation tend to regard "machine magic" as something both inevitable and beneficial, for others as well as themselves. This philosophy makes it seem natural for them to provide less-developed societies with technical missions to assist their progress in public health and agriculture, in housing and education. Although the activities of such missions will surely have some long-term effects on Guatemalan society, of much greater immediate importance is the fact that, even as the first missions were getting down to work during World War II, many Guatemalans were making up their minds that their country could not wait for these long-run effects to make themselves felt on what was in their eyes an anachronistic social and economic order.

Following the overturn of 1944, many individuals who had spent their formative years in exile returned to Guatemala; together with university students, they nourished dreams of social and political reform. Some of their aims were simply negative, directed against the existing state of things; others looked to positive goals, variously defined. A relatively few advocated patterns of social action copied from other nations, and of these Soviet Russia offered the most prominent prototype. Unlike the United States, where technology had historically led the way to social change, Russia has attempted the reverse; it first instituted violent social change and then followed up with technological progress and economic growth. In 1944, it must be remembered, opinions about Russia's path were not publicly a source of inter-American dissension, for both the United States and Guatemala were allied with Russia.

The leaders who emerged from these early days of ferment were not so much the returned exiles as younger men who had been university students at the time of Ubico's fall. The turn to communism, specifically to Russian-style communism, on the part of some of the students was not unnatural. In their student years they had been a special target of Communist propaganda, and they were now searching for an answer to a fundamental and baffling question: how can a people install a new social order without first building a new technological base? Uncritical approval of the Russian model, an export model that comes packaged with written "do-it-yourself" instructions, led many young intellectuals to accept communism as a philosophy of change, some others to look upon it as a suggestive program from which some useful points could be borrowed, and yet others to adhere to it as an infallible blueprint for action.

Between 1944 and 1948 Guatemala City was seething with new ideas, new experiments, new programs of action. Increasingly, nationalism became the channel through which ideas derived from a Russian model of social change were being introduced. As Soviet relations with the West deteriorated, U.S. activities in Guatemala also were on the downgrade. The emergent middle groups were pressing for drastic changes, while the cosmopolites, the local upper class, and the United States became increasingly the targets of social agitation. Only after Arbenz took over the presidency in 1951, however, did a clear-cut Guatemalan Communist party emerge. This marked the launching in earnest of overtly Communist activities.

The Communist Bid for Power and Its Aftermath

For the Guatemalan Communists, the only way to introduce their well-advertised model into Guatemala was to do it radically and swiftly. Few in number, they could not rely on the small Guatemalan army or on a large and well-organized reservoir of supporters. While fervidly preaching Marxist ideology in the hope of expanding and stiffening its basic cadres, the party relied more on the growing spirit of nationalism to "sell" its program of change to larger segments of the people. Quite naturally, the nationalist guise was most appropriate in Guatemala. For nearly a century foreigners had played a dominant role in developing the Guatemalan economy; Germans had an important place in coffee production, and the United States in the banana plantations. In view of Germany's postwar eclipse, the United States was the natural scapegoat. Ignoring the more enlightened behavior of American business concerns in recent years, the Communists and their allies found in their earlier policies the necessary fuel for inflammatory agitation.

One phase of the Communists' pattern of "planned"

social change called for infiltrating their supporters into key positions within the government. Special targets were the Guatemalan Congress, especially the presidency of the Congress, and the Department of Agrarian Reform, with its extensive opportunities to influence and even dominate the rural population. A second phase involved the setting up of new organizations in order to gain political control over important segments of the population, especially the laboring and emergent middle groups. Among these organizations the most effective were the labor unions of government workers, schoolteachers and urban workers, and, of particular importance, farm workers on family-owned and corporate farms. In addition, the party established mass organizations on the usual Communist pattern—for example, a National Peace Committee, a Women's Alliance, a Student Association—and gained control over a number of newspapers, including the official government paper.

Operating through this expanding structure, the party planned gradually to achieve a number of well-defined purposes. Caught between labor code requirements and slowdowns, strikes and excessive wage demands, farm owners could eventually be forced into an untenable position. Simultaneously, the agrarian reform program provided for building up a network of local agrarian committees throughout the country. The committees, directly patterned after Lenin's peasant soviets, could easily become an instrument of revolutionary rule. Of special importance, the agrarian reform program did not make the peasants the owners, but merely the tenants, of their new holdings. Thus the government retained its full control over the land even after it had been expropriated and redistributed. Failure of the recipients to conform to the demands of the government, and eventually of the Communist party, would mean eviction from the long-coveted allotments. In 1954, fearing that the army would not support him, President Arbenz attempted to arm the local agrarian committees and unions. With this showdown impending, the diverse opponents of Arbenz' increasingly

Communist-dominated regime joined forces to overthrow him and suppress the open and visible activities of the Communist party.

One significant feature of the Arbenz administration is that its policies represented an attempt to bring about drastic social changes without first tackling the problems of economic development. A second feature is that the Arbenz-Communist combination enlisted widespread support in Guatemala even though much of this support was ambivalent. Many people were not sure they liked the way Arbenz was doing things, but they felt that this was the only way to accomplish a great deal quickly. The belief that Communist policies could succeed in Guatemala was bolstered by the fact that they had succeeded in Russia. That the program was accomplishing many of its immediate purposes was confirmed by daily reports of "invasions" of estates by peasants, strikes successfully carried out, widespread expropriations, and so on. Although the overt Communist threat has been scotched since the Castillo Armas revolution, the Arbenz period had lasting effects on the process of social innovation. It set in motion changes that will be felt for a long time to come.

Among its effects, the Arbenz period destroyed any remnant of mutual interest between farm laborers and farm owners. The paternalism of the earlier pattern persists today mainly in the written provisions of the labor code. The farm labor groups are now acutely aware that a new type of relationship is possible between themselves and the cosmopolite, local upper, and middle classes. Similarly, the emergent middle mass is conscious of its own potential strength, once it has been consolidated through labor unions and similar organizations. It was the emergent middle that generally gave dynamic impetus to the Arbenz programs.

The elaborate forms of political control instituted by the Arbenz government have also resulted in creating new channels for introducing change into the Indian communities. Effective political action at the local level was bolstered by the establishment of new foci of power within each community. The individuals who came forward to staff the new organizations bypassed and brushed aside the older forms of Indian political organization in order to reach their goals. The traditional Indian structure was not compatible with the new political parties and agrarian committees. Indian communities had been dominated by a hierarchy based on age and respect for elders. Placing young men in the newer political channels of power cut across the older pattern of authority, which was forced to give way. Similarly, within many *Ladino* communities the local upper class lost its former dominance to the newer political organizations.[17]

The result of the turbulent post-1944 years has been to set in motion a whole chain of social innovations. Essentially, these changes have been spurred on by political action, and have not been accompanied by any basic changes in the pattern of technology and production. The Communist-led forces showed no strong interest in the problems of over-all economic development. Such economic steps as were taken, notably the agrarian reform and the opening of a highway to the Atlantic, plainly were undertaken primarily for their political effect.

However, the events of the Arbenz period have left behind some changes in the economic structure. One of these has been the expansion of speculative agriculture. The threatening behavior of labor under Arbenz' rule made this type of enterprise attractive, for it relieves the entrepreneur of any continuing responsibility of providing for the livelihood of a permanent labor force, and offers him mobility and a quick turnover on his investment. This trend has also encouraged other farmers, especially in coastal areas, to turn to mechanized methods to a degree previously unknown. With the threat of expropriation looming ahead, many cosmopolites had been fearful of investing in agriculture. After Arbenz' downfall, however,

---

[17] See Adams, *Political Changes in Guatemalan Indian Communities*, cited.

mechanization offered the added advantage of releasing the entrepreneur from commitments to provide for the needs of a large and stable labor force.

As a boost for the new government of Castillo Armas, the United Fruit Company turned over a large part of its Pacific coast properties to the colonization program, and similar though smaller gifts of land have been made by other landowners. The post-1954 governments have found it politically expedient to continue the agrarian reform program, though on a quite different basis. Under the new program, each land allotment becomes the outright property of the recipient, rather than a leasehold which can be revoked at will by the government of the day. The program has also been strengthened by providing improved credit facilities and expanding agricultural extension activities to help the new owners get on a firm footing.

The answer of technical-aid specialists to the post-Arbenz challenge has been to push ahead with economic development, while making a supplementary effort to promote limited social change. The colonization of farmers in newly available coastal lands is based on a new settlement pattern, similar to the individual homesteads of most North American farmers, in contrast to the more common *Ladino* pattern of the compact community, from which the farmer goes out to his fields each day. Social change, as a goal in itself, is still secondary for the North American specialists and technical missions. It is still regarded as something which must develop gradually out of changes in the technology of production.

The Castillo Armas government had one special problem. While held publicly responsible by public opinion for promoting and guiding social change, it did not have the same freedom of action as the Arbenz government had enjoyed. Committed to economic advance as well as to social evolution, it had to tread much more cautiously in order to satisfy a wider range of conflicting interests and ambitions. The priority of economic development over social change is doubtless more congenial to North Americans. But within Guatemala the Arbenz-launched social changes have stimulated new forces and new alignments which North American specialists are not well equipped to guide or even to understand. Their own sense of values, as well as the purposes of their technical missions, make it too easy for them to stand aside from problems of social action.

Needed: A Dynamic Policy of Social Change

Any dealer in the international game of power poker knows full well that the order of the deck is a major factor in determining who wins the hand. Domestic issues, which are frequently glossed over or inadequately understood, sometimes play the determining role in shaping a country's international behavior. In order to understand Guatemala's conduct in international politics, the outsider must examine objectively the social processes which are reshaping its society. Are there means by which the United States can better evaluate these processes so as to take more effective account of them in shaping its policies? In posing this question my concern is not with reviewing specific U.S. operations in Guatemala, or criticizing the activities of the various U.S. agencies, such as the embassy, the International Cooperation Administration, or the U.S. Information Agency. My concern is with a broader issue.

Since the downfall of the Arbenz regime the activities of the United States in Guatemala show evidence of a change in outlook and purpose. Since 1954 the newspapers no longer have occasion to report that the American ambassador has insulted the president of Guatemala. U.S. officials no longer reject even the principle of agrarian reform as dangerous to private property and American interests. Nor do U.S. technical-aid missions push through their programs in the face of contrary arguments advanced by Guatemalan officials. In the pre-Arbenz period, all these things were happening. Many North Americans would explain this change of approach by pointing out that the Guatemalan government is no longer communistic. This, however, is at best a dubious answer and certainly not the whole answer.

Perhaps because of the apparent threat posed to U.S. interests and to inter-American solidarity, the events of 1950-1954 made it plain that even a small country can be a threat when led by hostile forces, that such a drastic change as agrarian reform need not be a threat to American interests, while it may be of critical importance within the country. Fundamentally, these turbulent events made it evident that social change was a matter of vital importance to Guatemalans, so much so that some of them were willing to convert their country into a Soviet satellite in order to bring it about.

When more cordial relations between the two governments were resumed in 1954, the United States attempted to adjust its policies to the lessons it had learned. Technical-aid missions were rapidly expanded and new ones were set up, but they often languished for lack of firm support in Washington and of local Guatemalan leadership in setting up programs and getting them going. The flight into exile of many people who had served under previous governments also deprived the country of much of its experienced personnel, while many who joined in the undignified scramble for spoils were not well qualified for their new posts. The precise reasons for the lag of the Guatemalan government or the United States since 1954 in advancing a vigorous new economic program are far from clear. In any event, despite evidences of some change in U.S. attitudes toward programs of social action, the post-Arbenz attempt at a new adjustment has been far from successful.

If we grant that there has been some change in U.S. policy, has this gone far enough? The evidence indicates that it has not, even though the United States has initiated or supported a number of programs designed to answer some immediately pressing issues. Notably, it has supported the colonization of landless peasants, the expansion of education in rural areas, the development of urban housing, and the strengthening of farm extension services. The United States appears to have supported these policies less as part of an over-all national policy than as a concession to expediency or to Guatemalan demands for attention to politically wavering segments of the population. While recognizing at last that social change is of great importance, the United States is still without a definite policy for social change. Its activities resemble uncoordinated reflexes rather than a consciously planned and unified program of action.

Whether we realize it or not, U.S. activities in any foreign area are seen by the nationals of that area as a whole, as reflections of a general policy. Russia acts on a clear-cut policy toward other countries; the fact that its real purposes are often camouflaged is not directly relevant. In part as a result of Communist propaganda, the Soviet model is attractive to many Latin Americans, for the Russians state very positively why change should take place, what the goals of the utopian society are, and, of course, how to achieve them. The United States in turn can point to itself as a country that has grown strong and prosperous as a result of economic and social changes. However, the rags-to-riches propaganda of the Soviet Union is more effective just because the Russian development has taken place so recently, while the United States seems to outsiders always to have had an advance economic and social system.

U.S. propaganda holds up our democracy as the model political system, forged in blood many years ago. This way of life assumes that every man can enjoy his independence and that everyone benefits, though some more and some less, from the efficient operation of the North American variety of capitalism. Further, this progress can be achieved by other nations if certain puritan ideals are followed, and if education is taken seriously by all. An essential element of the American philosophy rests on this last point: education is essential for the democratic process, and, once education for all is achieved, democracy and prosperity will inevitably follow.

Many Latin Americans admire the United States for its genuine achievements, but few are deluded into thinking that the North American model of democracy can be made to work with clocklike precision in their own countries. Indeed, many are offended by the unspoken assumption that a utopian future should be so un-Latin. Their centuries of Latin heritage are treasured as much by them as our Anglo-American heritage is by us. From the viewpoint of a Latin, whatever policy the United States may have in the field of social change appears essentially one of making over his country in an image close to that of the United States. Furthermore, the politically sophisticated Latin Americans know from their own experience that education equips people to read Communist as well as North American propaganda.

If the policies of the United States are to be understandable and attractive in Guatemala and in other nations which are undergoing basic changes in their social order, the problem is how to identify those policies with their own best interests. It is, however, far from simple to define what those "best interests" are; the "best interests" of the cosmopolites or the Euro-American components in the Guatemalan population are not identical with those of the mobile rural laborers or the Indian laborers. From both a political and a practical point of view, the solution is to identify U.S. policy, not with all the conflicting desires of various groups, but with those changes that are likely to shape the new stage of an evolving social order. In the case of Guatemala, for example, the focus of U.S. interest, to be effective, must be on the emergent middle class and on those changes which are strengthening its role.

This is hardly an easy assignment. North Americans, including officials, usually find the cosmopolites and the Euro-Americans far more congenial than other groups. Their customs and ways of living are more attractive to foreigners. Because these groups do contribute importantly to the running of the government and the economy, it is useful, up to a point, to work closely with them. The emergent middle mass does not offer this same attraction in social intercourse, and its members are a hodgepodge of many backgrounds and divergent interests. This variety of background offers an important advantage to the United States—the possibility of choosing those policies that will appeal not only to a large proportion of the emergent middle groups but also to those segments of the society from which they spring. This last factor is of continuing importance. For years to come the new middle class will receive its more creative membership from the local upper, cosmopolite, and foreign-orientated groups, but its dynamic force is likely to stem from laboring groups and independent farmers, both modified Indian and *Ladino*.

The formulation of a well-defined policy for coping with the phenomena of social change, the lack of which has been evident in our policy toward Guatemala, also has major relevance for U.S. activities in many other parts of the world. The adjustment of policy to regional and national realities is one of the daily tasks of the State Department and other agencies of government. An even greater problem lies in the need for Americans to realize that to gain the good will of other peoples it is necessary both to understand the needs of those countries as their own spokesmen see them and to identify the segments of the population that produce these leaders and shape their outlook.

It is, of course, beyond the scope of one essay or many essays to lay down a policy by which the United States can identify itself with the emerging populations and classes in all or several parts of the world. Nevertheless the case of Guatemala may offer a few helpful suggestions, for its recent experiences make it clear that the new factor which is reshaping Guatemalan society is the novel process of continuous or open-ended change, and that Guatemalans have manifested a strong interest in strengthening their nation through political and social action. Communism, though fundamentally hostile to nationalism, has often mobilized wide support by identifying many of its short-run purposes with those of the national interest. There is certainly no reason why the United States cannot succeed even better in this, by making it clear that its policies are designed to support the development of national strength and self-respect.

Instead of boasting of U.S. achievements by lectures, posters, movies, and news accounts, the United States could emphasize the ways in which it is helping Guatemalans to achieve their own national goals and to build an integrated nation with the very tools the United States is offering: economic development, education, improved public health and housing, and so forth. Of course such a change in approach would require making over the usual outlook and habits of some American personnel abroad. Some would have to discard the practice of looking down on the people of the country and refusing to learn about their history.

Programs of assistance should allow for points of national pride. Whether or not they are desirable from the standpoint of economic development, some projects mean more than others to Guatemalans. An example of this was the completion of the highway to the Atlantic. The recognition of national pride would involve a greater emphasis on the exchange of Guatemalan nationals with those of the United States in the field of intellectual and artistic activities. The sponsoring of Guatemalan intellectuals at American centers of learning, not just for a month's quick trip but for a full semester or two, can have great long-run benefits for both countries.

Perhaps the basic element is the public recognition and encouragement by Americans, both as individuals and as a community, of Guatemalan national aspirations. Such public recognition obviously implies a respect for qualities of the Guatemalan culture. A constant stressing of American political stability, for example, is neither a convincing nor an ingratiating argument to offer Latins. They are aware of this stability; if it were readily transferable, they might have imported it long ago. Similarly, the characteristically hierarchical, somewhat authoritarian and paternalistic patterns of Latin American governments need not be compared unfavorably with the more decentralized North American system. For a foreign country, concerned with promoting its own political stability and economic development, it is hard to comprehend why an important bill may be put off for a year or more by the U.S. Congress because of a filibuster. Whether or not Americans believe that some aspects of Guatemalan culture are superior to their own, Guatemalans, in any case, believe this. And they know that their future will be cast in a mold of their own, not in that of the United States.

U.S. policy can be strengthened by giving greater recognition to Guatemala's place within Central America. The history of Guatemala has always been influenced by what happens in the neighboring countries of the isthmus. Its small size, a disadvantage in terms of economic development, can in considerable measure be offset by promoting more effective cooperation between it and its neighbors. Central American regional specialization is just starting,[18] but it has long been regarded as a promising line of development. The cheek-by-jowl proximity of the Central American countries provides special opportunities for the joint development of regional facilities and programs. Such a regional program of development has been considered by foreign-aid officials, but it has not been publicly approved as a national policy.

In much of Latin America, one of the recurring irritations centers on the emphasis on the role of U.S. business. To couch U.S. foreign policy primarily in terms of promoting U.S. business interests is as sure a way of losing friends and alienating people south of the border as could be devised. The question is not whether big business can and should play an effective role in development. In Latin

18 See Hoselitz, cited.

America, big business is the symbol of exploitation for leftist and nationalist leaders, and this symbol has considerable reality behind it in any review of the last half-century. Furthermore, in many parts of Latin America big business is mainly foreign-owned business. The issue is not one of discouraging business from moving to Latin America, but to encourage business leaders to face up to the political and social realities of Latin America and to show foresight in adapting their plans and operations to them, rather than to depend on U.S. influence in solving their local problems. A foreign policy must represent an interaction between sovereign states, not merely a projection of the desires of one country or of some segments within it. If the United States is not strong enough politically and economically to place its national foreign policy above the pressures of particular business interests, then it is perilously close to forfeiting its right to be called a nation.

Among all social groups in Guatemala, it is the urban and mobile rural laborers who have felt most directly the impact of North American business practices, and it is among them that leftist agitation and organizations were most successful during the Arbenz regime. The laborers of the wholly foreign-owned railroad and fruit plantations were the target of unremitting leftist efforts, and their favorable response was most vehement. A more promising type of business enterprise, which brings greater satisfaction to national pride, is one that provides for participation by local capital and ownership. And if local ownership draws into partnership a portion of the growing middle class, this may create a really significant commitment by this class to the capitalist system.

Americans would like to feel that the broad goals of U.S. foreign policy, the expansion of freedom and opportunity for all, are shared by most Latin Americans. One way of helping Latin Americans to understand these purposes better is to encourage a wider sharing of experiences with each other. For example, a new venture which has succeeded in one Latin American country may be worth testing in another. Mexico, Brazil, Venezuela, Chile, and El Salvador all offer case studies in development which can be useful to other countries. Some interchanges of ideas and experience between countries have taken place, as in the case of the improved farming methods and extension services developed in Mexico and the farmer education center at Turrialba, Costa Rica, but much more could be done. In its programs the United States also could profitably employ well-qualified nationals of other countries instead of drawing its personnel solely from American institutions. This raises a number of problems of administration, but none of them is insurmountable. This practice has been adopted on a small scale, but it has not become a part of policy.

Only a dynamic policy concerned with guiding the movement of social change into constructive channels, a policy that provides a model of ideas and a focus of aspirations, can compete effectively with the promises held out by Communist propaganda. But to enlist the cooperation of the country to which it is directed, it must be based on a recognition of that country's basic values as well as its specific features and problems. In formulating a long-range policy of modernization, social scientists have an essential contribution to make. Their insights can help the diplomats and technicians in many ways. For example, over the past decade or more U.S. policies have frequently failed to reach politically crucial elements of the Guatemalan population, or to take account of their interpretations of the changes which they are experiencing. If in 1945 the United States had had a clear-cut policy defining the positive role it could play in aiding Latin America through a period of many changes, it might have foreseen and averted the extreme anti-United States developments of the late 1940's, based as they were on the growing popularity of Communist doctrine and action in middle-mass circles and among laboring groups.

Today the Good Neighbor era is over. The United States and the Latin American countries are, in fact, neighbors, and whether the adjective "good" can be applied to that relationship depends upon with whom one is speaking. The stable and mobile laboring groups know little of the United States; when they come into contact with North Americans, it is usually through a weekly pay envelope or the lurid posters of nationalist or leftist-inspired anti-Americanism. The traditional Indians see us either not at all or perhaps as quaint tourists who, for unfathomable reasons, come to stare at them or purchase some item of Indian clothing. Urban laborers are familiar with many of the machines that come from the United States. The automobiles are flashy, the radios entertaining, the television visible through the window of a bar or a store; but these, as something unobtainable, carry no politically convincing argument. Like literacy, the automobile and radio can serve any brand of politician. The urban laborer, like his rural cousin, is also subjected to persistent propaganda against the "imperialist" designs of the United States and the "menace" of its economic policies to his welfare. The laborer sees the face of the United States in several profiles, and he admires, envies, and sometimes hates us for these glimpses.

When we look at the publicized slogans of U.S. policy in Latin America, it is not clear to whom they are directed. "Good Neighbors," "Good Partners," "People's Capitalism," even "Hemispheric Security" are remote concepts to most of the people who hear them; they are meaningless to those who know that partners must be equals, that capitalism requires capital, and that international security involves some restrictions of choice. The people whom it is most important to convince of the positive values of U.S. policy—the emergent middle mass—see things in terms of the daily changes they are witnessing. To reach people who are experiencing rapid social change, the United States needs a dynamic and progressive policy, one which expresses a positive interest in the new social world that is emerging. When we cooperate with other nations, we do not expect the French to become less French, the Indians less proud of India's distinctive role, or even the Egyptians to be less Arab. Yet, inadvertently or intentionally, we often convey the impression that Guatemalans and other Latin Americans ought to seek a gringo utopia. This impression has been created partly by positive actions, but perhaps more by a failure to define and follow through a policy toward social change that would demonstrate a genuine interest in and respect for the values which are cherished by the Latins themselves.

The future of the free world will depend on the real and not imagined relationships that exist among its members. As recent histories of Korea and Egypt, Israel, Indo-China, Cuba, and Guatemala have clearly indicated, events in small countries can be as crucial to peace as in the big ones, and a policy can be as disastrous when it fails to take account of their aspirations as when it disregards those of the major powers. Guatemala, one of the smaller Latin American republics, may indeed not attract the concentrated attention of U.S. foreign-policy planners. It would be a mistake, however, to assume that Guatemalans are a whit less ambitious to develop their country now than they were under the Arévalo and Arbenz administrations.

The United States has failed twice, once after World War II and again after the 1954 revolution, to understand the purport and direction of the changes that are under way in Guatemala and elsewhere in Latin America. It has failed to formulate a policy on social change that would carry conviction to the emerging leaders and measure up to the changes that are being experienced by major segments of the population. If we want to define and apply an effective policy on social change—and it is still not too late to do this—we must realize that in a country like Guatemala people do not see their problems solely in terms of technological aid and economic development. They are intimately involved in the painful emergence of a new society with its new sources of power. The United States must recognize the impact of these social and political developments and make this recognition an important factor in shaping its foreign policy. If it fails to do so, it may see the leadership over the forces of change gathered into other and hostile hands.

Six

MEXICO SINCE CÁRDENAS

by OSCAR LEWIS

THE YEAR 1940 is a particularly convenient bench mark for
the study of social and economic change in Mexico. The
last year of the Cárdenas administration, it marks the end
of the distinctively agrarian and revolutionary phase of the
Mexican Revolution and the beginning of a new phase,
which some have called the "industrial revolution" and
others "a shift to the right." [1] During the preceding thirty
years, after 1910, the primary emphasis had been upon

I wrote this paper in 1956 as a Guggenheim Fellow in Mexico, where
I was studying the process of urbanization. Many of the statistics have
since been brought up to date, thanks to the generous assistance of Helena
Stalson and William Diebold, Jr. An earlier version of this paper appeared
in "México desde 1940," *Investigación Económica,* 2d Quarter 1958, pp.
185-256. I am grateful to the Guggenheim Foundation for making this
study possible. I am also grateful to Professor Bert F. Hoselitz of the
University of Chicago for his critical reading of this manuscript and to
my research assistant William H. Holland for his help in collecting some
of the data.

[1] The Mexican economist, Manuel Germán Parra, in his book, *La in-
dustrialización de México* (Mexico City: Imp. Universitaria, 1954), writes:
"The agrarian revolution and the industrial revolution in Mexico are
not two opposed facts, but rather, two aspects of a single phenomenon.
The agrarian revolution had the objective of destroying the feudal and
slave system under which the country was living, in order to establish
capitalism. The objective of the industrial revolution is to establish the
capitalist regime throughout the length and breadth of the country"
(p. 187). For the turn to the right, see Sanford A. Mosk, *The Industrial
Revolution in Mexico* (Berkeley: University of California Press, 1950).

basic institutional changes, the remaking of a semifeudal
agrarian economy, the breaking up of large landholdings,
the distribution of land to the peasants, the establishment
of communal villages, or *ejidos,* the strengthening of the
power of organized labor, the reduction of foreign participation in and control over the economy, the emancipation of the Indians, and the spread of public education.
The basic objective was to improve the lot of the common
man.

Beginning with the Camacho administration in 1940, a
new emphasis began to make itself felt. The tempo of social change and land distribution was slowed down appreciably. Industrialization and increased production became
the immediate national goal, and foreign investment was
encouraged by the government. "Less attention has been
given in recent years to how the pie is sliced, and more
emphasis is being put on producing a bigger pie." [2]

Closely paralleling this shift in governmental emphasis
has been the increasing influence of the United States in
Mexican life. Never before in the long history of U.S.-
Mexican relations has there been such a varied and intense
interaction between the two countries. The close cooperation during World War II, the rapid tempo of U.S. investment, the remarkable influx of U.S. tourists into Mexico
and of Mexican visitors to the United States, the annual
migration of several hundred thousand Mexican agricultural workers to the United States, the exchange of
students, technicians, and professors, and the increasing
number of Mexicans who are becoming U.S. citizens, have
made for a new type of relationship between the two countries. What is the meaning of these major social, economic,
and cultural changes which have been taking place in
Mexico since 1940, and what are their implications for the
United States and its foreign policy?

---

2 James G. Maddox, *The Growth of the Mexican Economy,* report by
the American Universities Field Staff (New York, June 1956), p. 3. This
excellent study will be referred to hereafter as Maddox.

Population Growth and Urbanization

Since 1940 Mexico has experienced an unusually rapid rate of population increase, accompanied by a surge of urbanization.[3] Today, Mexico has one of the most rapidly growing populations in the world. This new trend is all the more remarkable because of its traditionally slow rate of growth and its large excess of emigrants over immigrants.

From 19.6 million in 1940, Mexico's population grew to 25.7 million in 1950; the estimate for 1960 is about 33.8 million. Between 1940 and 1950 the average annual rate of increase was 3.1 per cent as compared to 1.9 per cent for the previous decade. In absolute figures the increase from 1940 to 1950 was 6.1 million, more than the total increase in the previous twenty years and twice that of 1930-1940. The predominantly non-Indian regions of the north Pacific states and the north showed the highest rates of increase, urban and rural; the lowest rates were in the areas of greatest Indian concentration—the south Pacific states and the Gulf states.[4] Between 1950 and 1957 the rate of annual increase fell slightly, to 2.83 per cent, but in these years another 5.6 million Mexicans were added to the population.

The major source of population growth is the persistently high birth rate, 45.1 per thousand for the period 1946-1950 and 46.9 for 1957, combined with a sharp drop in the death rate as modern medicine and national health campaigns have reached more and more of the rural population. Some observers also stress the improvement of the general level of nutrition as an important contributing factor, pointing to this as one of the positive achievements of the Mexican Revolution.[5] In any case, the over-all death

---

[3] See Julio Durán Ochoa, *Población* (Mexico City: Fondo de Cultura Económica, 1955); also Floyd Dotson and Lilian O. Dotson, "Urban Centralization in Mexico," *Rural Sociology*, March 1956, pp. 41-49.

[4] Durán, cited, p. 197.

[5] Germán Parra, cited, p. 112. Population estimates for Mexico in 1980, as made by Luis J. Ducoff, range from a medium estimate of 53,309

rate dropped from 23.2 per thousand in 1940 to 16.2 in 1950, and to 12.9 by 1957. Infant mortality dropped even more sharply, from 125.7 per thousand in 1940 to 96.2 in 1950, and to an all-time low of 70.9 in 1956; in 1957 it was 79.1. The drop in the infant mortality rate from 1940 to 1950 was about five times greater than that between 1930 and 1940.[6]

As people have moved to the cities, the urban population has grown much more rapidly than the rural population. From 1940 to 1950 the average annual rate of increase of the urban population, as defined in the census, amounted to 5.9 per cent, compared to 1.6 for the rural areas.[7] During the same period the number of localities with a population of over 10,000 rose from 97 to 159, an increase of 62 per cent. In general, the larger cities have tended to grow more rapidly. The growth of Mexico City has been amazing—from about 1.4 million in 1940 to 2.2 million in 1950 and to an estimated 4 million in 1958. In that year Mexico City had nearly 13 per cent of the total population of the country as compared to 7.4 per cent in 1940 and 8.7 per cent in 1950. It is now the largest city of Latin America, and the second ranking city on the North American continent.

The increasing concentration of people in the large cities is due more to the growing population pressure on

---

million to a high of 61,794 million. See Gilberto Loya, "La población de México, 1950-1980," p. 29, reprinted from *Investigación Económica,* 1st Quarter, 1960.

6 Mexico, Secretaría de Economía, *Anuario estadístico de los Estados Unidos Mexicanos* (Mexico City: Author, 1954), p. 115; and Durán, cited, p. 120.

7 Durán, cited, p. 208. Durán follows the Mexican census definition of "urban" as referring to communities of over 2,500. Nathan L. Whetten's definition (*Rural Mexico* [University of Chicago Press, 1948], pp. 34-36) of urban communities as those of over 10,000 seems more realistic and, of course, gives a very different set of figures. According to the Mexican census definition, Mexico was 33.5 per cent urban in 1940 and 42.6 per cent urban in 1950. According to Whetten's definition, Mexico was 21.9 per cent urban in 1940 and 28.9 per cent urban in 1950. The proportion of the population residing in localities of over 25,000 rose from 16.8 per cent in 1940 to 22.5 per cent in 1950.

the land than to the attractions of urban life. Despite the expansion of Mexican agriculture since 1940, the rate at which new land is being brought under cultivation still lags far behind the rate of population increase. As might be expected, the heaviest migration from the land has occurred in the central states, where population density is greatest and improvements in agriculture have been fewest.

Another important factor has been the growth of industry, mostly concentrated in or near large urban areas. In Mexico, as in other underdeveloped countries, the cities are the major providers for industry's needs of skilled labor, technicians, adequate utilities, and transportation facilities. The concentration of the political and administrative bureaucracy in the cities provides a further incentive for the growth of industry. To the rural migrants the city offers the hope of better employment opportunities, better educational facilities, greater material conveniences, and a generally higher standard of living.

Despite the growth of its cities, Mexico remains a preponderantly rural country. In 1950, over 70 per cent of its people lived in communities of 10,000 or less, 65.4 per cent in communities of 5,000 or less.[8] Although the percentage of the total gainfully employed population engaged in agriculture dropped from 65.4 to 58.3 between 1940 and 1950, it did not decline further during the 1950's, and farming remains the basic occupation.

Mexico's Indian Population

Between 1940 and 1950 the Indian population, defined on a basis of languages spoken, decreased from 14.9 per cent to 11.5 per cent of the total. The number of persons speaking only an Indian language dropped from 1,237,018 in 1940 to 795,069 in 1950, a 35 per cent decrease. The number of persons speaking both Spanish and an Indian

---

[8] In 1940, 78.1 per cent of the population lived in communities of 10,000 or less, and 72.5 per cent in communities of 5,000 or less.

language increased from 1,235,891 to 1,652,540. Mexicans who previously spoke only an Indian language are becoming bilingual more rapidly than those who speak both an Indian language and Spanish are losing their native idiom. So long as there remains a sizable population speaking only an Indian language, the number of persons speaking both languages will continue to increase. If the rates of the 1940's continue few Mexicans will speak only an Indian language by the year 2000. Only afterwards will the bilingual population decrease.[9]

In terms of geography, the Indian problem is a limited and regional one. In 1950, 86 per cent of all persons speaking only an Indian language were concentrated in four southern states (Yucatán, Chiapas, Oaxaca, Guerrero) and three central states (Puebla, Veracruz, Hidalgo). In eleven states from 12 to 63 per cent of the population was bilingual.

The importance of the Indians is far greater than their relatively small numbers suggest. The Indian is a symbol of oppression, and the redemption of the Indian has been a major aim of the Mexican Revolution. In sentiment, most Mexicans identify their nation with the Indian rather than the Spanish heritage. Cuauhtemoc has displaced Las Casas as a symbol of the Indian's defender. This feeling was officially consecrated by the Mexican Congress in a decree of October 10, 1949, whose first article reads: "We hereby express categorically . . . that the heroic figure of Cuauhtemoc is the symbol of our nationality and therefore deserves the sincere devotion of the Mexican people." [10] This decree reflected the popular enthusiasm that followed the alleged discovery, about 1948, of the bones of

---

9 In estimating the Indian population, I have added 142,919 children under the age of six to the 795,069 persons who spoke only Indian languages in 1950, making a total of 937,988 persons. Similarly, in estimating the total number of persons speaking both an Indian language and Spanish, I have added 307,740 children to the number 1,652,540, giving a total of 1,960,280 bilinguals.

10 José E. Iturriaga, La estructura social y cultural de México (Mexico City: Fondo de Cultura Económica, 1951), p. 228.

the last Aztec emperor, "an enthusiasm which has not yet cooled, even after the official declaration that the remains were not really those of Cuauhtemoc." [11]

Even Mexican psychiatrists reflect the Indianist bias with their idealized characterizations of the Indian mother as the apogee of maternity, and the Spanish-colonial woman as cold and rejecting.[12] Widespread Mexican hostility toward the Spaniard, and by generalization toward most foreigners, is explained by the psychiatrists as hostility against the absent father figure.[13] The Spaniard is still the symbol of the oppressor, and no statues of Cortes are allowed in the country.

Immigration, Emigration, and the "Bracero" Movement

Population pressure on poor and limited agricultural resources, combined with employment opportunities in the United States, has made Mexico a country of emigration since the beginning of the century. Immigration, on the other hand, has been very small. At no time in the last sixty years has the foreign-born population of the country been over one per cent of the total. From 1939 to 1951 only about 8.6 per cent of those entering Mexico with the declared intention of establishing permanent residence stayed on.[14] However, the number of U.S. citizens residing in Mexico has increased from about 10,000 in 1940, to 32,000 in 1953, to 48,500 in 1956.

Legal Mexican emigration to the United States has increased steadily in the last few decades. From 1931 to 1940, an annual average of 2,200 Mexican nationals entered the United States for permanent residence. Between 1940 and 1950 the number increased to 6,000, and by 1955 it had

---

[11] Same.

[12] Santiago Ramírez, "Estructura psicológica del mexicano," *Revista de Cultura y Letras Potosina,* no. 115, 1952.

[13] Same.

[14] Durán, cited, p. 172.

jumped to 61,368.[15] The desire of so many Mexicans to leave their country is a blow to national pride, and their exodus at a time when the economy is apparently booming suggests that the prosperity does not extend far down the socio-economic ladder.

Increasing numbers of Mexicans have come to the United States as *braceros* (temporary agricultural workers). From 1955 through 1958 about 400,000 a year crossed the Rio Grande, perhaps four times as many as the average of the 1940's. Of the million and a half *braceros* who entered the United States legally between 1942 and 1955,[16] nine-tenths came from the central and northern regions of Mexico, with eight states, Coahuila, Chihuahua, Durango, Zacatecas, Guanajuato, the Federal District, Jalisco, and Michoacán, contributing about 80 per cent. Most of the *braceros* are young, unmarried, and landless. A study made in 1946 found their age range to be from fifteen to forty-nine, with over 80 per cent of them twenty-nine years old or less, and 70 per cent twenty-one years or less.[17]

The *bracero* movement has been of great importance for the Mexican economy in providing a source of income for the landless and for other poor sectors of the agricultural population. Also, it has considerably lessened the chronic under- and unemployment of rural Mexico, thereby serving as a partial, though temporary and inadequate, solution of the agrarian problem. In the central region from

15 Charles G. Sommer, *A Study of the Increase in Mexican Immigration to the U.S.*, U.S. Embassy Report (Mexico City, 1956), p. 14.

16 The million and a half figure is based on data supplied by the Mexican Department of Statistics. The illegal "wetback" movement reached very high proportions during the fifties. In the three years 1953-1955, 1.7 million Mexican aliens were arrested by the border patrol in Operation Wetback and returned to Mexico. In addition, unknown thousands left the country voluntarily to avoid arrest. See Gertrude D. Krichefsky, "Importation of Alien Laborers," *I and N Reporter* (U.S. Department of Justice), July 1956, pp. 4-9. In 1956-1958 over a million and a quarter *braceros* came into the United States legally.

17 Luis Argoytia, Guillermo Martínez, and Luis Fernández del Campo, *Los braceros* (Mexico City: Secretaría del Trabajo y Previsión Social, 1946), pp. 87-91, cited in *Proceso ocupacional* (Mexico City: Cámara Nacional de la Industria de Transformación, 1956), p. 132.

which the bulk of the *braceros* have come, traditional agricultural practices prevail and government efforts at irrigation, mechanization, and the distribution of land to the landless have been at a minimum. In other words, those sectors of the rural population which would otherwise have been abandoned to their own resources have turned to *bracerismo* for relief. But for this safety valve, the government's heavy emphasis upon industrialization since 1940 might have been accompanied by considerable unrest in the countryside. Were the United States suddenly to close its borders to the *braceros,* a major crisis would probably follow in Mexico.

As a cultural influence, the *bracero* movement has somewhat broadened the perspective of the Mexican rural population. Over a million and a half rural Mexicans from thousands of villages have seen some parts of the United States. Even in some of the most isolated hamlets in Mexico, an American may be greeted with a few words of English by peasants who feel a bond with the visitor because they have been in his country. Unfortunately, the rich potential for better understanding between Mexico and the United States has not been developed because of the conditions under which *braceros* work and live in the United States. Most *braceros* are isolated in work camps or on farms, speak no English, live on a Mexican diet, and on the whole learn very little about the United States and its way of life. Very few learn agricultural skills that can be applied in their own villages.

Often the *braceros* return to their villages only to rest for a few months before setting out for another period in the United States. The effect of this pattern on local agriculture is interesting. Villages like Tepoztlán, which suffered from an acute land shortage in the mid-1940's, in ten years developed a shortage of manpower, and many milpas go uncultivated because men have gone to the United States as *braceros* (approximately 500 in 1951-1955).

The *braceros* have been sending home more than 30

million dollars a year, a very large sum in Mexican pesos.[18] Judging from my restudy of Tepoztlán (1951) the *braceros* are investing their money wisely. Most of them have made improvements in their houses and have bought land and cattle. Many have brought home portable battery radios, mechanical toys, clothing, and U.S. cloth. The village now has four full-time tailors who are kept busy providing tailor-made pants for the peasants.

In the light of frequent reports on the poor treatment and bad living conditions of *braceros* in the United States, the findings of the study of Tepoztlán are interesting. In interviews with fifty *braceros* we found practically no complaints about their treatment in the United States. The few complaints that could be elicited were about overseers who were either Filipinos or Japanese. The general reaction reflected satisfaction with the experience and the hope that they could go back to stay for longer periods.

Culture Change and U.S. Influence

Most marked in large cities, U.S. influence has also been felt in rural areas. The proximity of the United States, improved means of communication and transportation, the power and prestige of the United States as a great industrial civilization, and the growth of a Mexican middle class that models itself after its northern counterpart, are largely responsible for this change. The mighty wave of "Americanisms," mostly related to an improved standard of living, has advanced unresisted except by a few intellectuals, nationalists, anti-gringos, Mexican businessmen, and isolated Indians.[19]

---

18 Banco de México, *Asamblea general ordinaria de accionistas* (Mexico City: Author, various years). From 1953 through 1958 the average annual remittances of *braceros* were $32 million, a sum equal to 4.5 or 5 per cent of Mexico's merchandise exports in most of these years.

19 A study of the image of the United States held by the Mexican child found that Mexican school children, when asked to choose some nationality other than their own, showed a preference for U.S. over Spanish, French, Italian, and German. Forty-two per cent of the boys

It is difficult to say how much of the change is due to direct U.S. influences, and how much is a natural concomitant of a developing, twentieth-century, industrial, urban civilization. Both processes have been occurring simultaneously and have been mutually reinforcing. Modern French, Spanish, German, or British influence, once more important than that of the United States, is today scarcely detectable. Italian influence has grown but remains minor. The countries of Central and South America have remarkably little influence on the economic and cultural life of Mexico. It cannot be doubted that much of the modernization has a specifically North American stamp.

U.S. citizens are now the largest single group of foreigners residing in the country. About 15,000 U.S. businessmen live and work in Mexico, attracted by its good investment opportunities, cheap living, and excellent climate.[20] Increasing numbers of foreigners are coming to Mexico as tourists, and a large number of these are North Americans. Annually more than 500,000 U.S. tourists appear, not only in the expensive hotels and resorts, but also in market towns, villages, and other out-of-the-way places. This great tourist trade has led to the establishment of modern hotels and motels, American-style restaurants, curio shops, tourist agencies and guide services, and special transport lines. The folk art, music, and dance of Mexico have been exploited and commercialized; celebrations which are supposedly "folk" or religious are advertised in advance and used to attract tourists. The consequences for the Mexican economy have been significant. In recent years tourist spending has averaged about 70 per cent of Mexican

and 29.4 per cent of the girls chose U.S. nationality. When asked simply whether they would like to be North Americans, 57.6 per cent of boys and 67.0 per cent of the girls answered affirmatively. (Paper presented at the Third Inter-American Psychological Congress, Austin, Texas, December 1955, by the Mexican Branch of the Inter-American Psychological Society.)

20 Daniel Seligman, "The Maddening, Promising Mexican Market," *Fortune*, January 1956, p. 103.

merchandise exports. "There is no doubt," says the UN Economic Commission for Latin America, "that . . . balance-of-payments difficulties were less acute in Mexico than elsewhere in Latin America largely because of the additional exchange resources provided by foreign travel." [21]

Advertisements, more than any other one thing, announce U.S. influence. "Everywhere signs proclaim U.S. companies: General Motors, Singer, Goodrich, Studebaker, RCA, Eastman Kodak—only the corporate suffix 'S.A.' (for Sociedad Anónima) attests plainly that the locale is other than Rahway, N.J." [22] Large-scale advertising arrived with recent U.S. investments, and advertisements in newspapers, radio, and television have a decidedly U.S. flavor. The major television programs are sponsored by foreign-controlled companies like Nestlé, Coca-Cola, General Motors, Proctor and Gamble, and Colgate. Only the use of the Spanish language and of Mexican artists distinguishes the commercials from those of the United States. On the Quaker Oats program one hears the Mexican lightweight idol, Ratón (the mouse) Macias recommend Quaker Oats as "the cereal of champions." Some commercials do not even trouble to translate phrases and have spread American linguistic forms or *pochismos*. Thus, beauty products are announced as "Touch and Glow," "Bright and Clear," and so forth.

A Mexican anthropologist, analyzing U.S. influence as seen in newspapers, writes as follows:

About 50 per cent of the total number of pages in the newspaper indicate the dependence of both the newspaper and

---

[21] *Economic Survey of Latin America, 1957*, 58.II.G.1 (New York: UN Department of Economic and Social Affairs, 1959), p. 69. The statement refers to the previous decade. According to this source, Mexico's gross earnings from tourism grew 20 per cent a year from 1946 to 1957. Mexican figures show a 272 per cent increase in annual expenditures of all tourists from 1946 to 1958. U.S. government figures for American tourists alone show only a 155 per cent increase, but this is almost certainly understated and does not include some visits (e.g., those of less than forty-eight hours).

[22] Seligman, cited, p. 103.

the readers on U.S. civilization for information and direction of public opinion, concepts of life, family conduct, health, child-training, recreation, transportation, travel, writing, forms of graphic expression, individual and national economy, domestic, office and factory equipment, and finally, the direction of interest in other people's business.[23]

Mexican newspapers use Associated Press and United Press bulletins as well as U.S. syndicated news, gossip and advice columns, and comics. In addition, the U.S. Embassy in Mexico publishes two four-page newspapers, *Gaceta de la Semana* and *Suplemento Semanal*, which are distributed free of charge to several hundred small newspapers in the country.

With the increase of wealth and the improvement of transportation facilities, Mexicans have traveled abroad in large numbers. The touring has shifted from Europe to the United States. There has been a great increase in spending abroad—from 64 million dollars in 1946 to 247 million in 1958. Domestic travel, also, has increased and changed in character, especially among the middle class.

. . . Mexican tourism . . . has consigned to history the Sunday custom of baths, going to the market, going to mass, drinking in the *cantinas* and *pulquerías,* and going on picnics to nearby country spots, all of which could be accomplished without great effort and without complicated means of transportation. Sunday has been radically transformed along secular lines into a day of excursion to some rather distant point. . . . Vacations, which were once used to work around the house or to visit distant relatives who could put up the whole family, have lost their patriarchal character and have been displaced by excursions organized by travel agencies.[24]

Increasing employment in factories and office buildings has led to the spread of the quick lunch, eliminating the midday meal at home as well as the traditional siesta. The American-style breakfast, consisting of fruit juice, cereal,

---

23 Julio de la Fuente, "La civilización 'pocha' de México," *Cambios Socio-Culturales en México: Acta Antropológica,* December 1948, p. 444.

24 Same, p. 445.

ham and eggs, and coffee, has become popular, displacing
the traditional breakfast, consisting of beans, chile sauce,
and tortillas. The practice of eating stuffed turkey on
Christmas Eve has been adopted by some middle-class
families. The same trend is seen in the substitution of the
Christmas tree for the customary Nativity scene, and the
exchange of gifts on December 25 instead of January 6,
the Day of the Kings. Drinking habits have also been
changing, with beer replacing pulque among the lower
and middle classes, and whiskey replacing cognac among
the middle and upper classes.

The spread of English is also noteworthy. English has
replaced French as a second language in the schools. Many
university technical texts are now in English, and at least
one important Mexican hospital, El Hospital de la Nu-
trición, requires English for its staff members, many of
whom have received graduate training in the United
States. The French tradition in medicine is slowly but
surely being replaced by U.S. medicine.

Leading U.S. texts in the social sciences, including many
works of anthropologists, for example, Benedict, Mead,
Linton, Kroeber, Kluckhohn, and Redfield, are now available in Spanish translation. The U.S. influence in anthropology has been predominant, and since 1940 the emphasis
in Mexican anthropology has shifted from a preoccupation
with archaeology toward a greater interest in social anthropology.

Because the Mexican film industry was still in its in-
fancy in 1940, over 95 per cent of all films shown in the
country in that year were made in the United States. From
1940 to 1955, Mexican films shown in the capital increased
from 2 to 33, but 54 out of 83 movie programs advertised
in 1955 still included U.S. films. Until 1950, very few films
from other countries were shown, but in 1955 we find 7
French films, 4 Italian films, and 3 British films. But in
Monterrey, Guadalajara, and Puebla, only one or two foreign films other than U.S. films were shown during the
same year.

The number of legitimate theaters in Mexico City increased from 4 to 30 (there are 77 in the whole country) in four years during the 1950's. Translations of Broadway hit plays attract large audiences. Spanish versions of "The Boy Friend" and "Bus Stop," for example, were popular in the mid-50's.

Interest in American sports, particularly football, has reached phenomenal proportions. In 1954, the number of soccer and U.S.-style games and also the number of baseball games played throughout Mexico exceeded that of bullfights and cockfights. In the Distrito Federal almost twice as many tickets were sold for football games as for bullfights. Boxing and wrestling, however, remain the most popular sports. A comparison of the 1940 and 1954 census figures on the number of games and matches of the various sports shows a startling growth.[25]

Economic Development

The remarkable growth of the Mexican economy since 1945 has set a record which can be matched by few countries. The gross national product doubled in volume from 1945 to 1957; the rate of increase in other leading Latin American countries was considerably smaller.[26] In this period per capita production in Mexico increased 44 per cent, in the United States only 6.5 per cent. All this was accomplished without any dramatic discoveries of unutilized natural resources, such as occurred in Venezuela. Moreover, all sectors of the Mexican economy appear to have grown at rates more uniform than those of other large Latin American countries. Many Mexicans believe they have found a formula for balanced growth which will soon lift Mexico out of the category of underdeveloped countries.

---

25 *Anuario Estadístico* . . . , cited (1940), pp. 295-300; same (1954), pp. 297-298.

26 Argentina, 45 per cent; Brazil, 87 per cent; Chile, 30 per cent; Colombia, 76 per cent; Peru, 73 per cent; Mexico, 100 per cent.

The strikingly even growth of the various sectors of the economy from 1945 to 1957 has resulted in a doubling of volume in all areas except mining and construction. The contribution of each sector to the total national product is shown in Table 1.

TABLE 1

National Product by Shares

	1945	1950	1957
		(in per cent)	
Agriculture, forestry, fishing	18.8	20.6	19.1
Mining	4.3	3.2	2.6
Crude petroleum	1.5	1.7	1.8
Manufacturing	20.2	20.0	20.9
Construction	2.4	2.1	2.0
Wholesale and retail trade	33.9	33.7	35.0
Transport	4.6	4.7	4.9
Other	14.3	14.0	13.7

Source: *Economic Bulletin for Latin America* (UN), October 1958, p. 47.

The largest increases have occurred in the generation of electrical energy, which in 1957 was nearly three times the 1945 volume, and in petroleum refining, which more than tripled in this period. The emphasis in the program of industrial expansion has been on economic development, and output of producer goods has increased at a far more rapid rate than output of goods for immediate consumption. Capital accumulation has amounted to about 15 per cent of the total national product; [27] nearly two-thirds of this investment in fixed capital has been undertaken by private enterprise, a proportion which has been growing in relation to the share provided by public investment.

The major factors responsible for the expansion and increasing industrialization of the economy since 1940 can

---

[27] Among the thirteen major Latin American countries, Mexico has had a progressively declining place in the proportion of output devoted to capital investment; in the early 1950's Mexico was a member of the upper half; in 1957 it tied with Ecuador for fourth place from the bottom.

be summarized as follows: use of increased amounts of land, labor, and capital; increased efficiency—the output per worker for the Mexican economy as a whole increased about 35 per cent from 1945 to 1957; government expenditures on public works programs, especially on road-building, irrigation projects, the rehabilitation of the railroad system, and improvement of airports; government encouragement to new industries through tax exemptions, protective tariffs, import controls, and direct subsidies (amounting to 496.9 million pesos in 1955); foreign investments, also encouraged by the government; a high level of savings (encouraged by government policies favoring the upper-income groups); increasing income from the U.S. tourist trade, between $500 and $600 million in 1957 and 1958; and remittances from the braceros.

Of the many factors listed above, the role of government has been of striking importance. Public investment has been concentrated in the expansion of basic economic activity—in transportation and communications, irrigation, petroleum, and electrical power. Since 1945 the government's share in new investment has ranged from 27 to 47 per cent per year, the public funds acting as a counterweight to sharp fluctuations in private investment, and also as a stimulus to it by creating a basic structure within which private enterprise could function. The government's investments for development in 1957 and 1958 accounted for nearly one-half its total budget. Out of a total investment in the public sector of 5.5 million pesos in 1958, 41 per cent was earmarked for transportation and communications, 24 per cent for petroleum and electrical power, and 14 per cent for agriculture (chiefly irrigation).

A comparison of the allocation of federal funds to the various departments over the four presidential administrations from Cárdenas to Ruiz Cortines reveals also some highly significant trends. Especially marked is the sharp decrease in the proportion of funds allocated to national defense, reflecting the demise of caudillismo as a serious factor in Mexican life. Adolfo Ruiz Cortines was the first president since the 1920's who did not depend heavily on either the national or a private army to maintain his control. Table 2 shows the declining proportion of funds de-

TABLE 2

Percentages of National Budget

	1935-1940	*1953-1956*
Defense	17.3	8.1
Communications	13.0	17.4
Hydraulic resources	7.7	10.5
Investment	5.8	10.0
Health and welfare	5.6	4.2
Education	12.7	12.3

Source: Official statistics of the Ministerio de Hacienda y Crédito Público.

voted to defense, the government's increased emphasis on industrialization and the development of commercial farming, and its relative neglect or de-emphasis of social welfare activities.[28]

In Mexico, one notable feature of government spending and investment is its heavy concentration in the federal system, in comparison with the miserly resources available

[28] However, public expenditures for social services took an increasing share of the federal budget in the late 1950's. The Banco Nacional de Comercio Exterior provides the following budget categories and proposed expenditures:

	Percentages of national budget			
	1957	*1958*	*1959*	*1960*
Economic development (including communications and transport, agriculture, industry)	47.3	48.1	42.1	42.6
Social investments (educational, cultural, health, welfare)	23.9	24.1	27.4	30.5
Defense [a]	10.4	10.4	10.3	10.6
All other	18.4	17.4	20.2	16.3

[a] A substantial part of the defense budget appears to have been expended by the navy for a program of harbor improvements; this share, properly speaking, should also be credited to "economic development."

Source: *Comercio Exterior de México*, January 1958, pp. 3-4; January 1959, p. 4; January 1960, p. 3.

to state and municipal governments. The budget of the Federal District alone usually equals that of all the thirty-two states and territories and the 2,361 *municipios*. In the early 1950's the latter spent only 10 per cent of the total, the states and territories 40 per cent, and the Federal District the remaining 50 per cent.[29] The small amount of income available to the *municipios* is one of the greatest handicaps to the strengthening of local government.

Foreign Investment

In 1897, direct private U.S. investment in Mexico amounted to about $200 million, primarily in mining and railroads.[30] British investment was considerably higher. By 1908, after thirty years of the Díaz open-door policy, U.S. direct investment had risen to $417 million, of which 57 per cent was in mining, 14 per cent in railroads, 12 per

29 Diego G. López Rosado, "La experiencia mexicana en materia de la intervención estatal," in Instituto de Investigaciones Económicas, *La intervención del estado en la economía* (Mexico City: Author, 1955), pp. 37-54.

30 The discussion of foreign investment has been based on the following sources: two studies of the Cámara Nacional de la Industria de Transformación, *Las inversiones extranjeras directas en México* (Mexico City: Author, 1955) and *Estudio general sobre las inversiones extranjeras* (Mexico City: Author, 1955); the Banco de México's recent annual reports, *Asamblea general* . . . cited; *Economic Bulletin for Latin America* (UN), October 1958; Great Britain, Board of Trade, *Mexico*, Overseas Economic Surveys (London: HMSO, 1956); two studies by Cleona Lewis, *America's Stake in International Investments* (1938) and *The United States and Foreign Investment* (1948), both published by the Brookings Institution in Washington; Pan American Union, *Foreign Investments: Recent Developments and Proposals for an Inter-American Financial Institution* (Washington: Author, 1957); J. Fred Rippy's *British Investments in Latin America, 1922-1949* (Minneapolis: University of Minnesota Press, 1959) and *Globe and Hemisphere* (Chicago: Regnery, 1958); *Survey of Current Business* (U.S. Department of Commerce), September 1958; UN Economic Commission for Latin America, *External Disequilibrium in the Economic Development of Latin America: The Case of Mexico*, E/CN.12/428 (New York: Author, 1957), v. 1; and four surveys of the U.S. Department of Commerce, *Investment in Mexico* (Washington: GPO, 1955), *American Direct Investments in Foreign Countries, 1940* (Washington: GPO, 1942), *Balance of Payments* (Washington: GPO, 1958), *Factors Limiting U.S. Investment Abroad* (Washington: GPO, 1953), pt. 1.

cent in petroleum, 5.3 per cent in public services, 2.4 per cent in manufactures, and 1 per cent in commerce. In the years just before the First World War, the United States moved ahead of Britain as the main source of private investment funds in Mexico. Portfolio investment, an important part of it in government securities, also began to be significant in those years. Private American investments in Mexico reached their peak in 1924 when they totaled slightly more than $1 billion, of which $735 million was direct investment.[31] During the 1930's, depression, sales, and nationalization sharply curtailed foreign private investment. Direct U.S. investments fell to about $480 million by 1936 and $267 million by 1939. At that time, the United States accounted for some 60 per cent of foreign direct investment in Mexico, Canada for 25 per cent, Britain 7 per cent, and Sweden 5 per cent. As in the past, the largest part of the American investment was in mining, transportation, public utilities, and—before nationalization—oil.

The postwar years brought a marked increase in foreign investment in Mexico. Private direct investment rose from $582.5 million in 1945 to $1.1 billion in 1957. The American share in the latter year was nearly 80 per cent. More important than the increase in amount was the dramatic change in the pattern of American investment. From 1940 to 1957, of the total U.S. private investment, the proportion invested in manufacturing and trade rose from 4.9 per cent to 58.5 per cent. The share of U.S. investment in mining and smelting, petroleum, transportation, communications, and public utilities dropped from 88.4 per cent of the total to 42 per cent.[32] Expropriation of the petroleum industry had started this shift, but after World War II American investors lost no time in taking advantage of the rapid development of the internal Mexican market.

31 Cleona Lewis, *America's Stake in International Investments*, cited, p. 606. Mexican sources give a billion dollars for U.S. private investment as early as 1912. See *Las inversiones extranjeras directas en México*, cited, p. 16.

32 *Factors Limiting U.S. Investment Abroad*, cited, p. 36; *Survey of Current Business*, September 1958, p. 18.

Measured in current dollars, U.S. direct investments had in 1957 surpassed the peak of the 1920's by $50 to $100 million, but this amounted to only about 3 per cent of total U.S. private investment abroad in contrast to the 9 per cent of 1929. The relative importance of foreign investment for Mexico is reflected in the fact that it amounted to 11.3 per cent of the total new investment in 1957 and 7.7 per cent in 1958.[33]

Although in the early 1950's, direct foreign investment participated in some 1,500 companies spread throughout the country, the bulk of it is concentrated in large enterprises. A survey showed that in 1953, of 31 business enterprises in Mexico with a gross annual income of over 100 million pesos, 19 were United States-owned or controlled, 5 were Mexican government projects—some taken out of foreign hands, for example, Petróleos Mexicanos and Ferrocarriles Nacionales—and only 7 were private Mexican firms.[34] These seven included two insurance companies, an iron and steel firm, a copper refinery, a paper company, and two breweries. The owners of the breweries were a Spaniard and a Frenchman, both of them naturalized.

There is a higher degree of Mexican ownership and control in the smaller companies. In the early 1950's, of 43 enterprises with annual average gross earnings of 50 to 100 million pesos, only 22 were foreign-owned or controlled; and of 168 with 20 to 50 million pesos in annual earnings, only 70 were controlled by foreigners.[35]

The twenty-five largest foreign concerns in Mexico in the early 1950's were subsidiaries of large U.S. corporations.[36] They operate in highly strategic areas of the econ-

---

[33] Banco de México, cited (1959), p. 48. It was a higher proportion of total private investment.

[34] José Luis Ceceña Gámez, "Política en materia de inversione extranjera, pp. 81-103, in *La intervención del estado en la economía*, cited, p. 83.

[35] Same. See also *Las inversiones extranjeras directas* . . . , cited, pp. 24-43.

[36] Of the 50 largest foreign concerns in Mexico, 46 were affiliates of foreign corporations and only 4 were independent in Mexico. (Ceceña Gámez, cited, p. 86.)

omy: mining, iron and steel, chemical products, cotton, electricity, telephones, aviation, automobiles, tires and tubes, cigarettes, commerce and finance (especially savings banks, insurance companies, and loan associations), and food products.[37] American Smelting, Anderson Clayton, General Motors, Ford, Chrysler, B. F. Goodrich, Goodyear Tire and Rubber, Colgate-Palmolive, General Electric, E. I. Du Pont de Nemours, American Power, Sears Roebuck, and Woolworth are some of the major companies.

Estimates of the rate of earnings on foreign investments in Mexico have ranged from about 10 per cent to over 20 per cent.[38] However, an examination of data published by the U.S. Department of Commerce shows that over the six-year period, 1950 to 1955, average profits on the annual U.S. investment in Mexico of about $500 million amounted to about 10 per cent, of which 6 per cent was withdrawn and 4 per cent reinvested.[39] In 1956, when earnings rose to nearly 12 per cent, the rate of reinvestment shot up to over 7 per cent while withdrawals came to 4.8 per cent. In the following year earnings fell below 10 per cent, withdrawals rose to 5.2 per cent and reinvestment fell to 4.6 per cent.[40]

The predominant position of U.S. investments in Mexico creates one of the most sensitive and potentially explosive points in U.S.-Mexican relations. The Mexican Chamber of Manufacturing Industries asserted bluntly: "The economic power of these large foreign enterprises constitutes a serious threat to the integrity of the nation

[37] Three U.S. corporations controlled the production and refining of minerals, two produced most of the electricity, three predominated in auto assembly, and two controlled cigarette production; for details, see Ceceña Gámez, cited, pp. 90-91.

[38] A report on foreign investments of the United Nations gives 21.8 per cent as the average annual earning on private investment in Latin America as a whole for the year 1951. Seligman, cited, p. 106, estimated a 15 per cent rate of profit.

[39] This conclusion is based on data in *Direct Private Foreign Investments* (Washington: Author, 1953); also, *Survey of Current Business*, August 1956.

[40] *Survey of Current Business*, September 1958, p. 19.

and to the liberty of the country to plan its own economic development." [41] In the late 1940's, Sanford Mosk, commenting on the unusual investment pattern whereby an American corporation, Mexican private capital, and the Mexican government were co-investors in the Celanese Corporation in Mexico, wrote:

The inflow of American capital into Mexican manufacturing in recent years has fostered the belief that the nation is allowing itself to be kept in a semi-colonial economic status rather than freeing itself from the remaining ties which have kept it dependent upon the United States. . . .

Mexicans are beginning to wonder whether they are returning to the days of Porfirio Díaz when the foreigner was better treated by the Mexican government than the Mexican.[42]

Almost a decade later, an article in *Fortune* sounded a similar note:

At present, though the nationalists are capable of harassing U.S. investors in Mexico, there is no visible danger of anything so serious as further expropriations. Yet the altered political climate may pose serious long-run problems for U.S. investors.

"The nationalists represent the sub-conscious mind of Mexico," was the gloomy estimate of one well-informed businessman.

Give them an issue to work on—one good issue, with the *Gringos* cast as villains—and they could be running the government.[43]

Suspicion about large foreign enterprises unites diverse sectors of Mexican opinion: industrialists, small businessmen, middle-class intellectuals, and a variety of nationalists. The argument made by the economists who work for the Mexican Chamber of Manufacturing Industries and for the Bank of Mexico sums up the Mexican nationalist case:

41 *Las inversiones extranjeras directas* . . . , cited, p. 30.
42 Cited, p. 138.
43 Seligman, cited, p. 176.

(1) Foreign investments, especially those establishing subsidiaries of large U.S. corporations, attempt to obtain absolute control of the market and eliminate competition.

(2) In addition to displacing Mexican firms, foreign-controlled firms do not always employ Mexican raw materials or semielaborated products—thereby retarding the development of local industry and the local market.

(3) When foreign-owned or controlled companies produce raw materials or semimanufactured goods, they tend to exert a monopoly over the Mexican industries depending upon these products.

(4) A great deal of the wealth produced with the aid of foreign investment leaves Mexico. According to the report of the Bank of Mexico, the earnings on foreign investments from 1939 to 1955 amounted to $813.7 million. During the same period $790.9 million were sent out of Mexico in the form of profits, patent fees, interest, and royalties.[44] The Mexican critics, viewing earnings as potential capital, conclude that the outflow of this "capital" represents a decapitalization of the country and is therefore harmful to national interests.[45] This argument does not take into consideration the benefits accruing to Mexico from foreign investment in the effects upon the industrial potential, increased employment, the training of native technicians, greater efficiency in production, and general stimulus to economic development. The alternative to dependence upon foreign investment, many economists and businessmen point out, would be a long, slow process of building up Mexican industry with little capital at its disposal, with little managerial or technical personnel available, and with very little twentieth-century know-how. The exclusion of foreign capital would also result in heavier

---

[44] Banco de México, cited (1956), p. 82. It is difficult, perhaps impossible, to reconcile these figures with other estimates of profits, their repatriation, and reinvestments (see above, p. 306).

[45] See *Estudio general sobre las inversiones extranjeras,* cited; see also José Domingo Lavin, *Inversiones extranjeras* (Mexico City: Ibero-Americana de Publicaciones, 1954).

taxation being imposed on native capital in order to support even a reduced program of development.

(5) The Mexican critics of foreign investment maintain that they are not opposed to all foreign loans; rather, they argue, foreign investment should be subject to stricter legal controls and should be accepted only when invested in fields which benefit the nation and do not compete with or displace already operating Mexican business interests. They do not explain exactly what Mexican interests have been displaced or to what degree foreign firms do, in fact, enjoy monopolistic positions. These critics would prefer intergovernmental loans to direct private investment and maintain that they want no strings attached; that is, they would reject any conditions governing the expenditure of the loans.

Industrial Expansion; Transportation and Communication

From 1939 to 1957 Mexico's volume of industrial production increased 130 per cent.[46] Most of the increases resulted from the fuller use of equipment and the expansion of facilities in already established industries such as iron and steel, cement, chemicals, paper, sugar, and glass. However, many new industries were created during and after the 1940's—such as rayon and acetates, alkalis, plywood, fertilizer, electrical equipment, aluminum products, tin containers, and automobile assembly plants, to name a few.

The production increases of heavy industry are particularly significant and suggest that Mexico is on its way to becoming an industrial nation. By 1957 the volume of output in several major industries had increased enormously over 1945. Steel ingot production was over 1 million tons (an increase of nearly 500 per cent); crude petroleum production was 91 million barrels (109 per cent increase); electrical energy generation was 8.5 billion kilowatt hours

---

[46] Banco de México, cited (1956 and 1958).

(175 per cent); and cement output was 3 million tons (270 per cent). The output of the construction industry in 1957 was nearly seven times that of 1939. Rubber, paper, and alcohol industries also grew greatly. Food processing nearly tripled between 1938 and 1957, and only such older industries as textiles, clothing, and tobacco-processing showed increases of less than 100 per cent during this period.[47]

Mexicans are proud of the progress made by Petróleos Mexicanos (known as Pemex) because of its symbolic value to their efforts toward national economic independence. Oil production in 1957 was about twice what it had been in the late 1930's. Except for the shortage of refineries it would suffice to meet the growing internal demand. The production of petroleum derivatives has been rising and they have become important export items. During the twelve years in which Senator Bermúdez was its director, Pemex was generally regarded as being remarkably free from graft and typical government inefficiency. However, when a new management came in at the beginning of López Mateos' presidency, it publicized a series of unfavorable allegations about its predecessors and instituted several changes in policy. Along with the expansion of Pemex' production has gone an increase in the revenues it has turned over to the government. Wages and working conditions for the oil workers are far better than those of workers in most industries. The oil workers enjoy the special status of a labor aristocracy, and new jobs are restricted to the sons of oil workers.

Improvements in transportation and communication since 1940 have more than kept pace with the growth of industry. As indicated earlier, the increased proportion of government expenditures on communications and transport has been one of the major changes since Cárdenas.

From 1939 to 1959, Mexico increased its national highways from 9,929 kilometers to over 43,000 kilometers. In addition, many farm-to-market roads are being built

---

[47] *Comercio Exterior de México*, May 1959, p. 21.

throughout the country under the direction of an autonomous authority, the National Committee for Rural Communications. Various Indianist organizations, also, are directing the building of "roads of penetration" into isolated Indian areas as part of the program of incorporating the Indian within the nation.[48]

Highway transportation has grown in importance. It is estimated that well over 40 per cent of all freight carried in Mexico is now transported by truck. Registered trucks increased from about 42,000 in 1940 to about 240,000 in 1956. During the same period the number of buses increased from 10,141 to 21,000 and automobiles from 93,632 to 320,400. In the early 1950's the Federal District alone had about 38 per cent of all the automobiles, 36 per cent of the buses, and 13 per cent of the trucks.

Aviation facilities have been greatly expanded and improved. Mexico had 236 registered landing fields in 1956. Domestic and international airlines carried over 1.8 million passengers. The field and facilities at Mexico City are rated among the best in the world.

In 1956, Mexico had 391,360 telephones (compared to 206,517 in 1944) of which about one-half were in Mexico City. However, only 5,102 are listed as private phones. In order to meet the great demand, the Ministry of Communications and Public Works, by agreement with Teléfonos de México, undertook to establish 25,000 new telephones each year for five years.

There were 266 commercial radio stations in 1954 and three official government stations operated for cultural purposes. Daily telecasting services were introduced in Mexico in 1950. Commercial telecasting is carried on by private enterprise and is dominated by two wealthy families. In 1957, ten stations were in operation, five of them in the Federal District. At the end of 1956 there were an estimated 150,000 television sets in the country, the vast majority of them in or around Mexico City.

---

48 See Julio de la Fuente, "Carreteras de penetración," *Novedades,* February 19, 1956.

Agricultural Development

The advances in Mexican agriculture since 1940 seem even more impressive than those in industry, all the more so since terrain, climate, and weather put obstacles in the way of expanding production. Mexico is one of the most mountainous countries of the world. Its climate ranges from tropical to cool temperate. Nearly one-half of the total land area is intensely arid and another 15 per cent is extremely hot and humid. Even when rainfall and temperature are relatively favorable for farming, countless slopes of more than 25 degrees make it impossible to cultivate large areas. It has been estimated that Mexico has only half a hectare of land per capita under cultivation; by comparison, the United States has 4 hectares, Canada 2.2, and Argentina 1.7. According to the Mexican census of 1950, a little more than half the tillable land is planted, while nearly half is left fallow because of lack of rainfall. Of the area planted, about 15 per cent, on the average, results in crop failure, and about three-fourths of all crop failures are due to lack of rain.

In these circumstances, few would have predicted the rapid and far-reaching changes that have occurred in Mexican agriculture in the last twenty years. Agriculture has held its own in the expanding economy, contributing about one-fifth of the gross national product during the whole period (not counting subsistence agriculture). Between 1945 and 1957 agricultural production more than doubled while population grew by 40 per cent. While farming still occupies more Mexicans than all other pursuits put together—and two million more in 1957 than in 1940—agriculture maintained its share of the gross national product with a declining proportion of the labor force. The drop in numbers was particularly sharp during the war, as the figures in Table 3 show. Industry and construction, in contrast, have been absorbing a larger proportion of the labor force though their relative contribution to the gross national product has remained stable.

TABLE 3

Gainfully Employed Population

	1940		1946		1957	
	mil-lions	% of total	mil-lions	% of total	mil-lions	% of total
Agriculture, forestry, fishing	3.831	65.4	4.	59.2	5.878	57.8
Manufacturing, construction	0.64	10.9	0.8	11.8	1.459	14.3
Total employment	5.858		6.755		10.169	

Sources: 1940—International Labor Office, *Year Book of Labour Statistics, 1953* (Geneva: Author, 1953), p. 15;

1946—UN Economic Commission for Latin America, *Economic Survey of Latin America, 1949,* 1951.II.G.1 (New York: UN Department of Economic Affairs, 1951), p. 401;

1957—International Labor Office, *Year Book of Labour Statistics, 1958* (Geneva: Author, 1958), p. 29.

Mexico has gone a long way in the last twenty years toward changing from a predominantly subsistence economy in agriculture to a market economy. This has been accomplished by bringing new land under cultivation, by the expansion of irrigation, by the increasing use of fertilizer and improved seed varieties, by increased mechanization, and by the concentration of most of these improvements on larger holdings. In doing this, Mexico has practically bypassed the older subsistence areas of agriculture which continue to specialize in the production of corn and beans, using traditional primitive methods on small holdings. The contrast between the new and old agriculture is thus becoming sharper and in some measure parallels the contrast between the *mestizo* and the Indian, the north and the south.

This contrast is clearly seen when we compare the type of power used in agriculture. Whereas the number of tractors increased from 4,620 in 1940 to 22,711 in 1950 and

55,000 in 1955, about 34 per cent of all private holdings of five hectares or less were still being worked in 1950 by the ancient pre-Hispanic hoe culture (cutting and burning) and without benefit of plow and oxen.[49] Though cereals, chiefly corn, occupied nearly three-quarters of the tilled acreage, they accounted for less than one-third of the total value of agricultural production in 1953-1955. [50]

PRODUCTION, HARVESTED AREAS, AND YIELDS

The total volume of agricultural production rose by some 155 per cent between 1939 and 1954.[51] The Mexican Secretary of Economy classifies crops into four groups: industrial, food, fruit, and feeds. According to their figures, by far the greatest production increase was registered in industrial products (309 per cent), followed by food products (113 per cent), fruit (48 per cent), and feeds (49 per cent).

Most of the big increases in production occurred in export crops. Agricultural products have displaced oil and minerals as Mexico's leading export. These shipments, as the UN Economic Commission for Latin America has pointed out, "did much to speed up economic development, because they considerably increased Mexico's capacity to import." In this and other respects Mexico is one of

---

49 *Censo agrícola y ganadero* (Mexico City: Secretaría de Economía, 1950), p. 15.

50 UN Economic Commission for Latin America, *Economic Survey of Latin America, 1956,* 1957.II.G.1 (New York: UN Department of Economic and Social Affairs, 1957), pp. 179-181.

51 Annual fluctuations in output, due largely to the weather and differing from crop to crop, make comparisons between individual years somewhat risky. There are also differences in coverage and compilation of statistics which make comparison of sources difficult. The figures used in this section are drawn largely from official sources and illustrate major trends even though the choice of other years or other sources would somewhat alter the picture. For instance, the FAO estimates that in 1956-1957 Mexican agricultural output was 109 per cent above prewar and food production 91 per cent above prewar, while the Chase Manhattan Bank records a 150 per cent increase in agricultural production between 1935-1939 and 1956-1957. Comparing 1945 and 1957 the Economic Commission for Latin America gives a 103 per cent increase in agriculture, forestry, and fishing production.

the few Latin American countries in which agriculture
"has played the dynamic role expected of it." [52] From 1950
to 1957 coffee production increased 48 per cent and cotton
81 per cent. During the period 1952-1955 the value of the
cotton crop was higher than that of any other crop, although it occupied only 11 per cent of the total harvested
area. With the exception of wheat and beans, which increased by 132 per cent and 80 per cent respectively, between 1950 and 1957, the increase in food production has
been at a much slower pace than that of industrial crops.
Corn, the most important subsistence crop, occupying
nearly one-half the total harvested area, increased by only
44 per cent from 1950 to 1957. This expansion exceeded
the population increase but did not eliminate the need
for imports.

From 1940 to 1954, the harvested area increased by 69
per cent or 4,128,949 hectares. Here again, the greatest
percentage of increase was in land used for the production
of export crops. There were marked regional differences
in this expansion. The central states, the breadbasket of
the nation, accounted for about one-third of the increase,
but their share of the total harvested area fell from 48 to 42
per cent between 1940 and 1954. The next most important producer, the north, held its relative position at 22 per
cent. The biggest increase came in the north Pacific region
(from 8 to 13 per cent) while the Gulf states showed some
gain and the south Pacific states about an equivalent drop.

An examination of the relationship between the increase in the number of harvested hectares and the size and
types of holdings, as reported in the censuses of 1940 and
1950, reveals a definite trend toward larger holdings and
a decline in the relative importance of *ejidos*. Although
the increase in the total harvested area for the country was
1,934,774 hectares or 28 per cent, 48 per cent of this increase occurred in the larger private holdings, compared
to 20 per cent in small private holdings and 21 per cent in

---

[52] *Economic Survey of Latin America, 1957,* cited, p. 242.

ejidal or communal holdings. The increased importance of the larger landholders is also reflected in the rise from 39 to 43 per cent of all harvested land owned in holdings over 5 hectares. However, in both years the *ejidos* accounted for the largest share of the harvested area.

Compared with U.S. standards, yields of most crops are still low. Corn, much of it grown by traditional methods, yields less per acre in Mexico than anywhere else in Latin America, a region of low corn yields in comparison with the rest of the world. On irrigated land, and with the application of fertilizer and improved seed, yields can be doubled and quadrupled. Yields of cotton are relatively high because nearly all is irrigated and is produced by much more modern methods.[53] In fact, Mexican cotton yields in 1953-1955 were 20 per cent higher than those of the United States, and in all Latin America they were exceeded only by Peru.[54] Over the years, Mexican yields have risen for the most part, but at very uneven rates. From 1925 to 1956 the bean yield has increased by 59 per cent; corn by 20 per cent; cotton by 93 per cent; tomatoes by 9 per cent; tobacco by 106 per cent; wheat by 103 per cent; and rice by 13 per cent. In coffee, henequen, oranges, and bananas there has been a decline in yields.

SPREAD OF IRRIGATION

More than any other single factor, irrigation has been transforming Mexican agriculture. By it crop production has been increased and the development of a new type of intensive commercial agriculture, based on the use of farm machinery, fertilizers, and improved seed varieties, has been stimulated. It has also raised land values, increased income and purchasing power, and has been an important new source of wealth. Moreover, the irrigation projects pay for themselves within a relatively short time. Annual government revenues from the collection of taxes and the

---

[53] *Boletín Mensual de la Dirección de Economía Rural* (1947), pp. 740-741.

[54] *Economic Survey of Latin America, 1956*, cited, p. 182.

sale of water and electricity are estimated to equal nearly 12 per cent of the total cost of irrigation projects which therefore can be said to pay for themselves in 8.5 years.

From 1940 to 1955, 1,368,000 hectares of irrigated land were added to the crop area, making for a total of 3.1 million hectares under irrigation. This represents a 79 per cent increase over 1940. The irrigated portion of the harvested area rose from about 28 per cent in 1940 to 33 per cent in 1955. Moreover, well over 60 per cent of all new land brought under cultivation between 1950 and 1955 was irrigated land, mostly in the north and north Pacific regions.

The area under irrigation in the mid-1950's represented approximately 45 per cent of the maximum potential for irrigation according to official estimates. Studies by engineers of the Secretary of Hydraulic Resources suggest that 7.4 million additional hectares could be irrigated and another 2 million hectares could be brought under cultivation in the lowland coastal areas. In other words, Mexico might eventually count on a maximum tillable area of approximately 30 million hectares.[55]

In the mid-1950's nearly two-thirds of all irrigation facilities in the country consisted of large, federally constructed projects involving dam and storage facilities which could also be used for hydroelectric power. In addition, there were about 31,000 wells used for irrigation. About 60 per cent of the irrigated land was in cotton and wheat in 1955. Most of Mexico's cotton and about 80 per cent of its wheat are produced on irrigated land. Sugar cane, rice, alfalfa, vegetables, flax, and tobacco are also grown extensively in irrigated areas.

MECHANIZATION AND AGRICULTURAL CREDITS

In the last fifteen years considerable progress has been made in the mechanization of agriculture on large irri-

---

[55] See the excellent article by Jorge L. Tamayo, "Influencia de las condiciones fisiográficas de México en su desarrollo económico," *Investigación Económica*, 3d Quarter, 1955, pp. 363-377.

gated holdings. As noted earlier, the number of tractors increased from 4,620 in 1940 to 55,000 in 1955. In 1950 nearly three-quarters of the tractors were used in the north and the north Pacific area which provided roughly one-third of the agricultural output. In other regions tractors are also used, principally on sugar *haciendas*. Tractors are being concentrated increasingly on larger private holdings. While there was a considerable increase between 1940 and 1950 in the use of tractors on *ejidos,* the rate of increase was much higher on private holdings larger than five hectares. Small holdings, however, are worked with plow and oxen or by hand. Out of a million such holdings in 1950, not a one had a tractor.

Although the volume of agricultural credit has increased continuously since 1940, there seem to have been no major shifts in policy. Trends noted by Whetten in the early 1940's have continued. The north and north Pacific regions still receive the bulk of agricultural credit despite the fact that these areas contain a relatively small percentage of *ejidatarios* and private farmers.

In 1945 Whetten found that only 14 per cent of all *ejidatarios* received loans.[56] By 1954 the Ejido Bank had managed to extend its credit facilities to reach 25 to 30 per cent of all *ejidatarios.*[57] Nevertheless, a frankly business psychology seems to dominate the motif in agricultural credit policy. This contrasts sharply with the ideals of the Cárdenas regime which regarded the Ejido Bank as a device for facilitating social reforms. The current policy of the Ejido Bank was summed up by its director of research:

We lend to about one-third of all *ejidatarios,* those that have the richest and best lands. We prefer risks that have fertile soil and preferably irrigation. We do not have enough money

---

56 Cited, p. 195.

57 Banco Nacional de Crédito Ejidal (Mexico City), *Informe,* Ejercicio de 1954, pp. 30, 216.

for loans to subsistence farmers most of whom have the poorest lands.[58]

In 1955, 3,219 million pesos were invested in agricultural loans throughout the country. Sixty-nine per cent of this money went to private farmers and 31 per cent to the *ejidatarios*. Thirty-five per cent of the total was loaned by national banks, including the Ejido Bank and the Agricultural Bank; 32 per cent by private banks; and 33 per cent by private lenders.[59] Approximately 90 per cent of the agricultural loans made by the Ejido Bank and the Agricultural Bank were invested in five crops: three major export crops—cotton, coffee, and rice—and two major domestic crops—corn and wheat. About 50 per cent of all loans were for cotton alone and another 20 per cent for corn and beans. In the past few years a great investment has been made in wheat with the result that Mexico has achieved self-sufficiency in this crop.

On the whole, the Agricultural Bank makes loans to larger landowners whereas the Ejido Bank makes loans to *ejidatarios,* who are by definition small landowners. The great mass of the small peasant landholders—those with private holdings of less than five hectares (1,004,835 in 1950) [60] and about 75 per cent (roughly 1,030,330) [61] of the *ejidatarios* are simply not reached by existing government credit facilities and continue to be victims of local money lenders.

Exports and Imports

From just before World War II up to 1957, the volume of Mexico's exports increased 143 per cent while the volume of imports increased 265 per cent. From 1925 to 1944

---

[58] Ramón Fernández y Fernández of the Ejido Bank, Mexico City; personal communication.

[59] Ramón Fernández y Fernández, "México y su crédito agrícola," Banco Nacional de Crédito Ejidal, *Boletin de Estudios Especiales*, v. 6 (July 1956), p. 78.

[60] *Censo agrícola y ganadero,* cited, p. 5.

[61] *Tercer censo ejidal* (Mexico City: Secretaría de Economía, 1950), p. 5.

Mexico had a favorable balance of merchandise trade; since 1944 the value of imports has consistently exceeded that of exports. The deficit has been made up by large receipts from tourist trade, remittances from *braceros,* and foreign loans and investments.

Important changes have occurred in the structure of exports and imports. Although Mexico is still an exporter of raw materials, which accounted for two-thirds of all exports in 1957, there has been a sharp shift from the export of minerals to that of agricultural products. Before the war agricultural exports were only one-third of the total; in the 1950's they were more than one-half.[62] By contrast, minerals, metals, and petroleum products now account for about one-fifth of all exports. This change from the export of nonrenewable to renewable materials is hailed by Mexicans as a step forward in the transformation of a colonial economy.

Approximately one-half of agricultural exports are food products (coffee, fish, meat, vegetables, peanuts, etc.). Cotton, the leading export, accounted in the mid-1950's for one-fourth of the total value of all merchandise exports, and coffee is second with nearly 15 per cent. About three-fourths of the cotton and, in good years, even more of the coffee produced are shipped abroad. Mexico is the world's second largest exporter of cotton and the fourth largest exporter of coffee.

The composition of Mexico's imports shows a relative decline in imports of agricultural products, from 10.3 per cent in 1937-1941 to 7.3 per cent in 1952-1956. In volume, however, these imports have more than doubled; even on a per capita basis, imports of agricultural products were 40 per cent higher in 1952-1956 than before the war. The imports are chiefly foodstuffs since the greatest gains in the expansion of Mexican agricultural output have been in crops for export, not in foods for domestic consumption. The major exception is wheat, which was traditionally

---

62 *Economic Survey of Latin America, 1957,* cited, p. 288.

one of the large import items; in 1956 and 1957 domestic production was sufficient for the country's requirements. However, two staple foods in the Mexican diet, corn and beans, must be imported in years of extensive crop failures. For example, foreign shipments of these foods amounted to 1 per cent of total Mexican imports in 1956; in 1957 and 1958 they were nearly 5 per cent. Other significant food imports are livestock and poultry products and vegetable oils. Although largely self-sufficient in agricultural commodities, Mexico continues to rely on imports in years of poor harvests.

As might be expected from what has been said of the growth of the Mexican economy, imports of capital goods have grown significantly. In 1937-1940 they averaged 31.5 per cent of Mexico's imports; in 1954-1957, 42.6 per cent.[63] They are the most important broad category of Mexican imports. "Raw and semi-processed materials are next (nearly 30 per cent), and consumption goods of all kinds, including food, are in third place (18 per cent). These figures emphasize the relatively small proportion that consists of finished manufactures for consumption." [64]

Income Distribution

Even a brief review of Mexico's recent great increases in production and national wealth makes it clear that, as a nation, the Mexican people have made remarkable progress since 1940. But what has been its impact upon the various sectors of the society? How has this increasing wealth been divided? Can it be said that most Mexicans are living better today than they did fifteen years ago?

Most available data indicate that the distribution has

---

[63] UN Economic Commission for Latin America, *Economic Survey of Latin America, 1949*, 1951.II.G.1 (New York: UN Department of Economic Affairs, 1951), p. 413; . . . *1957*, cited, p. 214. The highest figure in the first group of years was 36.7 per cent in 1937 and in the latter 46.1 per cent in 1956. Other sources give figures ranging from 34 to 48 per cent for 1957, because of differences in definition.

[64] *Investment in Mexico*, cited, p. 102.

been extremely uneven and has been weighted heavily in favor of the owners of capital and generally of the upper-income groups. A report of the U.S. Department of Commerce states:

There appears to have been a considerable increase in the real per capita income since 1939. However, most of the increase was in the form of commercial and industrial profits, and large sectors of the population apparently derived little if any benefit from the enlarged national product.[65]

In his annual report to the nation in September 1956, President Ruiz Cortines said:

Yes, we have made progress; but the progress obtained by the country as a whole enables us to see with greater clarity those who have still not benefited by this progress, or at least have not benefited as much as we fervently hoped for . . . I think, with much emotion, of the great masses who are still suffering ignorance, illness and poverty. . . . So long as these great masses do not progress at the same pace as the rest of the country, we will have to say to those who are satisfied with the present situation, "We have done very little indeed, the essential promise has yet to be fulfilled."

From 1939 to 1950 the share of the national income going to profits rose from 26.2 per cent to 41.4 per cent, while that of wages and salaries dropped from 30.5 per cent to 23.8 per cent.[66] The Economic Commission for Latin America [67] found that, "Whereas wages, salaries and incomes of the small entrepreneurs increased at an annual rate of 4.4 per cent between 1939 and 1952, profits, inter-

---

[65] *Investment in Mexico,* cited, p. 10. The uneven distribution of income is especially marked in some fields. "No less than 80 per cent of income payments from commerce go to capital and only 16 per cent to labor." (Adolf Sturmthal, "Economic Development, Income Distribution, and Capital Formation in Mexico," *Journal of Political Economy,* June 1955, p. 189.)

[66] International Bank for Reconstruction and Development, *The Economic Development of Mexico: Report of the Combined Mexican Working Party* (Baltimore: Johns Hopkins Press, 1953), p. 178.

[67] *Economic Survey of Latin America, 1951-52,* 1953.II.G.3 (New York: UN Department of Economic Affairs, 1954), p. 86.

ests, and rent rose 10.1 per cent." One Mexican economist, Manuel Germán Parra, finds a greater inequality in 1955 than in 1940 in the distribution of the national income and urges the social and economic necessity of bringing about a more equitable pattern, closer to that which prevails in the United States and Britain. He comments ironically that after forty-five years of struggle by the Mexican Revolution for social justice, the distribution of income in Mexico is so lopsided as to make the most conservative British or U.S. capitalist blush.[68]

The more or less chronic inflation which has been going on in Mexico since 1940 has squeezed the real income of the poor. During the latter years of the Cárdenas administration, prices rose at an average annual rate of 6 per cent; under Camacho, at 22 per cent; under Alemán, at 12 per cent; and under Ruiz Cortines at 7.3 per cent. Studies of real wages in agriculture, industry, and government employment show decreases of 27 to 46 per cent over the period 1939-1950.[69] Between 1952 and 1958 minimum wage levels were raised about 30 per cent, but the level of real wages in the country as a whole was still below that of 1939. Index figures published by the Mexican Secretaría de Economía showed that the cost of living for workers in Mexico City was nearly seven times greater in 1958 than in 1939.[70] Of course, in a country where so large a portion of the working population lives on the land, wage rates cannot be relied on as the sole measure of the welfare of the poorer classes. Difficult as it is to measure the real changes over a long period, the evidence about the poverty of most Mexicans is very clear.

In the 1950 census figures, incomes for 4.5 million families were classified by source, wages and salaries or other

[68] "Un programa reaccionario para la Revolución Mexicana," *Siempre,* October 3, 1956, p. 16.

[69] Diego G. López Rosado and Juan F. Noyola Vásquez, "Los salarios reales en México, 1939-1950," *El Trimestre Económico,* April-June 1951, p. 206.

[70] *Memoria de la secretaría de economía* (Mexico City: Author, 1956), p. 221.

income (rent, dividends, etc.). Of these families, 89 per cent received less than 600 pesos a month ($70 at the 1950 rate of exchange), and 71 per cent received less than 300 pesos a month ($35). Only 4 per cent of the families had monthly incomes of 1,000 pesos ($115) or more (see Table 4). The 1950 census also reported that 605,013 families had "mixed incomes." Although this group represented only 12 per cent of the total number of families, its income from several sources amounted to nearly 20 per cent of total family incomes.

TABLE 4

Monthly Income by Families or Persons Living Alone, Mexico, 1950

Monthly Income (pesos)	Number of Families	Per Cent of Families
1-149	1,510,613	33.6
150-299	1,677,471	37.3
300-599	824,649	18.3
600-999	309,785	6.9
1,000-2,999	156,832	3.5
3,000 or more	20,424	0.4
Total	4,499,774	100.0

Note: This table excludes 605,013 families whose incomes were not broken down in census statistics. Their total income in 1950 was 374.8 million pesos per month and that of the 4.5 million families shown here was 1,594.9 million pesos.

Source: Mexico, Dirección General de Estadística, *Séptimo censo general de población,* 6 de junio de 1950, *Parte Especial* (Mexico City: Author, 1955), p. 68.

The 1950 census data on the distribution of income among workers and employers for the various sectors of the economy further underlines the poverty of most Mexicans. Approximately 63 per cent of all workers earned less than 200 pesos a month; of these, 50 per cent were in agriculture, 18 per cent in industry, and 30 per cent in commerce. Approximately 80 per cent of the employees and employers reported an annual income of less than 4,000 pesos. This suggests that the category *patrón,* or employer, included many small-scale operators in addition to *ejidatarios,* small landholders, vendors of all kinds, and as well all those self-employed. About three-fourths of the 3 per cent of the nation's workers who earn 9,600 pesos a year are occupied in industry, commerce, and services, as opposed to only 3 per cent of these high earners employed in agriculture. However, 1,773 or one-fourth of all employer incomes of 50,000 to 250,000 pesos and over were derived from agriculture.

In a recently published study by the Mexican economist, Ifigenia M. de Navarrete, we learn that, in 1957, 2,665,000 families (46 per cent) had a monthly income of less than 500 pesos and received 14 per cent of the total income. By contrast, 286,686 families (5 per cent) had a monthly income of over 3,000 pesos and received 37 per cent of the total national income.

Between 1950 and 1957 family income in the nation as a whole rose by 23 per cent. However, the distribution of this increase was uneven. The alarming fact is that the 20 per cent of the families at the lower end of the income scale showed both a relative and an absolute decrease in

TABLE 5

Total Families and Total Income
(in per cent)

Economic class	Mexico				United States				England	
	1950		*1957*		*1935*		*1952*		*1952*	
	F	I	F	I	F	I	F	I	F	I
Lower class	70	31	65	25	47	18	40	15	40	17
Middle class	18	17	19	18	35	33	40	39	40	39
Well-to-do	7	12	11	20	11	18	10	15	10	14
Wealthy	5	40	5	37	7	31	10	31	10	30

Note: F = Families; I = Income.

Source: Ifigenia M. de Navarrete, *La distribución del ingreso y el desarrollo económico de México* (Mexico City: Instituto de Investigaciones Económicas, Escuela Nacional de Economía, 1960), p. 88.

income, whereas the families which occupied the seventh, eighth, ninth, and tenth places in the scale, i.e., the upper 40 per cent, showed by far the greatest income gains. The essential data are shown in Table 5.

In commenting upon the increasing inequality of income distribution in Mexico and the suffering caused by inflation, a *Fortune* study noted:

Indeed, it might correctly be said that the true hero of the Mexican investment boom is the ordinary Mexican worker, whose acceptance of a declining real income has in effect "subsidized" much of the nation's building.

It is a token of Mexico's political stability that this program of chronic inflation has been accompanied by no political disorders or even by any noticeable diminution in the popularity of the party in power. The Party of Revolutionary Institutions, which elected Ruiz Cortines in 1952, appears to remain the overwhelming favorite of Mexican voters. In a nation with a long and violent history of religious warfare, the P.R.I. gets the votes of both Catholics and anti-clericals. It is supported by labor and by large numbers of businessmen too; and above all it is supported by the *campesinos,* the Mexican peasant.[71]

Levels of Living

The great majority of Mexicans are still living on what Cline has called the "impoverished level" or the "survival level and below." [72] Whetten, writing in 1950, summarized the situation in these words:

. . . the vast majority of the Mexican people . . . live near the subsistence level, have received little or no education, are confronted with lack of sanitation, ill health, a high death rate and general poverty.[73]

71 Seligman, cited, p. 173.

72 Howard F. Cline, *The United States and Mexico* (Cambridge: Harvard University Press, 1953).

73 Nathan L. Whetten, "The Rise of the Middle Class in Mexico," *La clase media en Bolivia, Brasil, Chile y Paraguay,* v. 2 of Theo R. Crevenna, ed., *Materiales para el estudio de la clase media en la América latina* (Washington: Pan American Union, 1950; 6 v.).

Later a young Mexican industrialist noted:

Since 1945 our economy has improved by 50 per cent but not-withstanding . . . 50 per cent of all Mexicans have a level of living equal to or inferior to what they had 50 years ago.[74]

In the course of my village and urban studies I have found many peasants, once Zapatistas, who are embittered by the high cost of living and now look back with nostalgia to the "good old Díaz days" when living was cheap. As one villager put it, "Yes, we have freedom now, but we can't eat it. There are villagers here who are suffering hunger." I have found similar attitudes expressed among the very poor in the city slums.

There is also evidence, however, of a considerable improvement in some aspects of the levels of living of the population taken as a whole. To some degree the increased national wealth has seeped down to the lower classes in both city and country. According to the population censuses of 1940 and 1950, we find an increase in the number of the population wearing shoes, from 9.7 to 13.5 million; an increase in the number wearing *huaraches,* from 4.6 to 6.6 million; and a decrease in the number going barefoot from 5.2 to 4.7 million. The proportion of the total population eating wheat bread rose by 7.8 per cent. These figures reflect important changes in rural areas. They tell us relatively little, however, about changes in living conditions in the cities, where items like bread and shoes have long been customary.

In my own study of several *vecindades,* or settlements, in a poor section of Mexico City made in 1956, I have found clear evidence of a rise in the standard of living, most of which had taken place in the last five years. Many modern conveniences have found their way into the already crowded one-room homes, sometimes forcing the residents to build little balconies or *tapancos* for sleeping space, which they reach by ladder. Most of the new items are

---

[74] Alfonso Noriega, *Mexico debe bastarse a si mismo* (Mexico City: Confederación de Cámaras Industriales, 1956).

bought on the installment plan and more than half of the families are deeply in debt. One-third of all the families with television sets in one *vecindad* were from two to three months in arrears on the rent.

In a sample of 70 out of 157 households in one poor *vecindad,* I found 56 radios, 39 gas stoves, 33 sewing machines, 44 wristwatches, 35 families who used knives and forks (spoons are common, but most eating is done with the tortilla and the hands), 26 who used aluminum pans as well as clay pots, 16 blenders (informants referred to the traditional stone mortar and pestle as the Mexican blender), 15 television sets, 7 washing machines, and 4 cars. Radios have, in fact, become so common as no longer to serve as an indicator of income level. Gas stoves, TV sets, and the use of *cubiertos* or silverware in eating are now the most useful indices.

The one aspect of living standards that has improved very little, if any, is housing. On the contrary, under the pressure of the rapidly rising population and growing urbanization, crowding and slum conditions in the large cities, especially Mexico City, are getting worse day by day. Of the 5.2 million dwellings in Mexico in 1950, 60.2 per cent had only one room and 24.1 per cent had two rooms.[75] In the same year, 70 per cent of all houses were made of adobe, wood, poles and rods, or rubble; only 18.4 per cent were of brick and masonry. Only 17 per cent of the homes had individual piped water; only 26 per cent even shared a piped-water supply with other families. The remaining 57 per cent used wells, cisterns, or tanks—or had no water supply. Conditions in Mexico City were little different. In 1950, 46 per cent of the 626,262 dwellings had only one room and 23 per cent had two rooms. Only 45 per cent had private piped-water supplies, and 47 per cent shared water supplies with other families, probably in the form of a communal tap.[76]

---

[75] *Compendio estadístico, 1954,* p. 104.
[76] Same, p. 114.

Between 1940 and 1952 the population of Mexico City increased by 92 per cent while the area of the city grew by only 38 per cent. Meanwhile, between 1947 and 1952, its slum areas had increased from 3.8 to 12.7 per cent of the total city area. It is estimated that from 1940 to 1954 there was an increase of 296,000 families in Mexico City; during this period 176,596 houses were constructed, leaving a deficit of 119,404 houses.[77] The same situation is true of the country as a whole: to meet housing needs, it is estimated that 150,000 houses a year would have to be built for many years to come.

The building boom in Mexico since 1940 has benefited principally the middle and upper classes. Most building has been of elegant, private homes, apart from a dozen or so large modern apartment buildings constructed for government workers in the past ten years.

Education

Facilities for education and the number of children attending school have increased steadily in Mexico since 1940. The number of primary schools increased by 17 per cent between 1940 and 1954, and the number of children registered by 76 per cent.[78] In 1953 there were over 500 secondary schools counted (a growth of 82 per cent since 1946), most of them in urban centers. Between 1946 and 1955, the number of kindergartens also increased by almost 100 per cent. A larger proportion of urban children than rural go to school, and the urban advantage is steadily increasing. For example, in 1955 the Federal District reported that 80.3 per cent of its children were registered in schools; in the same year the Federal District alone had about one-third of the nation's primary-school children

---

77 Ramón Ramírez Gómez, "El problema de la habitación y los niveles de vida," in Escuela Nacional de Economía, *Niveles de vida y desarrollo Económico* (Mexico City: Universidad Nacional Autónoma de México, 1953), p. 225.

78 Exclusive of kindergarten enrollment. UNESCO, *World Survey of Education*, v. 2: *Primary Education* (Paris: Author, 1958), p. 714.

and teachers. For the country as a whole, the estimated proportion of children between five and fourteen attending primary school rose from 40 per cent in 1940-1944 to 47 per cent in 1950-1954.[79]

Technical schools, under the jurisdiction of the Instituto Politécnico Nacional, have more than doubled in number and enrollments since 1940. In 1954 there were 46 such schools with 21,218 students; the number of students had jumped to 26,800 in 1956. By contrast, agricultural schools declined in number, from 17 in 1940 to 12 in 1954, and registration remained about the same. The Mexican National University grew 19 per cent from 1951 to 1954, attaining a registration of 32,813 in the latter year. Professional degrees awarded in federal and state colleges and universities throughout the country increased by 134 per cent between 1950 and 1954, reaching a high of 13,658 in 1954.

Within the educational system standards for the teaching profession have become more rigorous—more teachers are receiving degrees from normal schools. To meet the problem of upgrading undertrained teachers, a Teacher Training Institute was established in Mexico City in 1954; by 1956, 5,414 teachers were taking in-service training. The U.S. government program has also helped by awarding grants to Mexicans for study in the United States; a total of 237 grants was made between 1949 and 1955.[80]

---

[79] Same. The Mexican Secretaría de Educación reports that the proportion of children six to fourteen years old attending school rose from 41 per cent in 1940 to 56 per cent in 1954. (*Educación*, October 1958, p. 80.)

[80] I talked with the cultural attaché and staff at the U.S. embassy and, on the basis of their data, it seems the educational exchange program of the United States has not appreciably expanded since 1955. On the contrary, it seems not to have expanded at all. In view of the need for this program, I consider this state of affairs lamentable. In 1960 the total budget for the exchange program was $210,000, of which only $137,000 was available for Mexicans (professors and students, etc.) to visit the United States. From 1956 to 1960 there were only 179 grants. Some of these were for student groups of as many as 30 students. I might add that the exchange programs have been growing on a university-to-university basis. The University of Texas has an exchange with the Technological Institute of Monterrey, and Montana State College has a special program for training

Although the advances in education have been substantial, many serious problems remain. Rising costs have meant that the fivefold increase in the federal budget for education between 1941-1953 made a much smaller real contribution to educational resources. The rise in the cost of education, combined with the rapid rise in population, makes it very difficult for Mexico to solve its educational problem. In 1956, 42 per cent of Mexican children of school age were still not going to school. In 1953, only 8 per cent of the children between ages five and six were attending kindergarten. In 1954, 81.7 per cent of the rural schools taught only through the third grade or less, and a mere 5.1 per cent of the children of primary-school age reached the sixth grade. Secondary-school education is still a luxury; in 1953, only 3.9 per cent of the youth between the ages of fifteen and twenty-four attended secondary, vocational, or normal schools. The proportion attending colleges and universities was far smaller. Over 40 per cent of the Mexican population was still illiterate in the mid-1950's.[81]

Despite these handicaps the many-pronged attack on backwardness and illiteracy in Mexico is admirable and must be greatly expanded. The lack of well-trained personnel, particularly in rural areas where the conditions of life are often difficult, seriously impedes progress. Work is further handicapped by inadequate budgets, a continually expanding population, and resistance to attending schools due to the pressure of poverty and other cultural factors. The greatest progress in education has been made among urbanized groups, especially the middle class. The rate of expansion of post-primary schools and in the field

---

in industry. The University of Chicago and Harvard have research programs going on in Chiapas in cooperation with the National Indian Institute. Antioch College has set up a branch at Guanajuato. This is just an example of the growing interaction between the two countries on the intellectual plane.

[81] The illiteracy rate for people six years old and over fell from 66.6 per cent in 1930 to 58 per cent in 1940 and 43.2 per cent in 1950. UNESCO, *World Illiteracy at Mid-Century* (Paris: Author, 1957), p. 95.

of higher education has been much more rapid than that of primary schools.

Perhaps more significant than the quantitative changes have been the shifts in the conception of the role of the school in society and the attitudes of teachers toward their work. The earlier revolutionary concept of the school as a major instrument of cultural change and social reform seems to have given way to a more prosaic emphasis on the three R's with little reference to integrating the content of education with local community needs. Except for a few Indianists, who still show some glimmer of the old dedication, the passionate idealism and desire for service of the 1930's also seem to have died out. Today, most teachers and administrators seem to be primarily concerned with improving their own working conditions and prospects.

Religion

Since 1940, the Catholic Church has regained much of the influence it had lost in the Revolution. The constitution of 1917, which severely restricted the educational, political, and economic activities of the church and the clergy, apparently has not been seriously enforced by the Camacho or succeeding administrations. In 1941, Camacho became the first president since the Revolution to declare publicly that he was "a believer." His precedent was followed by President Alemán. President Ruiz Cortines declared only that "I am respectful," but relations between government and church continue to be amicable.

The recovery of its influence by the church has continued apace. In an interview given to *Time* magazine (May 9, 1955) the late Archbishop Martínez could say: "The only thing that now remains is to change the constitution. Today the church's schools which until recently had to develop their activities secretly, function openly [although they still carry the names of Mexican patriots instead of saints]. There are thirty-four seminaries preparing about 2,000 young priests. In Mexico City alone, about twenty churches have been built in the past year, with twenty-three more under construction. Never have we seen such afflux to the temples. . . ."

The number of priests has multiplied significantly, although the proportion of growth is still far below that of other Catholic countries. In 1955, there was one priest for each 6,450 inhabitants.[82] In 1935, there were "less than 500 ecclesiastics in the country and in half the states they did not permit any priest to officiate. . . ."[83] The Eleventh National Assembly of the Mexican Catholic Action, held on August 2, 1955, reported that there were 5,777 catechism centers in Mexico, imparting religious instruction to 250,000 children and 32,516 adults.[84]

The church has greatly increased its organizational activity. Since the early 1950's there has been a noticeable increase in the number of congresses and conferences of prelates, public ceremonials, dedications, parades, and pilgrimages. The church has also carried on an intense program of the glorification of the Virgin Mary and of the Virgin of Guadalupe, both highly effective symbols. Organized groups of the faithful from trade-unions, shops, housing settlements, villages, and towns make regular pilgrimages to the shrine of the Virgin of Guadalupe, in Mexico City, on a scale greater than at any time since the days of Díaz. At the five hundredth anniversary of the coronation of the Virgin of Guadalupe, the church initiated a series of celebrations which brought worshipers and high clergy to the Basilica of Guadalupe from all over the hemisphere. The Pope sent a special representative and a message, in which he designated the Virgin Mary as the Universal Patron Saint of Latin America.

Once again the church has made some attempt to emerge as a political force in the country. In the election

---

82 La Iglesia en América Latina: Problemas de Latinoamérica, no. 2, 1956, p. 42.

83 Stephen S. Goodspeed, "El papel del jefe del ejecutivo en México," Problemas Agrícolas e Industriales de México, January-March 1955.

84 Excelsior, August 28, 1955.

of deputies on July 3, 1955, two Catholic leaders, one the president of Juventud Católica, the other the president of Acción Católica and Pax Romana, ran for office. An ex-president of the Asociación Católica de la Juventud Mexicana was a member of the Cámara de Diputados in 1955.[85] In the election of 1955, the combined vote of the religious *partidos confesionales* (Partido de Acción Nacional) accounted for 32.7 per cent of the total in the Federal District, compared with 16.2 per cent in 1946.[86]

The Changing Social Structure

The class structure of contemporary Mexico is still in a process of steady change, and although the basic patterns are evident, clear-cut lines cannot always be drawn. The problem of describing the changes is complicated by the lack of careful social, economic, and psychological studies of each of the major social groupings and of the criteria that mark one off from the other. We know most about some sectors of the rural population, thanks to community studies made by anthropologists. However, we know relatively little about the non-Indian rural areas and even less about the large rural proletariat. Our knowledge of the urban class structure is superficial, at best, and much work needs to be done, particularly to trace the rapid pace of urbanization and industrialization.

To understand Mexican social structure we must take into account rural-urban differences, class divisions and subdivisions, and also Indian, transitional, and modern culture types.

The present social structure is more complex than that of prerevolutionary days, when class lines were more sharply drawn. The upper class today consists of the remnants of the old, aristocratic families and of a new class of bankers, industrialists, and big businessmen who managed to rise up out of the middle and lower classes during

---

85 *Últimas Noticias,* September 3, 1955.
86 *La Iglesia* . . . , cited, pp. 55-56.

the turbulent postrevolutionary days. Many of them got their start because of connections with the revolutionary leaders, who then became high officials in the government and army. The new upper class is essentially a nonaristocratic group, interested in fostering social change and economic growth. Individual annual incomes here range from 50,000 to 250,000 pesos and over, but the class makes up less than one per cent of the population. The majority reside in cities and live in a manner similar to that of wealthy people elsewhere in the Western world.

Of this entrepreneurial group, Maddox writes:

Few of its members had inherited the traditional, status-burdened concepts of the old landholding group, in which change either in technological processes of production or in economic and social relationships was suspect and something to be handled with care and "proper" guidance. As a result, risk-taking entrepreneurship received an important "shot-in-the-arm" from the change in political power.[87]

The growth of the middle class over the last fifteen years is one of the important developments. This process had, it is true, received its first impetus under Díaz, when foreign companies invested in mines, railroads, and oil, and encouraged the training of technicians, managers, clerical workers, scientists, and professionals. It was this group that led the Revolution, gave it its ideology, and carried out much of the constructive work in the postrevolutionary period.

Between 1895 and 1940, the middle class as a whole grew from 7.8 to 15.9 per cent of the total population and increased in numbers from less than one million to over three million, or by 215 per cent. Although the upper and lower classes both declined in rural areas, the middle class increased there by no less than 125.9 per cent. The urban middle class likewise increased by almost 100 per cent.[88] Since 1940, the middle class has grown even more rapidly

---

87 Cited, p. 31.
88 Iturriaga, cited, p. 28.

as a by-product of industrialization and urbanization and now probably constitutes about 20 per cent of the total population.

This new middle class is varied in membership and difficult to define. Lines between the middle class, on the one hand, and the upper and lower classes on the other, are tenuous, and recruits enter the middle class from above and below. Most observers include in it government workers, teachers, small businessmen, storekeepers, skilled laborers, small industrialists, intellectuals and professionals, and, in addition, small landowners and *ejidatarios*. There is a wide range in the income and standard of living; families in this group may earn between 5,000 and 50,000 pesos a year. They live in houses ranging from the mansions of the Lomas de Chapúltepec to the slum dwellings of small merchants. Cline has described the middle class as "mainly . . . defined by its economic dependence on personal work which requires education, technical training, or administrative abilities—equipment the individual has developed for himself." [89]

Iturriaga divides the middle class into two major groups: the autonomous or self-employed and the dependent or salaried workers. Table 6 shows the changes in these groups in both the rural and urban middle class from 1895 to 1940:

Table 6

Changes in the Middle Class, 1895-1940

	1895		1940	
Group	Per Cent Rural	Per Cent Urban	Per Cent Rural	Per Cent Urban
Autonomous	91.03	60.93	50.82	30.09
Dependent	8.97	39.07	49.18	69.91

Source: José E. Iturriaga, *La estructura social y cultural de México* (Mexico City: Fondo de Cultura Económica, 1951), p. 70.

[89] Cited, p. 84.

There has been, as we can see, a notable increase in the number of salaried workers in both rural and urban areas. The breaking up of the *haciendas* with their few administrators into smaller holdings with more employees, the development of municipal governments, and the growth of large cotton and sugar mills account for the increase of salaried employees in rural areas. In the cities, the growth of governmental activities and of business and industry is responsible for the increase of salaried workers. Many marginal businesses, industries, and shops have been squeezed out by firms with larger capital and modernized techniques. In effect, the middle class has changed from being primarily autonomous to being largely dependent on salaried employment.

Some intellectuals and bureaucrats tend to eulogize the middle class, seeing in it the hope and future of Mexico. Thus, Lucio Mendieta y Núñez writes that the middle class places great value upon education, science, and culture, has a high ethical and religious sense, derives moral satisfaction from work, has a stable economic base, and is conservative and progressive at the same time:

Taken as a whole, the Mexican middle class has moral habits. The success of businesses selling articles, furniture, and automobiles on the installment plan is a clear demonstration that the middle class fulfills its contracts, guided by a high sense of social responsibility. The large number of marriages, the low number of divorces, the increase of life insurance, the private primary and preparatory schools, the enormous number of students in the universities and polytechnic institutes, are additional signs that Mexico's middle class is undoubtedly concerned with the stability of the family and the well-being and future of its children.[90]

Also, he writes, "The middle class in Mexico seems to be in addition the possessor and conserver of all the national

---

[90] "La clase media en México," *Revista Mexicana de Sociología*, nos. 2-3, 1955, p. 529.

qualities; it must therefore be consolidated and strengthened. . . ." [91]

The "popular class" or the lower class, like its counterparts all over the world, has the lowest incomes and the lowest standard of living, performs the most laborious manual work, and has the highest death rate. In Mexico, this is accompanied by the highest incidence of illiteracy and scanty educational opportunities. Some significant changes, however, have occurred in its situation over the past half-century. The proportion of the lower class in the total population declined from 90.8 per cent in 1895 to 83.08 per cent in 1940. In 1895, the lower class was preponderantly rural; only 14.2 per cent lived in the cities. In 1940, 22.4 per cent were urban. Before the Revolution, the vast majority (80.7 per cent) of the lower class were landless agricultural workers; after the *ejidos* were established, the number of *peones* decreased approximately 17 per cent and a new class of *ejidatarios,* many of whom can be classified as middle class, formed 26.4 per cent of the total population. During this period the number of small landowners, rural artisans, small traders, and people engaged in other occupations in rural areas also decreased by about 10 per cent.[92]

In the cities the number of workers, industrial and other, has increased markedly, whereas lower-class artisans and traders have decreased. In 1895, workers constituted only 20.3 per cent of the lower class; in 1940, 61.3 per cent.[93] The industrial workers in urban centers are more class-conscious than other sectors of the lower class, especially rural workers. Despite this class feeling, in 1948 only 3.2 per cent of the Mexican population were unionized.[94]

The census of 1940, under the influence of the Indianists, included a number of items, such as shoes, beds, wheat

---

91 Same, p. 531.
92 *Iturriaga,* cited, p. 34.
93 Same, p. 41.
94 Same, p. 56.

bread, knowledge of Spanish, which were considered indices of the level of living and of Indian-*mestizo*-modern
differences. Following this suggestion, Cline describes the
Indian world:

At the bottom of Mexican cultural strata are nearly two
million Indians who live in abject squalor and travel about
barefoot. Plagued by diseases, exploited by their fellows and
more modernized Mexicans, they exist but do not live. . . .
Just above the barefoot group are those who wear *huaraches*
but retain native costumes, in whole or part; numbering
nearly half a million, they often have *ranchos* of their own
or subsist in village communities that are generally inadequately supplied with elementary cultural equipment. More
changed, and sometimes happier, are still another group of
nearly equal size who have given up their native costumes for
the characteristic peasant dress of rural workers—white pajama-
like pants and blouses and straw hats; many now even wear
overalls like the unskilled laborers of towns and cities. Except
for their ignorance of Spanish they are Mexican; they are Indian only in language, and even that sometimes is shared. . . .
there are more than 100,000 Indians who live better than the
great majority of more culturally "modern" people. By cling-
ing to their native costumes, but combining them with the
use of shoes—a sign of affluence in Mexico—they really complicate the definition of an Indian. . . .
Much the same socially and economically are more than
150,000 individuals who speak Indian tongues habitually, but
have a knowledge of Spanish and have forsaken native dress.[95]

The transitional world is made up of the 85 per cent of
the population who do not use or know any native tongue
and who speak Spanish exclusively. "All the transitional
world speaks Spanish, is Roman Catholic, customarily eats
maize rather than wheat, and looks to modern centers for
many of its values and equipment, physical and cultural. It
is the backbone of rural Mexico and is now flooding the
cities." [96] Over three million of these still go barefoot and
live at as miserable a level as the poorest Indian. Over a

95 Cited, pp. 78-79.
96 Same, p. 81.

million still wear Indian dress but combine this with the use of *huaraches* or shoes. Some, such as independent land-owners, merchants, political leaders, and villagers have a higher social and economic status and have long been ex-posed to European culture. The rest of the transitional world is made up of about three million people in the city and country who take on new ways quickly while still re-taining many Indian traits.

The modern world of Mexico includes persons on every socio-economic level. Their unifying bond is the use of Spanish, the wearing of modern dress, and their identifica-tion with Mexico as a nation, rather than with a native village or state. In other words, they consider themselves "Mexicans" rather than Tepoztecans or Yucatecans.

These three cultural divisions are distributed among the total population as shown in Table 7:

TABLE 7

Major Mexican Groups, 1940

Cultural Divisions	Persons (millions)	Per Cent
The Indian world	2.945	15.0
The transitional world	7.268	37.0
The modern world	9.441	48.0
Total	19.654	100.0

Source: Howard F. Cline, *The United States and Mexico* (Cambridge: Harvard University Press, 1953), p. 76.

*   *   *

Mexico has made great progress on many fronts since 1940. The economy has been expanding and the country has become production-conscious as never before. Leading newspapers daily headline record-breaking achievements in agriculture and industry. The spurt toward industrial-ization which began with World War II has not been a temporary phenomenon, as some observers of the Mexican scene had expected. Indeed, the expansion of the economy since 1950 has been greater than that in the preceding ten years. A boom spirit has been created reminiscent of the great expansion in the United States at the turn of the century. Further, this rapid increase in Mexican production has been accomplished with relatively little assistance from abroad. The difficult undertaking of industrialization has been aided by several advantages derived from Mexico's position as a neighbor of the United States. For one thing, the *bracero* movement, by giving employment to surplus labor, has helped the process of industrialization. Similarly, the U.S. tourist trade provides many needed dollars to pay for imports of machinery and other equipment required for industrializing the country.

Despite a rapidly growing population, Mexico has managed to produce enough food to meet its needs except in drought years. Bringing another nine million hectares of new land under cultivation through irrigation should take care of further population increases in the next fifty or one hundred years. In addition, Mexico's new export agriculture is providing an important source of national income, indirectly helping the country to industrialize. Like the *ejidatarios,* the new commercial farmers may soon become a political force to be reckoned.

The modernization of agriculture, however, is only a limited phenomenon, concentrated mainly in the north and north Pacific regions. Elsewhere the great mass of the peasantry, both *ejidatarios* and owners of private holdings, continue to work their tiny subsistence holdings with traditional backward methods. The contrast between the new and the old agriculture in Mexico is becoming ever sharper. Thus, whereas less than 1 per cent of the cultivated land is worked with the aid of 50,000 tractors, about 20 per cent of the cultivated land is still worked by the pre-Hispanic method of cutting and burning. Indeed, in many areas the peasants are abandoning the plow and reverting to the more primitive hoe culture, in an effort to avoid the devastating effects of inflation.

Improved standards of living, a general trend since 1940,

are reflected in a variety of ways. More and more rural people sleep on beds instead of on the ground, wear shoes instead of *huaraches* or instead of going barefoot, use store-made pants instead of the home-made white cotton *calzones,* eat bread in addition to tortillas, grind their corn in the mill instead of by hand, drink beer instead of pulque, resort to doctors instead of *curanderos,* and travel by bus or train instead of on foot or by burro. In the towns and cities the trend has been from adobe to cement, from clay pots to aluminum, from cooking with charcoal to cooking with gas, from eating with tortillas to eating with tableware, from phonographs to radios and TV, from cottons to nylons, and from cognac to whiskey.

One of the most impressive gains since 1940 has been the growth of political democracy and a much greater sense of national unity. The role of the military in political life has been markedly reduced, and Mexico has enjoyed years of stability and peaceful elections. Mexico has a free press, freedom of speech, and freedom of worship. There are no political prisoners and the country is a haven for political refugees from countries throughout the Western Hemisphere.[97] The atmosphere of greater liberty can be measured in the fact that an occasional presidential adviser has published criticism of his government without losing his post.

The present government is also much more representative of the various sectors of the Mexican population than was the paternalistic government under Díaz, although its base of popular participation is less broad than it was under Cárdenas. The new upper class, though small and not well organized, has become increasingly influential in determining national policy, while the influence of organized labor and the *ejidatarios* has declined sharply. Neverthe-

---

[97] This paragraph, optimistic when I wrote it in 1956, is now out of date. The jailing of the leaders of the unsuccessful railroad strike in 1958 and of the renowned painter and avowed Communist David Alfaro Siqueiros in 1960, because of his support of an antigovernment student demonstration, has given Mexico more than a few political prisoners.

less, in the event of a political crisis, the government could probably count on the mass support of the two latter groups.

In spite of its great advances since 1940, Mexico is not yet a modern industrial nation. It still exhibits some characteristics of an agrarian colonial and underdeveloped country. Among key weaknesses are: the predominant role of foreign investment in certain basic industries, such as mining, and in strategic utilities, such as telephones and electricity; the continued dependence upon U.S.-controlled corporations for its automobiles and trucks, which are assembled but not manufactured in Mexico; the great lag in the modernization of its national railroad system; and its dependence upon the export of raw materials to pay for the importation of manufactured goods.

Even more serious, in terms of potential political consequences, is the failure to realize fully many of the social objectives of the Mexican Revolution. In 1960, over 60 per cent of the population are still ill fed, ill clothed, and ill housed, over 40 per cent are illiterate, and some 45 per cent of the nation's children are not being schooled. The national wealth has greatly increased since 1940, but the disparity between rich and poor is even more striking than before, despite some rise in the general standard of living. Some Mexicans are worried by this concentration of wealth and fear the possibility of political unrest unless the trend is corrected. However, given the high threshold for suffering of the Mexican people, it seems safe to predict that the present political stability will continue for some years to come.

Relations between the United States and Mexico have improved greatly since 1940. The traditional fear of the United States has been reduced, and Mexicans seem more confident of their national sovereignty and of their ability to cope with their many problems. Mexico's own economic and cultural progress makes its people more self-reliant and therefore more relaxed in its dealings with its northern neighbor. This change, together with increased contact with U.S. citizens and generally broadened horizons, has reduced anti-gringoism. There is little evidence of anti-U.S. sentiment among the rural population or among the urban poor, except where the Sinarquistas have been active over a long period. Anti-U.S. feeling on the whole is strongest among the small Mexican industrialists who feel threatened by the giant U.S. corporations and their subsidiaries. This group has sought to influence government policy toward more stringent controls over foreign investment. Left-wing groups likewise attack foreign investment as further evidence of U.S. imperialism. However, unlike the old imperialism that carried with it the threat of armed force, the new type of dependency offers a much more diffuse target to nationalist and leftist attacks. It is significant, though, that the major actual or potential points of tension between the two countries do result from the dependency relationship: for example, reliance upon tourist income, seasonal employment for unemployed agricultural workers, the inflow of U.S. capital, and subjection to the ups and downs of U.S. markets. These factors, along with the increasing exodus of Mexicans to become permanent U.S. residents and citizens, arouse some old sensitivities among many Mexicans, giving rise to resentment and insecurity. Many thoughtful Mexicans who value highly the traditional Mexican culture also view with apprehension the increasing spread of a wide variety of U.S. culture traits, ranging from Santa Claus to psychoanalysis.

Because of the long and now more intimate association between the two countries, Mexico and its strenuous ambitions for self-advancement offer a special challenge to U.S. policy. Here, the United States can, with respect for Mexico's cultural differences and sympathy for its expanding aspirations, help an ambitious and energetic Latin American people complete its emergence into the world of modern nations. Here, private business and cultural initiatives are understood and supported by an increasingly influential and active middle and professional class. Here, aid, cultural and economic, can flow through numerous and already established channels of communication, demonstrating the reality of mutual respect and reciprocal interests. And because of Mexico's prestige among Latin American nations as a people that has carried out an authentic national revolution of its own, Mexico can also be, more than any other Latin neighbor, both a testing-ground and an interpreter of the value and advantages of friendship and cooperation with the United States.

INDEX

347

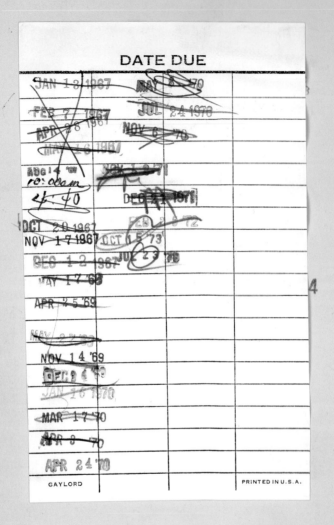

DATE DUE

JAN 13 1967	MAY 8 70	
FEB 7 1967	JUL 24 1970	
APR 28 1967	NOV 6 70	
MAY 16 1967		
AUG 14 '68	NOV 1 2 71	
re: obain		
4 40	DEC 21 1971	
OCT 20 1967	FEB 2 9 72	
NOV 17 1967	OCT 15 73	
DEC 12 1967	JUL 23 78	
MAY 17 68		
APR 25 '69		
MAY 2 '69		
NOV 14 '69		
DEC 8 4 '69		
JAN 16 1970		
MAR 17 70		
APR 3 70		
APR 24 70		